BERLITZ®

Dutch
PHRASE BOOK
& DICTIONARY

D0557154

Easy to use features

- Handy thematic colour coding
- Quick Reference Section – opposite page
- Tipping Guide – inside back cover
- Quick reply panels throughout

How best to use this phrase book

● We suggest that you start with the **Guide to pronunciation** (pp. 6–9), then go on to **Some basic expressions** (pp. 10–15). This gives you not only a minimum vocabulary, but also helps you get used to pronouncing the language. The phonetic transcription throughout the book enables you to pronounce every word correctly.

● Consult the **Contents** pages (3–5) for the section you need. In each chapter you'll find travel facts, hints and useful information. Simple phrases are followed by a list of words applicable to the situation.

● Separate, detailed contents lists are included at the beginning of the extensive **Eating out** and **Shopping guide** sections (Menus, p. 39, Shops and services, p. 97).

● If you want to find out how to say something in Dutch, your fastest look-up is via the **Dictionary** section (pp. 165–189). This will give you the word cross-referred to its use in a phrase on a specific page.

● If you wish to learn more about constructing sentences, check the **Basic grammar** (pp. 159–164).

● Note the **colour margins** are indexed in Dutch and English to help both listener and speaker. And, in addition, there is also an **index in Dutch** for the use of your listener.

● The symbol ☞ suggests phrases your listener can use to help you. Hand this phrase book to the Dutch-speaker to encourage pointing to an appropriate answer.

Contents

4

Acknowledgments
We are particularly grateful to Marianne Bielders-Bergmans and
Catheline Bijleveld-Gevaerts for their help in the preparation of
this book, and to Dr. T. J. A. Bennett who devised the phonetic transcription.

Guide to pronunciation

You'll find the pronunciation of the Dutch letters and sounds explained below, as well as the symbols we use in the transcriptions. The imitated pronunciation should be read as if it were English, with exceptions as indicated below. It is based on Standard British pronunciation, though we have tried to take into account General American pronunciation as well.

Letters that appear in bold type in the transcriptions should be read with more stress than the others. In the more unusual diphthongs, we print the weaker element in a raised position, e.g. oa^{ee} means that the **oa** element is the more prominent sound in the diphthong and the **ee** sound is short and fleeting.

Consonants

Letter	Approximate pronunciation	Symbol	Example	
f, h, k, l, m, n, p, q, t, x, y, z	as in English			
b	as in English but, when at the end of a word, like **p** in cup	b p	**ben** **heb**	behn hehp
c	1) before a consonant and **a, o, u,** like **k** in **k**een	k	**inclusief**	inklewseef
	2) before **e** and **i,** always like **s** in **s**it	s	**ceintuur**	sehntewr
ch	1) generally like **ch** in Scottish lo**ch**	kh	**nacht**	nahkht
	2) in words of French origin like **sh** in **sh**ut	sh	**cheque**	shehk
chtj	like Dutch **ch** followed by Dutch **j**	khy	**nichtje**	nikhyer
d	as in English, but, when at the end of a word, like **t** in hit	d t	**doe** **avond**	doo aavont

g	1) at the end of a word and before a strong consonant, like ch in Scottish loch	kh	**deeg** **liegt**	daykh leekht
	2) in a few words borrowed from French, like s in pleasure	zh	**genie**	zher**nee**
	3) otherwise (often at the beginning of a word), like a softer voiced version of ch in Scottish loch	gh	**groot** **zagen**	ghroat zaaghern*
j	1) like y in yes	y	**ja**	yaa
	2) in certain words borrowed from French, like s in leisure	zh	**lits-** **jumeaux**	lee- zhewmo^{ow}
ng	ng is pronounced as in English sing	ng	**toegang**	tooghang
nj	like ñ in Spanish señor or ni in onion	ñ	**oranje**	oarahñer
r	always trilled, either in the front or the back of the mouth	r	**warm**	√ahrm
s	like s in sit or ss in pass	s ss	**stoel** **roos**	stool roass
sj, stj	like sh in shut	sh	**meisje**	maiysher
sch	like s followed by a Dutch ch	skh	**schrijven**	skhraiy- vern*
th	like t in tea	t	**thee**	tay
tj	like ty in hit you	ty	**katje**	kahtyer
v	basically as in English, but is often harder and not voiced, it sounds almost like f	v	**hoeveel** **van**	hoovayl vahn
w	quite like English v, but with the bottom lip raised a little higher	√	**water**	√aaterr

---

* The final n of a word is not usually heard during a fast conversation; it is heard, however, when words are spoken slowly.

Note: When two consonants stand next to each other, one will often influence the other even if it is not in the same word, e.g. *ziens* is pronounced *zeenss,* but in the phrase *tot ziens,* it is pronounced *seenss* under the influence of the t before it.

PRONUNCIATION

Uitspraak

Vowels

Dutch vowels are long when followed by a single consonant that is, in turn, followed by a vowel, or when written double, or in most cases when at the end of a word.

a	1) when short, between **a** in cat and **u** in cut	ah	**kat**	kaht
	2) when long, like **a** in cart	aa	**vader**	**vaa**derr
e	1) when short, like **e** in bed	eh	**bed**	beht
	2) when long, like **a** in late, but a pure vowel, not a diphthong	ay	**zee**	zay
	3) in unstressed syllables, like **er** in other	er*	**zitten**	**zit**tern
eu	approximately like **ur** in fur, but pronounced with rounded lips	ur*	**deur**	durr
i	1) when short, like **i** in bit	i	**kind**	kint
	2) when long (also spelt **ie**) like **ee** in bee	ee	**zien**	zeen
	3) sometimes, in unstressed syllables, like **er** in other	er*	**monnik**	**mon**nerk
ij	sometimes, in unstressed syllables, like **er** in other; see also under "Diphthongs"	er*	**lelijk**	**lay**lerk
o	1) when short, like a very short version of **aw** in lawn	o	**pot**	pot
	2) when long, something like **oa** in road, but a pure vowel, with rounded lips	oa	**boot**	boat
oe	(long) like **oo** in moon and well rounded	oo	**hoe**	hoo
u	1) when short, something like **ur** in hurt, but with rounded lips	ur*	**bus**	burss
	2) when long, like **u** in French sur or **ü** in German für; say **ee**, and without moving your tongue, round your lips	ew	**nu**	new

---

* The r should not be pronounced when reading this transcription.

Diphthongs

ai	generally like **igh** in s**igh**	igh	**ai**	igh
ei, ij	between **a** in l**a**te and **igh** in s**igh**	aiy	**reis** **ijs**	raiyss aiyss
au, ou	Dutch short **o** followed by a weak short **u**-sound; can sound very much like **ow** in n**ow**	o°ʷ	**koud**	ko°ʷt
aai	like **a** in c**a**rt followed by a short **ee** sound	aaᵉᵉ	**draai**	draaᵉᵉ
eeuw	like **a** in l**a**te (but a pure vowel), followed by a short **oo** sound	ayᵒᵒ	**leeuw**	layᵒᵒ
ieuw	like **ee** in fr**ee**, followed by a short **oo** sound	eeᵒᵒ	**nieuw**	neeᵒᵒ
ooi	like **oa** in r**oa**d (but a pure vowel) followed by a short **ee** sound	oaᵉᵉ	**nooit**	noaᵉᵉt
oei	like **oo** in s**oo**n, followed by a short **ee** sound	ooᵉᵉ	**roeit**	rooᵉᵉt
ui	like **ur** in h**ur**t followed by a Dutch **u** sound, as described in **u** 2), but shorter	urᵉʷ*	**huis**	hurᵉʷss
uw	like the sound described for **u** 2), followed by a weak **oo** sound	ewᵒᵒ	**duw**	dewᵒᵒ

Pronunciation of the Dutch alphabet							
A	aa	H	haa	O	oa	V	vay
B	bay	I	ee	P	pay	W	vay
C	say	J	yay	Q	kew	X	iks
D	day	K	kaa	R	ehr	Y	aiy
E	ay	L	ehl	S	ehss	Z	zehd
F	ehf	M	ehm	T	tay		
G	ghay	N	ehn	U	ew		

---

* The r should not be pronounced when reading this transcription.

Some basic expressions

Yes.	**Ja.**	yaa
No.	**Nee.**	nay
Please.	**Alstublieft.** *	ahlstew**bleeft**
Thank you.	**Dank u.**	dahnk ew
Thank you very much.	**Hartelijk dank.**	**hahr**terlerk dahnk
That's all right/ You're welcome.	**Graag gedaan.**	ghraakh gher**daan**

Greetings *Begroetingen*

Good morning.	**Goedemorgen.**	ghooder**morghern**
Good afternoon.	**Goedemiddag.**	ghooder**middahkh**
Good evening.	**Goedenavond.**	ghooder**naavont**
Good night.	**Goedenacht.**	ghooder**nahkht**
Goodbye.	**Tot ziens.**	tot seenss
See you later.	**Tot straks.**	tot strahks
Hello/Hi!	**Hallo!**	hah**loa**
This is Mr./Mrs./ Miss...	**Dit is mijnheer/ mevrouw/juffrouw** ...	dit iss mer**nayr**/ mervro^{ow}/yurfro^{ow}
How do you do? (Pleased to meet you.)	**Hoe maakt u het?**	hoo maakt ew heht
How are you?	**Hoe gaat het?**	hoo ghaat heht
Very well, thanks. And you?	**Heel goed, dank u. En u?**	hayl ghoot dahnk ew. ehn ew
How's life?	**Hoe gaat het ermee?**	hoo ghaat heht ehr**may**
Fine.	**Uitstekend.**	ur^{ew}t**staykernt**

---

* In Dutch, *alstublieft* is a courtesy word often added to the end of a sentence. It has no real English equivalent.

I beg your pardon?	**Wat zegt u?**	√aht zehkht ew
Excuse me. (May I get past?)	**Neemt u mij niet kwalijk/Pardon.**	naymt ew maiy neet k√aalerk/pahrdon
Sorry!	**Het spijt mij/Sorry!**	heht spaiyt maiy/sorry

Questions *Vragen*

Where?	**Waar?**	√aar
How?	**Hoe?**	hoo
When?	**Wanneer/Hoe laat?**	√ahnayr/hoo laat
What?	**Wat?**	√aht
Why?	**Waarom?**	√aarom
Who?	**Wie?**	√ee
Which?	**Welk/Welke?**	√ehlk/√ehlker
Where is...?	**Waar is...?**	√aar iss
Where are...?	**Waar zijn...?**	√aar zaiyn
Where can I find...?	**Waar kan ik... vinden?**	√aar kahn ik vindern
Where can I get...?	**Waar kan ik... krijgen?**	√aar kahn ik kraiyghern
How far?	**Hoever?**	hoovehr
How long?	**Hoelang?**	hoolahng
How much/How many?	**Hoeveel?**	hoovayl
How much does this cost?	**Hoeveel kost dit?**	hoovayl kost dit
When does the next bus leave?	**Wanneer vertrekt de volgende bus?**	√ahnayr verrtrehkt der volghernder burss
When does... open/ close?	**Hoe laat gaat... open/dicht?**	hoo laat ghaat... oapern/dikht
What do you call this/that in Dutch?	**Hoe noemt u dit/dat in het Nederlands?**	hoo noomt ew dit/daht in heht nayderrlahnts
What does this/ that mean?	**Wat betekent dit/dat?**	√aht bertaykernt dit/daht

Do you speak ...?   *Spreekt u...?*

Do you speak English?	**Spreekt u Engels?**	spraykt ew **ehng**erlss
What foreign languages do you speak?	**Welke vreemde talen spreekt u?**	√**vehl**ker **vrehm**der **taa**lern **sprehkt** ew
Does anyone here speak English?	**Is hier iemand die Engels spreekt?**	iss heer **ee**mahnt dee **ehng**erlss spraykt
I'm a foreigner.	**Ik ben buitenlander (buitenlandse).**	ik behn bu**ew**ternlahnterr (bu**ew**ternlahntser)
I don't speak Dutch.	**Ik spreek geen Nederlands.**	ik sprayk ghayn **nay**derrlahnts
I speak a little Dutch.	**Ik spreek een beetje Nederlands.**	ik sprayk ern **bay**tyer **nay**derrlahnts
Could you speak more slowly?	**Kunt u wat lang-zamer spreken?**	kurnt ew √aht **lahng**-zaamerr **spray**kern
Could you repeat that?	**Kunt u dat herhalen?**	kurnt ew daht hehr**haa**lern
Could you spell it?	**Kunt u het spellen?**	kurnt ew heht **speh**lern
How do you pronounce this?	**Hoe spreekt u dit uit?**	hoo spraykt ew dit ur**ew**t
Could you write it down, please?	**Kunt u het op-schrijven, alstublieft?**	kurnt ew heht **op**-skhraiyvern ahlstew**bleeft**
Can you translate this for me?	**Kunt u dit voor mij vertalen?**	kurnt ew dit voar maiy verr**taa**lern
Could you point to the... in the book, please?	**Kunt u... in het boek aanwijzen, alstublieft?**	kurnt ew... in heht book **aan**√aiyzern ahlstew**bleeft**
answer	**het antwoord**	heht **ahnt**√oart
phrase	**de uitdrukking**	der ur**ew**tdrurking
sentence	**de zin**	der zin
word	**het woord**	heht √oart
Just a moment.	**Een ogenblik.**	ern **oa**ghernblik
I'll see if I can find it in this book.	**Ik zal kijken of ik het in dit boek kan vinden.**	ik zahl **kaiy**kern off ik heht in dit book kahn **vin**dern
I understand.	**Ik begrijp het.**	ik ber**ghraiyp** heht
I don't understand.	**Ik begrijp het niet.**	ik ber**ghraiyp** heht neet
Do you understand?	**Begrijpt u het?**	ber**ghraiypt** ew heht

Can/May...? *Kunnen/Mogen...?*

Can I have...?	**Mag ik... hebben?**	mahkh ik... **hehbern**
Can we have...?	**Mogen wij... hebben?**	**moaghern** √aiy... **hehbern**
I can't...	**Ik kan niet...**	ik kahn neet
Can you tell me...?	**Kunt u mij zeggen...?**	kurnt ew maiy **zehghern**
Can you help me?	**Kunt u mij helpen?**	kurnt ew maiy **hehlpern**
Can I help you?	**Kan ik u helpen?**	kahn ik ew **hehlpern**
Can you direct me to...?	**Kunt u mij de weg wijzen naar...?**	kurnt ew maiy der √ehkh √aiyzern naar

Do you want...? *Wenst u...?*

I'd like to...	**Ik wil graag...**	ik √il ghraakh
I'd like a/an...	**Ik wil graag een... (hebben).**	ik √il graakh ern... (hehbern)
We'd like some...	**Wij willen graag...**	√aiy √illern ghraakh
What do you want?	**Wat wenst u?**	√aht √ehnst ew
Could you give me...?	**Kunt u mij... geven?**	kurnt ew maiy... **ghayvern**
Could you bring me...?	**Kunt u mij... brengen?**	kurnt ew maiy... **brehngern**
Could you show me...?	**Kunt u mij... laten zien?**	kurnt ew maiy... **laatern** zeen
I'm looking for...	**Ik zoek...**	ik zook
I'm hungry.	**Ik heb honger.**	ik hehp **hongerr**
I'm thirsty.	**Ik heb dorst.**	ik hehp dorst
I'm tired.	**Ik ben moe.**	ik behn moo
I'm lost.	**Ik ben verdwaald.**	ik behn verrd√aalt
It's important.	**Het is belangrijk.**	heht iss berl**ahng**raiyk
It's urgent.	**Het is dringend.**	heht iss **dring**ernt

It is/There is... *Het is/Er is...*

It is...	**Het is...**	heht iss
Is it...?	**Is het...?**	iss heht

It isn't...	**Het is niet...**	heht iss neet
Here it is.	**Hier is het.**	heer iss heht
Here they are.	**Hier zijn zij.**	heer zaiyn zaiy
There it is.	**Daar is het.**	daar iss heht
There they are.	**Daar zijn zij.**	daar zaiyn zaiy
There is/There are...	**Er is/Er zijn...**	ehr iss/ehr zaiyn
Is there/Are there...?	**Is er/Zijn er...?**	iss ehr/zaiyn ehr
There isn't/ There aren't...	**Er is geen/ Er zijn geen...**	ehr iss ghayn/ ehr zaiyn ghayn
There isn't any/ There aren't any.	**Er is er geen/ Er zijn er geen.**	ehr iss ehr ghayn/ ehr zaiyn ehr ghayn

It's... *Het is...*

beautiful/ugly	**mooi/lelijk**	moa^ee/laylerk
better/worse	**beter/slechter**	bayterr/slehkhterr
big/small	**groot/klein**	ghroat/klaiyn
cheap/expensive	**goedkoop/duur**	ghootkoap/dewr
early/late	**vroeg/laat**	vrookh/laat
easy/difficult	**gemakkelijk/moeilijk**	ghermahkerlerk/moo^ee^lerk
free (vacant)/ occupied	**vrij/bezet**	vraiy/berzeht
full/empty	**vol/leeg**	vol/laykh
good/bad	**goed/slecht**	ghoot/slehkht
heavy/light	**zwaar/licht**	z√aar/likht
here/there	**hier/daar**	heer/daar
hot/cold	**warm/koud**	√ahrm/ko^o^w^t
near/far	**dichtbij/ver**	dikhtbaiy/vehr
next/last	**volgende/laatste**	volghernder/laatster
old/new	**oud/nieuw**	o^o^w^t/nee^oo
old/young	**oud/jong**	o^o^w^t/yong
open/shut	**open/dicht**	oapern/dikht
quick/slow	**snel/langzaam**	snehl/lahngzaam
right/wrong	**juist/verkeerd**	yur^ew^st/verrkayrt

Quantities *Hoeveelheden*

a little/a lot	**een beetje/veel**	ern baytyer/vayl
few/a few	**weinig/enkele**	√aiynikh/ehnkerler
much/many	**veel**	vayl
more/less	**meer/minder**	mayr/minderr
more than/less than	**meer dan/minder dan**	mayr dahn/minderr dahn

| enough/too much | **genoeg/te veel** | ghernookh/ter vayl |
| some/any | **wat/enige** | √aht/aynergher |

A few more useful words *Nog een paar nuttige woorden*

above	**boven**	boavern
after	**na**	naa
and	**en**	ehn
at	**te**	ter
before	**voor**	voar
behind	**achter**	ahkhterr
below	**onder**	onderr
between	**tussen**	tursern
but	**maar**	maar
down	**neer**	nayr
downstairs	**beneden**	bernaydern
during	**tijdens**	taiydernss
for	**voor**	voar
from	**van**	vahn
in	**in**	in
inside	**binnen**	binnern
near	**nabij**	nahbaiy
never	**nooit**	noaᵉᵉt
next to	**naast**	naast
none	**geen**	ghayn
not	**niet**	neet
nothing	**niets**	neets
now	**nu**	new
on	**op**	op
only	**slechts**	slehkhts
or	**of**	off
outside	**buiten**	burᵉʷtern
perhaps	**misschien**	mersskheen
since	**sedert**	sayderrt
soon	**spoedig**	spooderkh
then	**dan**	dahn
through	**door**	doar
to	**naar**	naar
too (also)	**ook**	oak
towards	**naar**	naar
under	**onder**	onderr
until	**tot**	tot
up	**op**	op
upstairs	**boven**	boavern
very	**zeer**	zayr
with	**met**	meht
without	**zonder**	zonderr
yet	**nog**	nokh

Arrival

Passport control *Paspoortcontrole*

Here's my passport.	**Hier is mijn paspoort.**	heer iss maiyn **pahs**poart
I'll be staying...	**Ik blijf hier...**	ik blaiyf heer
a few days	**een paar dagen**	ern paar **daag**hern
a week	**een week**	ern √ayk
2 weeks	**2 weken**	t√ay √aykern
a month	**een maand**	ern maant
I don't know yet.	**Ik weet het nog niet.**	ik √ayt heht nokh neet
I'm here on holiday.	**Ik ben hier met vakantie.**	ik behn heer meht vaa**kahn**see
I'm here on business.	**Ik ben hier voor zaken.**	ik behn heer voar **zaa**kern
I'm just passing through.	**Ik ben op doorreis.**	ik behn op **doar**rayss

If things become difficult:

I'm sorry, I don't understand.	**Het spijt mij, ik begrijp het niet.**	heht spaiyt maiy ik berghraiyp heht neet
Does anyone here speak English?	**Is er iemand hier die Engels spreekt?**	iss ehr **ee**mahnt heer dee **ehng**erlss spraykt

---

DOUANE
CUSTOMS

After collecting your baggage at the airport (*luchthaven*—**lurkht**haavern) you have a choice: use the green exit if you have nothing to declare. Or leave via the red exit if you have items to declare (in excess of those allowed).

aangifte goederen goods to declare	**niets aan te geven** nothing to declare

The chart below shows what you can bring in duty-free.*

Entering the Netherlands from:	Cigarettes		Cigars		Tobacco	Spirits		Wine
1)	200	or	50	or	250 g.	1 l.	and	2 l.
2)	300	or	75	or	400 g.	1½ l.	and	5 l.
3)	400	or	100	or	500 g.	1 l.	and	2 l.

1) EEC countries with goods bought tax free, and other European countries
2) EEC countries with goods not bought tax free
3) countries outside Europe

I have nothing to declare.	**Ik heb niets aan te geven.**	ik hehp neets aan ter ghayvern
I have...	**Ik heb...**	ik hehp
a carton of cigarettes	**een slof siga- retten**	ern sloff seeghaarehtern
a bottle of whisky	**een fles whisky**	ern flehss √iskee
It's for my personal use.	**Dit is voor mijn persoonlijk gebruik.**	dit iss voar maiyn pehr- soanlerk gherbrur^ew'k
It's a gift.	**Het is een cadeau.**	heht iss ern kaadoa

☞   ☜

Uw paspoort, alstublieft.	Your passport, please.
Hebt u iets aan te geven?	Do you have anything to declare?
Wilt u deze tas even open maken?	Please open this bag.
U moet hiervoor invoer- rechten betalen.	You'll have to pay duty on this.
Hebt u nog meer bagage?	Do you have any more luggage?

---

* All allowances are subject to change.

Baggage—Porter *Bagage—Kruier*

You will normally see porters only at airports and larger railway stations. Where there are none available, you'll find luggage trolleys (carts).

Porter!	**Kruier!**	krur^{ew}yerr
Please take this/my ...	**Wilt u deze/mijn ... ... meenemen, alstublieft.**	√ilt ew dayzer/maiyn... maynaymern ahlstewbleeft
luggage	**bagage**	baaghaazher
suitcase	**koffer**	kofferr
(travelling) bag	**(reis)tas**	(raiyss)tahss
That one is mine.	**Die is van mij.**	dee iss vahn maiy
Take this luggage to the...	**Breng deze bagage naar de...**	brehng dayzer baaghaazher naar der
bus	**bus**	burss
luggage lockers	**bagagekluizen**	baaghaazherklur^{ew}zern
taxi	**taxi**	tahksee
How much is that?	**Hoeveel is het?**	hoovayl iss heht
There's one piece missing.	**Er ontbreekt een stuk.**	ehr ontbraykt ayn sturk
Where are the luggage trolleys (carts)?	**Waar zijn de bagagewagentjes?**	√aar zaiyn der baaghaazher√aagherntyeress

Changing money *Geld wisselen*

Where's the currency exchange office?	**Waar is het wissel-kantoor?**	√aar iss heht √isserlkahntoar
Can you change these traveller's cheques (checks)?	**Kunt u deze reis-cheques wisselen?**	kurnt ew dayzer raiysshehks √isserlern
I'd want to change some...	**Ik wil enige... wisselen.**	ik √il aynergher... √isserlern
dollars	**dollars**	dollahrss
pounds	**ponden**	pondern
Can you change this into...?	**Kunt u dit tegen... wisselen?**	kurnt ew dit tayghern... √isserlern
guilders	**guldens**	ghurldernss
Belgian francs	**Belgische franken**	behlgheeser frahnkern
What's the exchange rate?	**Wat is de wissel-koers?**	√aht iss der √isserlkoorss

BANK – CURRENCY, see page 129

Where is ...? *Waar is ...?*

Where is the...?	**Waar is...?**	√aar iss
booking office	**het reserverings-bureau**	heht rayzehrvayrings-bewroa
duty (tax)-free shop	**de duty-free winkel**	der "duty-free" √inkerl
hotel information desk	**de hotel informatie-balie**	der hoatehl informaatsee-baalee
newsstand	**de kiosk**	der keeyosk
railway station	**het station**	heht stahtsyon
restaurant	**het restaurant**	heht rehstoarahnt
Where are the conference rooms?	**Waar zijn de ver-gaderzalen?**	√aar zaiyn der vehr-ghaaderrzaalern
How do I get to...?	**Hoe kom ik naar...?**	hoo kom ik naar
Is there a bus into town?	**Gaat er een bus naar de stad?**	ghaat ehr ern burss naar der staht
Where can I get a taxi?	**Waar kan ik een taxi vinden?**	√aar kahn ik ern tahksee vindern
Where can I hire (rent) a car?	**Waar kan ik een auto huren?**	√aar kahn ik ern oᵒᵂtoa hewrern

Hotel reservation *Hotelreservering*

Do you have a hotel guide (directory)?	**Hebt u een hotel-gids?**	hehpt ew ern hoatehl-ghits
Could you reserve a room for me?	**Kunt u voor mij een kamer reserveren?**	kurnt ew voar maiy ern kaamerr rayzehrvayrern
in the centre	**in het centrum**	in heht sehntrum
near the airport	**dichtbij de lucht-haven**	dikhtbaiy der lurkhthaavern
a single room	**een éénpersoons-kamer**	ern aynpehrsoanskaamerr
a double room	**een tweepersoons-kamer**	ern t√aypehrsoanskaamerr
not too expensive	**niet te duur**	neet ter dewr
I'll be staying from... to...	**Ik blijf hier van... tot...**	ik blaiyf heer vahn... tot
Where is the hotel?	**Waar is het hotel?**	√aar iss heht hoatehl
Can you recommend a guesthouse?	**Kunt u een pension aanbevelen?**	kurnt ew ern pehnsyon aanbervaylern
Do you have a street map?	**Hebt u een platte-grond?**	hehpt ew ern plahterghront

HOTEL/ACCOMMODATION, see page 22

Car hire (rental) *Autoverhuur*

To hire a car you must produce a valid driving licence (held for at least one year) and your passport. Some firms set a minimum age of 21, others 25. Holders of major credit cards are normally exempt from deposit payments, otherwise you must pay a substantial (refundable) deposit.

I'd like to hire (rent) a car.	Ik wil graag een auto huren.	ik vil ghraakh ern oowtoa hewrern
small	klein	klaiyn
medium-sized	middelgroot	middelghroat
large	groot	ghroat
automatic	met automaat	meht oowtoamaat
I'd like it for...	Ik wil het graag voor...	ik vil heht ghraakh voar
a day	een dag	ern dahkh
a week	een week	ern vayk
Are there any weekend arrangements?	Zijn er ook weekend-arrangementen?	zaiyn ehr oak "weekend-" ahrahngzhermehntern
Do you have any special rates?	Hebt u speciale tarieven?	hehpt ew spaysyaaler taareevern
What's the charge per day/week?	Wat is het tarief per dag/week?	vaht iss heht taareef pehr dahkh/vayk
Is mileage included?	Is het aantal kilometers inbegrepen?	iss heht aantahl keeloamayterrss inberghraypern
What's the charge per kilometre?	Wat is het tarief per kilometer?	vaht iss heht taarief pehr keeloamayterr
Are there any extra costs?	Zijn er nog extra onkosten?	zayn ehr nokh ehkstraa onkostern
I'd like to leave the car in...	Ik wil de auto graag in... achterlaten.	ik vil de oowtoa ghraakh in... ahkhterrlaatern
I'd like full insurance.	Ik wil graag een all-risk verzekering.	ik vil ghraakh ern "all risk" vehrzaykerring
How much is the deposit?	Hoeveel bedraagt de waarborgsom?	hoovayl berdraakht der vaarborkhsom
I have a credit card.	Ik heb een credit card.	ik hehp ern "credit card"
Here's my driving licence.	Hier is mijn rijbewijs.	heer iss maiyn raiybervaiyss

CAR, see page 75

Taxi *Taxi*

It is not common practice to hail a taxi. You'll find taxi ranks at airports, railway stations and scattered throughout the cities. All taxies are metered, but rates may vary a little from place to place; there is no extra charge for luggage.

Where can I get a taxi?	**Waar kan ik een taxi vinden?**	√aar kahn ik ern **tahksee** vindern
Where is the taxi rank (stand)?	**Waar is de taxi-standplaats?**	√ar iss der **tahksee** stahnt-plaats
Could you get me a taxi?	**Wilt u een taxi voor mij bestellen?**	√ilt ew ern **tahksee** voar maiy berstehlern
What's the fare to...?	**Wat kost het naar...?**	√aht kost heht naar
How far is it to...?	**Hoever is het naar...?**	hoovehr iss heht naar
Take me to...	**Brengt u mij naar...**	brehngt ew maiy naar
this address	**dit adres**	dit **aadrehss**
the airport	**de luchthaven**	der **lurkht**haavern
the town centre	**het stadscentrum**	heht **stahts**sehntrurm
the... Hotel	**het... hotel**	heht... hoatehl
the railway station	**het station**	heht stahsyon
Turn... at the next corner.	**Sla bij de volgende hoek...-af**	slaa baiy der **volg**hernder hook...-ahf
left/right	**links/rechts**	links/rehkhts
Go straight ahead.	**(Rijdt) rechtdoor.**	(raiyt) **rehkht**doar
Please stop here.	**Wilt u hier stoppen, alstublieft.**	√ilt ew heer stoppern ahlstewbleeft
I'm in a hurry.	**Ik heb haast.**	ik hehp haast
Could you...?	**Kunt u..., alstublieft?**	kurnt ew... ahlstewbleeft
drive faster	**wat sneller rijden**	√aht snehlerr raiydern
drive more slowly	**wat langzamer rijden**	√aht lahngzaamerr raiydern
Could you help me with my luggage?	**Wilt u mij met mijn bagage helpen, alstublieft?**	√ilt ew maiy meht maiyn baaghaazher hehlpern ahlstewbleeft
Could you wait for me?	**Kunt u op mij wachten, alstublieft?**	kurnt ew op maiy √ahkhtern ahlstewbleeft
I'll be back in 10 minutes.	**Ik ben in 10 minuten terug.**	ik behn in 10 meenewtern terrurkh

TIPPING, see inside back-cover

Hotel — Other accommodation

Early reservation and confirmation are essential in most major tourist centres during high season. Most towns and arrival points have a tourist information office, *Vereniging voor Vreemdelingen Verkeer* (VVV—vay vay vay), and that's the place to go if you're stuck for a room.

Hotel (hoatehl)	There is a wide range of hotels available from luxury international (in the bigger towns) to small family hotels. The Netherlands National Tourist offices abroad or the local VVV offices can provide you with a hotel list.
Motel (moatehl)	Motels are becoming more popular and are usually found near motorways and other major roads.
Pension (pehnsyon)	Many guesthouses are family run. They normally offer *vol pension* (full board) or *half pension* (half board). The local VVV offices will supply you with addresses.
Jeugdherberg (yurkhthehrbehrkh)	Youth hostels are generally open all year round to members of youth hostel organizations or holders of an international youth hostel card.
Vakantiehuisje (vaakahnseehur^ew sher)	Holiday cottages can be rented in many tourist resorts, but you must book well in advance.

Can you recommend a guesthouse?	**Kunt u mij een pension aanbevelen?**	kurnt ew maiy ern pehnsyon aanbervaylern
Are there any... vacant?	**Zijn er... vrij?**	zaiyn ehr... vraiy
flats (apartments) holiday cottages	**appartementen** **vakantiehuisjes**	ahpahrtermehntern vaakahnseehur^ew sherss

KAMERS VRIJ VACANCY	**VOLGEBOEKT** NO VACANCIES

HOTEL RESERVATION, see also page 19

Checking in—Reception *Receptie*

My name is...	**Mijn naam is...**	maiyn naam iss
I have a reservation.	**Ik heb gereserveerd.**	ik hehp gherrayzehrvayrt
We've reserved 2 rooms.	**Wij hebben 2 kamers gereserveerd.**	√aiy hehbern 2 **kaamerrss** gherrayzehrvayrt
Here's the confirmation.	**Hier is de bevesti-ging.**	heer iss der bervehster-ghing
Do you have any vacancies?	**Hebt u nog kamers vrij?**	hehpt ew nokh **kaamerrss** vraiy
I'd like a...	**Ik wil graag een...**	ik √il ghraakh ern
single room	**éénpersoonskamer**	aynpehrsoanskaamerr
double room	**tweepersoonskamer**	t√aypehrsoanskaamerr
We'd like a room...	**Wij willen graag een kamer...**	√aiy √illern ghraakh ern **kaamerr**
with twin beds	**met lits-jumeaux**	meht lee-zhewmoa
with a double bed	**met een twee-persoonsbed**	meht ern t√ay-pehrsoansbeht
with a bath	**met badkamer**	meht bahtkaamerr
with a shower	**met douche**	meht doosh
with a balcony	**met balkon**	meht bahlkon
with a view	**met uitzicht**	meht ur^{ew}tzikht
at the front	**aan de voorkant**	aan der voarkahnt
at the back	**aan de achterkant**	aan der ahkhterrkahnt
facing the sea	**met uitzicht op zee**	meht ur^{ew}tzikht op zay
It must be quiet.	**Het moet er rustig zijn.**	heht moot ehr rursterkh zaiyn
What floor is my room on?	**Op welke verdieping is mijn kamer?**	op √ehlker verrdeeping iss maiyn **kaamerr**
Is there...?	**Is er...?**	iss ehr
a laundry service	**een wasserij**	ern √ahsserraiy
a private toilet	**een eigen toilet**	ern aiyghern t√aaleht
a radio/television in the room	**een radio/televisie op de kamer**	ern raadeeyoa/taylerveezee op der **kaamerr**
air conditioning	**air-conditioning**	"air-conditioning"
heating	**verwarming**	verr√ahrming
hot water	**warm water**	√ahrm √aaterr
room service	**bediening op de kamer**	berdeening op der **kaamerr**
running water	**stromend water**	stroamernt √aaterr
May I see the room?	**Mag ik de kamer zien?**	mahkh ik der **kaamerr** zeen

CHECKING OUT, see page 31

Could you put... in the room?	**Kunt u... op de kamer bijzetten?**	kurnt ew... op der kaamerr baiyzehtern
a cot	**een kinderbed**	ern kinderrbeht
an extra bed	**een extra bed**	ern ehkstraa beht

How much? *Hoeveel?*

How much does it cost...?	**Hoeveel kost het...?**	hoovayl kost heht
per night	**per nacht**	pehr nahkht
per week	**per week**	pehr √ayk
for bed and breakfast	**voor overnachting met ontbijt**	voar oaverrnahkhting meht ontbaiyt
excluding meals	**zonder maaltijden**	zonderr maaltaiydern
for full board (A.P.)	**voor vol pension**	voar vol pehnsyon
for half board (M.A.P.)	**voor half pension**	voar hahlf pehnsyon
Does that include...?	**Is dat inclusief...?**	iss daht inklewseef
breakfast	**ontbijt**	ontbaiyt
service	**bediening**	berdeening
value-added tax (VAT) *	**B.T.W.**	bay-tay-√ay
Is there any reduction for children?	**Is er een reductie voor kinderen?**	iss ehr ern rerdurksee voar kinderren
Do you charge for the baby?	**Berekent u iets voor de baby?**	berraykernt ew eets voar der baybee
That's too expensive.	**Dat is te duur.**	daht iss ter dewr
Do you have anything cheaper?	**Hebt u niets goedkopers?**	hehpt ew neets ghootkoaperrss

How long? *Hoelang?*

We'll be staying...	**Wij blijven...**	√aiy blaiyvern
overnight only	**alleen vannacht**	ahlayn vahnnahkht
a few days	**een paar dagen**	ern paar daaghern
a week (at least)	**(minstens) een week**	(minsternss) ern √ayk
I don't know yet.	**Ik weet het nog niet.**	ik √ayt heht nokh neet

---

* Americans note: a type of sales tax, called *B.T.W.* in Holland and Belgium. It's always included in purchases, rentals, meals, etc.

NUMBERS, see page 147

Decision *Beslissing*

That's fine. I'll take it.	**Deze is prima.** **Die neem ik.**	**day**zer iss **pree**mah. dee **naym** ik
No. I don't like it.	**Nee. Die bevalt mij niet.**	nay. dee ber**vahlt** maiy neet
It's too...	**Het is te...**	heht iss ter
cold/hot	**koud/warm**	ko°ᵂt/√ahrm
dark/small	**donker/klein**	**donk**err/**klaiyn**
noisy	**lawaaierig**	laa√aaᵉᵉyerrerkh
I asked for a room with a bath.	**Ik heb om een kamer met bad gevraagd.**	ik hehp om ern **kaa**merr meht baht gher**vraakht**
Do you have anything...?	**Hebt u iets...?**	hehpt ew eets
better/bigger	**beters/groters**	**bay**terrss/**ghroa**terrss
cheaper/quieter	**goedkopers/rustigers**	ghoot**koap**errss/**rus**tergherrss
Do you have a room with a better view?	**Hebt u een kamer met een beter uitzicht?**	hehpt ew ern **kaa**merr meht ern **bay**terr urᵉᵂt**zikht**

Registration *Inschrijven*

Upon arrival at a hotel or guesthouse you'll be asked to fill in a registration form (*aanmeldingsformulier—***aan**mehldingsformewleer).

Naam/Voornaam	Name/First name
Naam/Voornaam	Name/First name
Woonplaats/Straat/Nummer	Home town/Street/Number
Nationaliteit/Beroep	Nationality/Occupation
Geboortedatum/-plaats	Date/Place of birth
Datum van aankomst	Arrived on
Paspoortnummer	Passport number
Plaats/Datum	Place/Date
Handtekening	Signature

| What does this mean? | **Wat betekent dit?** | √aht ber**tay**kernt dit |

Mag ik uw paspoort even zien?	May I see your passport, please?
Zoudt u zo vriendelijk willen zijn dit formulier in te vullen?	Would you mind filling in this registration form?
Hier tekenen, alstublieft.	Please sign here.
Hoelang bent u van plan te blijven?	How long will you be staying?

What's my room number?	**Wat is mijn kamer-nummer?**	√aht iss maiyn **kaamerr**-nurmerr
Will you have our luggage sent up?	**Wilt u onze bagage naar boven laten brengen?**	√ilt ew **onzer baaghaa**zher naar **boavern laatern brehng**ern
Where can I park my car?	**Waar kan ik mijn auto parkeren?**	√aar kahn ik maiyn o^ow^toa **pahrkayr**ern
Does the hotel have a garage?	**Heeft het hotel een garage?**	hayft heht hoa**tehl** ern ghaa**raa**zher
I'd like to leave this in the hotel safe.	**Ik wil dit graag in de hotelkluis deponeren.**	ik √il dit ghraakh in der hoa**tehlklur**^ew^ss daypoa**nayr**ern

Hotel staff *Hotelpersoneel*

hall porter	**portier**	por**teer**
maid	**kamermeisje**	**kaamerrmaiy**sher
manager	**directeur**	deerehk**turr**
porter	**kruier**	krur^ew^yerr
receptionist	**receptionist**	raysehptsyonist
switchboard operator	**telefoniste**	taylerfoanister
waiter	**kelner**	**kehl**nerr
waitress	**serveerster**	seh**rvayr**sterr

To attract the attention of staff members say *juffrouw* (**yur**fro^ow^)—Miss, or *mevrouw* (mer**vro**^ow^)—Madam, and *mijnheer* (mer**nayr**)—Sir. Address the waiter as *ober* (**oa**berr) when calling for service.

TELLING THE TIME, see page 153

General requirements *Algemene inlichtingen*

The key to room..., please.	**De sleutel van kamer ..., alstublieft.**	der slurterl vahn kaamerr... ahlstewbleeft
Could you wake me at... please?	**Kunt u mij om... wekken, alstublieft?**	kurnt ew maiy om... √ehkern ahlstewbleeft
When is breakfast/lunch/dinner served?	**Hoe laat is het ontbijt/de lunch/het diner?**	hoo laat iss heht ontbaiyt/der "lunch"/heht deenay
May we have breakfast in our room, please?	**Kunnen wij in onze kamer ontbijten?**	kurnern √aiy in onzer kaamerr ontbaiytern
Where's the shaver socket (outlet)?	**Waar is het stopcontact voor het scheerapparaat?**	√aar iss heht stopkontahkt voar heht skhayrahpaaraat
What's the voltage?	**Wat is het voltage?**	√aht iss heht voltaazher
Can you find me a...?	**Kunt u mij aan een... helpen?**	kurnt ew maiy aan ern... hehlpern
babysitter	**babysitter**	"babysitter"
secretary	**secretaresse**	serkrertaarehsser
typewriter	**schrijfmachine**	skhraiyfmaasheener
May I have a/an/some...?	**Kan ik... krijgen?**	kahn ik... kraiyghern
bath towel	**een badhanddoek**	ern bahthahndook
(extra) blanket	**een (extra) deken**	ern (ehkstraa) daykern
envelopes	**enveloppen**	ehnverloppern
hangers	**kleerhangers**	klayrhahngerrss
hot-water bottle	**een kruik**	ern krur^{ew}k
ice cubes	**ijsblokjes**	aiysblokyerss
needle and thread	**naald en draad**	naalt ehn draat
(extra) pillow	**een (extra) kussen**	ern (ehkstraa) kursern
reading lamp	**een leeslampje**	ern layslahmpyer
soap	**zeep**	zayp
writing paper	**schrijfpapier**	skhraiyfpaapeer
Where's the...?	**Waar is...?**	√aar iss
bathroom	**de badkamer**	der bahtkaamerr
dining room	**de eetzaal**	der aytzaal
emergency exit	**de nooduitgang**	der noatur^{ew}tgahng
hairdresser's	**de kapper**	der kahperr
lift (elevator)	**de lift**	der lift
Where are the toilets?	**Waar zijn de toiletten?**	√aar zaiyn der t√aalehtern

BREAKFAST, see page 38

HOTEL

Telephone—Post (mail) *Telefoon—Post*

Can you get me London 123-45-67?	**Kunt u mij verbinden met London 123 45 67?**	kurnt ew maiy verrbindern meht londern 123 45 67
Do you have any stamps?	**Hebt u postzegels?**	hehpt ew postzaygherlss
Would you post this for me, please?	**Wilt u dit voor mij postem, alstublieft?**	√ilt ew dit voar maiy postern ahlstewbleeft
Is there any mail for me?	**Is er post voor mij?**	iss ehr post voar maiy
Are there any messages for me?	**Heeft iemand een boodschap voor mij achtergelaten?**	hayft eemahnt ern boatskhahp voar maiy ahkhterrgherlaatern
How much are my telephone charges?	**Wat zijn mijn telefoonkosten?**	√aht zaiyn maiyn taylerfoankostern

Difficulties *Moeilijkheden*

The . . . doesn't work.	**. . . werkt niet.**	. . . √ehrkt neet
air conditioning	**de airconditioning**	der "air conditioning"
heating	**de verwarming**	der verr√ahrming
light	**het licht**	heht likht
radio	**de radio**	der raadeeyoa
shower	**de douche**	der doosh
television	**de televisie**	der taylerveezee
The tap (faucet) is dripping.	**De kraan blijft druppelen.**	ker kraan blaiyft drurperlern
There's no hot water.	**Er is geen warm water.**	ehr iss ghayn √ahrm √aarterr
The washbasin is blocked.	**De wastafel is verstopt.**	der √ahstaaferl iss verrstopt
The window is jammed.	**Het raam klemt.**	heht raam klehmt
The curtains are stuck.	**De gordijnen zitten vast.**	der ghordaiynern zittern vahst
The bulb is burned out.	**De lamp is gesprongen.**	der lahmp iss ghersprongern
My bed hasn't been made up.	**Mijn bed is niet opgemaakt.**	maiyn beht iss neet opghermaakt

POST OFFICE AND TELEPHONE, see page 132

Hotel

The... is broken.	... is kapot.	... iss kahpot
blind	de jaloezie	der yaaloozee
lamp	de lamp	der lahmp
plug	de stekker	der stehkerr
shutter	het luik	heht lur^{ew}k
switch	de schakelaar	der skhaakerlaar
Can you get it repaired?	Kunt u het laten repareren?	kurnt ew heht laatern raypaarayrern

Laundry—Dry cleaner's   *Wasserij—Stomerij*

I'd like these clothes...	Ik wil deze kleren laten...	ik √il dayzer klayrern laatern
cleaned	stomen	stoamern
ironed	strijken	straiykern
pressed	persen	pehrsern
washed	wassen	√ahsern
When will they be ready?	Wanneer zijn ze klaar?	√ahnayr zaiyn zer klaar
I need them...	Ik heb ze... nodig.	ik hehp zer... noaderkh
today	vandaag	vahndaakh
tonight	vanavond	vahnaavont
tomorrow	morgen	morghern
before Friday	voor vrijdag	voar vraiydahkh
Can you... this?	Kunt u dit...?	kurnt ew dit
mend	repareren	raypaarayrern
patch	verstellen	verrstehlern
stitch	naaien	naa^{ee}yern
Can you sew on this button?	Kunt u deze knoop aanzetten?	kurnt ew dayzer knoap aanzehtern
Can this be invisibly mended?	Kan dit onzichtbaar gestopt worden?	kahn dit onzikhtbaar gherstopt √ordern
Can you get this stain out?	Kunt u deze vlek verwijderen?	kurnt ew dayzer vlehk verr√aiyderrern
Is my laundry ready?	Is mijn was klaar?	iss maiyn √ahss klaar
This isn't mine.	Dit is niet van mij.	dit iss neet vahn maiy
There's something missing.	Er ontbreekt iets.	ehr ontbraykt eets
There's a hole in this.	Hier zit een gat in.	heer zit ern ghaht in

Hairdresser—Barber *Dameskapper—Herenkapper*

Is there a hair-dresser/beauty salon in the hotel?	**Is er een kapper/ schoonheidssalon in het hotel?**	iss ehr ern **kahperr**/ **skhoanhaiytssaalon** in heht **hoatehl**
Can I make an appointment for...?	**Kan ik een afspraak voor... maken?**	kahn ik ern **ahfspraak** voar... **maakern**
Could you... my hair, please?	**Kunt u mijn haar..., alstublieft?**	kurnt ew maiyn haar... **ahlstewbleeft**
blow-dry/cut dye/tint	**föhnen/knippen verven/tinten**	**furnern/knippern vehrvern/tintern**
with a fringe (bangs)	**met pony**	meht ponnee
I'd like a/some...	**Ik wil graag...**	ik √il ghraakh
colour rinse	**een kleurspoeling**	ern **klurrspooling**
face pack	**een gezichtsmasker**	ern **gherzikhts**mahskerr
manicure	**een manicure**	ern maaneekewrer
permanent wave	**een permanent**	ern pehrmaanehnt
setting lotion	**een haarversteviger**	ern **haarverrstayvergherr**
shampoo and set	**wassen en water-golven**	√ahssern ehn √aaterr-gholvern
I'd like a shampoo for... hair.	**Ik wil een shampoo voor... haar.**	ik √il ern **shampoa** voar... haar
normal/dry/ greasy (oily)	**normaal/droog/vet**	normaal/droakh/veht
Do you have a colour chart?	**Hebt u een kleuren-kaart?**	hehpt ew ern **klurrernkaart**
I don't want any hairspray.	**Ik wil geen haarlak.**	ik √il ghayn **haarlahk**

... and at the barber's:

I'd like a haircut, please.	**Ik wil graag mijn haar laten knippen.**	ik √il ghraakh maiyn haar laatern knippern
Don't cut it too short.	**Knipt u het niet te kort.**	knipt ew heht neet ter kort
A little more off the...	**Nog iets korter...**	nokh eets korterr
back	**van achteren**	vahn **ahkh**terrern
neck	**in de nek**	in der nehk
sides	**aan de zijkanten**	aan der **zaiy**kahntern
top	**bovenop**	**boavernop**

DAYS OF THE WEEK, see page 151

I'd like a shave.	**Ik wil mij laten scheren.**	ik √il maiy laatern skhayrern
Would you trim my..., please.	**Wilt u mijn... bijknippen?**	√ilt ew maiyn... baiyknippern
beard	**baard**	baart
moustache	**snor**	snor
sideboards (sideburns)	**bakkebaarden**	bahkerbaardern

Checking out   *Vertrek*

May I have my bill, please?	**Mag ik mijn rekening, alstublieft?**	mahkh ik maiyn raykerning ahlstewbleeft
I'm leaving early in the morning.	**Ik vertrek morgen-ochtend vroeg.**	ik verrtrehk morghern-okhternt vrookh
Please have my bill ready.	**Wilt u mijn rekening klaarmaken, alstublieft.**	√ilt ew maiyn raykerning klaarmaakern ahlstewbleeft
We'll be checking out around noon.	**Wij vertrekken om-streeks 12 uur.**	√aiy verrtrehkern omstrayks t√aalf ewr
I must leave at once.	**Ik moet onmiddellijk vertrekken.**	ik moot onmidderlerk vertrehkern
Is everything included?	**Is alles inbegrepen?**	iss ahlerss inberghraypern
Can I pay by credit card?	**Kan ik met een credit card betalen?**	kahn ik meht ern "credit card" bertaalern
I think there's a mistake in the bill.	**Ik geloof dat er een vergissing in de rekening gemaakt is.**	ik gherloaf daht ehr ern verrghissing in der raykerning ghermaakt iss
Can you get us a taxi?	**Kunt u een taxi voor ons bestellen?**	kurnt ew ern tahksee voar onss berstehlern
Could you have our luggage brought down?	**Kunt u onze bagage naar beneden laten brengen?**	kurnt ew onzer baaghaazher naar bernaydern laatern brehngern
Here's the forward-ing address.	**Hier is mijn volgende adres.**	heer iss maiyn volghernder aadrehss
You have my home address.	**U hebt mijn huis-adres.**	ew hehpt maiyn hur^ewss-aadrehss
It's been a very enjoyable stay.	**Het is een erg prettig verblijf geweest.**	heht iss ern ehrkh prehtikh verrblaiyf gher√ayst

TIPPING, see inside back-cover

Camping *Kamperen*

There are many excellent camp sites in Holland and Belgium. No special permit is required. Charges vary from place to place. The Netherlands National Tourist Office and local VVV offices will provide you with a list of camp sites. Camping is only permitted on specially designated sites.

Is there a camp site near here?	**Is hier een kampeerterrein in de buurt?**	iss heer ern kahmpayrtehraiyn in der bewrt
Can we camp here?	**Mogen wij hier kamperen?**	moaghern √aiy heer kahmpayrern
Do you have room for a tent/caravan (trailer)?	**Hebt u plaats voor een tent/caravan?**	hehpt ew plaats voar ern tehnt/"caravan"
What's the charge...?	**Wat kost het...?**	√aht kost heht
per day	**per dag**	pehr dahkh
per person	**per persoon**	pehr perrsoan
for a car	**voor een auto**	voar ern oᵒʷtoa
for a tent	**voor een tent**	voar ern tehnt
for a caravan (trailer)	**voor een caravan**	voar ern "caravan"
Is tourist tax included?	**Is de verblijfsbelasting inbegrepen?**	iss der verrblaiyfsberlahsting inberghraypern
Is there/Are there (a)...?	**Is er/Zijn er...?**	iss ehr/zaiyn ehr
cooking facilities	**kookgelegenheid**	koakgherlayghernhaiyt
drinking water	**drinkwater**	drink√aaterr
electricity	**elektriciteit**	aylehktreeseetaiyt
playground	**een speelplaats**	ern spaylplaats
restaurant	**een restaurant**	ern rehstoarahnt
shopping facilities	**winkels**	√inkerls
swimming pool	**een zwembad**	ern z√ehmbaht
Where are the...?	**Waar zijn...?**	√aar zaiyn
showers	**de douches**	der doosherss
toilets	**de toiletten**	der t√aalehtern
Where can I get butane gas?	**Waar kan ik butagas krijgen?**	√aar kahn ik bewtaaghahss kraiyghern
Is there a youth hostel near here?	**Is hier een jeugdherberg in de buurt?**	iss heer ern yurkhthehrbehrkh in der bewrt

CAMPING EQUIPMENT, see page 106

Eating out

Bar
(bahr)

A sophisticated establishment where all sorts of drinks are served.

Bistro
(beestroa)

A cosy place to eat, where tasty meals are served.

Broodjeswinkel
(broatyers√inkerl)

A sandwich shop; serves a wide variety of sandwiches made of *broodjes* (rolls) with different types of meat, fish and cheese. This is one of the Dutchman's favourite places for lunch or a quick snack.

Café
(kahfay)

This is the place where the Dutch go to have a drink and to play billiards.

Cafetaria
(kahfertaareeyaa)

Serves hot meals and is often self-service.

Croissanterie
(krwahsahngterree)

A place serving different types of French *croissants* and open sandwiches of French bread with ham and cheese, shrimps, mushrooms or onions; coffee, tea and soft drinks are also available.

Hotel
(hoatehl)

Most hotel restaurants are open to the public.

Koffieshop
(koffeeshop)

A coffee house where the Dutch go for their *kopje koffie* (cup of coffee) and *gebak* (pastries).

Motel
(moatehl)

Eating place along main roads; international choice of food.

Pannekoekhuisje
(pahnerkookhur^ewsher)

A pancake house serving a wide variety of *flensjes* (a thin type of pancake) and *pannekoeken* (pancakes). You could also try *poffertjes* (a kind of small round pancake) served with icing sugar.

Proeflokaal
(proofloakaal)

A bar/shop where you can sample various local drinks. Here you can try *jenever* (Dutch gin). There are also lemon- and blackcurrant-flavoured jenevers.

Restaurant
(rehstoarahnt)

Many restaurants in Holland specialize in French, Italian, Indonesian, Greek, Japanese, Indian and Turkish cooking. A few of them even advertise *Dutch restaurant,* in English, on the door.

Snackbar ("snackbar")	Useful for a bite on the run. For snacks see page 62.
Tea-room ("tea-room")	These serve tea and coffee. The Dutch like to take their tea between 3 and 5 p.m. with *koekjes* (biscuits) or *gebak* (pastry).
Wegrestaurant (**v**ehghrehstoarahnt)	Eating place along main roads; international choice of food.

Meal times

Breakfast (*ontbijt*—ont**bayt**) is served between 7 and 10 a.m.

Lunch *(lunch)* or the Dutch *koffietafel* (see below) is served from noon until 2 p.m.

Dinner (*diner*—dee**nay**) is usually served between 6 and 8 p.m.

Eating habits

If you start your day the Dutch way, your breakfast will consist of three or four kinds of bread or rolls, ham, sliced cheese and maybe an egg, plus a delicious breakfast cake called *ontbijtkoek*. After such a hearty meal you probably won't want a three-course lunch, so try a *koffietafel* (**ko**ffeetaaferl), a lunch consisting of soup or salad followed by a selection of bread, cold cuts, cheese and possibly a warm dish; coffee, milk or tea is included in the meal. You can, of course, also just have a quick sandwich at a sandwich shop, *broodjeswinkel,* or go to a street stall and buy a salt-cured herring. To eat it like any true Dutch person you should hold the fish by the tail, dip it in chopped onions, tip back your head and then bite a piece off. In the afternoon you'll be tempted by pastries and *poffertjes* (**po**ffertyes), a kind of pancake—but try to save some space for a Dutch or Indonesian meal in the evening.

Many restaurants throughout Holland offer a tourist menu, consisting of a set-price, three course meal. This is generally good simple fare, and cheaper than à la carte. These restaurants can be recognized by the emblem shown here.

TOURIST
MENU

Dutch cuisine   *De Hollandse keuken*

Typical Dutch cooking is very filling: the Dutch like hearty meals, especially when the weather is cold. Strangely enough it is hard to find a Dutch restaurant that serves authentic local cuisine. In most restaurants you'll find on the menu a choice of international dishes and a number of Dutch specialities.

Centuries of Dutch colonial presence in what is now Indonesia have added another dimension to the cuisine of the Netherlands. Rice-based, sometimes spicy, Indonesian- and Chinese-influenced food is found in many restaurants throughout the country.

Although Indonesian and Chinese restaurants abound, there is also a large selection of ethnic restaurants serving French, Italian, Greek, Yugoslavian, Japanese and even Thai food.

Wat wenst u?	What would you like?
Ik kan u dit aanbevelen.	I recommend this.
Wat wilt u drinken?	What would you like to drink?
Wij hebben geen...	We don't have...
Wilt u...?	Would you like...?

Hungry?   *Hongerig?*

I'm hungry/I'm thirsty.	**Ik heb honger/Ik heb dorst.**	ik hehp **hong**err/ik hehp dorst
Can you recommend a good restaurant?	**Kunt u een goed restaurant aan-bevelen?**	kurnt ew ern ghoot rehstoa**rahnt** aanbervay**lern**

If you want to be sure of getting a table in a popular restaurant, it may be better to book in advance.

I'd like to reserve a table for 4.	**Ik wil graag een tafel reserveren voor 4 personen.**	ik √il ghraakh ern taaferl rayzehrvayrern voar 4 pehrsoanern
We'll come at 8.	**Wij komen om 8 uur.**	√aiy koamern om 8 ewr
Could we have a table...?	**Kunnen wij een tafel... krijgen?**	kurnern √aiy ern taaferl... kraiyghern
in the corner	**in de hoek**	in der hook
by the window	**bij het raam**	baiy heht raam
outside	**buiten**	bur**ew**tern
on the terrace	**op het terras**	op heht tehrahss
in a non-smoking area	**in een niet-roken gedeelte**	in ern neet roakern gherd**aiy**ter

Asking and ordering *Vragen en bestellen*

Waiter/Waitress!	**Ober/Juffrouw!**	oaberr/yurfro**ow**
I'd like something to eat/drink.	**Ik wil graag iets eten/drinken.**	ik √il ghraakh eets aytern/drinkern
May I have the menu, please?	**Mag ik de kaart hebben, alstublieft?**	makhk ik der kaart hehbern ahlstewbleeft
Do you have...?	**Hebt u...?**	hehpt ew
a children's menu	**een kindermenu**	ern kinderrmernew
a set menu	**een menu van de dag**	ern mernew vahn der dahkh
local dishes	**speciale gerechten van deze streek**	spaysyaaler gherrehkhtern vahn dayzer strayk
What do you recommend?	**Wat kunt u aanbevelen?**	√aht kurnt ew **aan**-bervaylern
Do you have anything ready quickly?	**Hebt u iets dat snel klaar is?**	hehpt ew eets daht snehl klaar iss
I'm in a hurry.	**Ik heb haast.**	ik hehp haast
Could we have a/an..., please?	**Kunnen we een... krijgen?**	kurnern √er ern... kraiyghern
ashtray	**asbak**	ahsbahk
cup	**kopje**	kopyer
fork	**vork**	vork
glass	**glas**	ghlahss
knife	**mes**	mehss
napkin (serviette)	**servet**	sehrveht
plate	**bord**	bort
spoon	**lepel**	layperl

NUMBERS, see page 147

I'd like...	**Ik wil graag...**	ik √il ghraakh
May I have some...?	**Mag ik... hebben?**	mahkh ik... hehbern
bread/butter	**brood/boter**	broat/boaterr
oil/vinegar	**olie/azijn**	oalee/aazaiyn
salt/pepper	**zout/peper**	zoᵒwt/payperr

Some useful expressions for those with special requirements:

I'm on a diet.	**Ik ben op dieet.**	ik behn op deeayt
I'm a vegetarian.	**Ik ben vegetariër.**	ik behn vayghaytaareeyerr
I don't drink alcohol.	**Ik drink geen alcohol.**	ik drink ghayn ahlkoahol
I don't eat meat.	**Ik eet geen vlees.**	ik ayt ghayn vlayss
I mustn't eat food containing...	**Ik mag geen gerechten die... bevatten.**	ik mahkh ghayn gherrehkhtern dee... bervahtern
fat/flour	**vet/meel**	veht/mayl
salt/sugar	**zout/suiker**	zoᵒwt/surᵉwkerr
Do you have... for diabetics?	**Hebt u... voor diabetici?**	hehpt ew... voar deeyaabayteesee
cakes	**koekjes**	kookyers
fruit juice	**vruchtesap**	vrurkhtersahp
a special menu	**een speciaal menu**	ern spaysyaal mernew
Do you have any vegetarian dishes?	**Hebt u vegetarische gerechten?**	hehpt ew vayghaytaareeser gherrehkhtern
Could I have... instead of dessert?	**Kan ik... krijgen in plaats van dessert?**	kahn ik... kraiyghern in plaats vahn dehsehrt
Can I have an artificial sweetener?	**Kan ik kunstmatige zoetstof krijgen?**	kahn ik kurnstmaatergher zootstof kraiyghern

And...

Can I have more..., please?	**Kan ik wat meer... krijgen, alstublieft?**	kahn ik √aht mayr... kraiyghern ahlstewbleeft
Just a small portion.	**Slechts een kleine portie.**	slehkhts ern klaiyner porsee
Nothing more, thanks.	**Niets meer, dank u.**	neets mayr dahnk ew
Where are the toilets?	**Waar zijn de toiletten?**	√aar zaiyn der t√aalehtern

Breakfast *Ontbijt*

The Dutch breakfast, or *ontbijt,* consists of coffee or tea, three or four types of bread or rolls and a kind of honey cake (*ontbijtkoek*—ont**baiyt**kook), as well as cheese, ham, jam and sometimes a boiled egg. Many of the larger hotels, however, also provide an English or American breakfast.

I'd like breakfast, please.	Ik wil graag een ontbijt, alstublieft.	ik √il ghraakh ern ont**baiyt** ahlstew**bleeft**
I'll have a/an/some...	Ik wil graag...	ik √il ghraakh
bacon and eggs	spiegeleieren met ontbijtspek	**spee**gherlaiyyerrern meht ont**baiyt**spehk
boiled egg	een gekookt ei	ern gher**koakt** aiy
hard boiled	hardgekookt	**hahrt**gherkoakt
soft boiled	zachtgekookt	**zahkht**gherkoakt
cereal	cornflakes	**korn**flayks
eggs	eieren	**aiy**yerrern
fried eggs	spiegeleieren	**spee**gherlaiyyerrern
scrambled eggs	roerei	**roor**aiy
fruit juice	vruchtesap	**vrurkht**ersahp
grapefruit juice	grapefruitsap	,,grapefruit''sahp
ham and eggs	ham en eieren	zahm ehn **aiy**yerrern
jam	jam	zhehm
marmalade	marmelade	mahr**mer**laader
slices of bread	een paar sneden brood	ern paar **snay**dern broat
toast	toast	,,toast''
May I have some...?	Mag ik... hebben?	mahkh ik... **heh**bern
butter	boter	**boat**err
(hot) chocolate	(warme) chocolademelk	(√**ahr**mer) shoakoa**laa**dermehlk
cheese	kaas	kaass
coffee	koffie	**kof**fee
decaffeinated	cafeïnevrije	kahfayeenervraiyer
black/with milk	zwart/met melk	z√ahrt/meht mehlk
honey	honing	**hoan**ing
(cold/hot) milk	(koude/warme) melk	(ko**ow**der/√**ahr**mer) mehlk
pepper	peper	**pay**perr
rolls	een paar broodjes	ern paar **broat**yers
salt	zout	zo**ow**t
tea	thee	tay
with milk/lemon	met melk/citroen	meht mehlk/see**troon**
(hot) water	(warm) water	(√ahrm) √**aat**err

What's on the menu? *Wat staat er op het menu?*

Restaurants now often display a menu *(menukaart* or *spijskaart)* outside. Besides ordering à la carte, you can usually order a set menu *(menu van de dag)*. Some restaurants offer a dish of the day *(dagschotel)* at a modest price. Menus are often printed in two or three languages, almost always including English.

Under the headings below you'll find alphabetical lists of items that might be offered on a Dutch menu, with their English equivalent. You can simply show the book to the waiter. If you want some vegetables, for instance, let *him* point to what's available on the appropriate list. Use pages 36 and 37 for ordering in general.

Reading the menu *De menukaart bekijken*

Dagschotel	Dish of the day
Menu van de dag	Set menu/Menu of the day
Kindermenu	Children's menu
Toeristenmenu	Tourist menu
Specialiteit van het huis	Speciality of the house
Speciaal aanbevolen...	We recommend...
Eigengemaakt	Home-made
Naar keuze...	Choice of...
Indien voorradig	When available
Op bestelling	Made to order
Voor twee personen	For two
Bereidingstijd: 15 min.	Waiting time: 15 minutes
...bij de prijs inbegrepen	...included in the price
Toeslag	Extra charge

aardappelen	aardahperlern	potatoes
bier	beer	beer
bijgerechten	baiygherrehkhtern	side dishes
drankjes	drahnkyers	drinks
eiergerechten	aiyyergherrehkhtern	egg dishes
fruit/vruchten	frur^{ew}t/vrurkhtern	fruit
gegrilde gerechten	gherghrilder gherrehkhtern	grills
geroosterd	gherroasterrt	grilled
gevogelte	ghervoaghehlter	poultry
groenten	ghroontern	vegetables
hoofdgerecht	hoaftgherrehkht	main course
mineraalwater	meenerraalvaaterr	mineral water
nagerecht	naagherrehkht	dessert
salades	saalaaders	salads
schaal- en schelpdieren	skhaal- ehn skhehlp-deerern	seafood
soepen	soopern	soups
vis	viss	fish
vlees	vlayss	meat
voorgerechten	voargherrehkhtern	starters (appetizers)
wijn	√aiyn	wine
wild	√ilt	game

Starters (appetizers) *Voorgerechten*

The Dutch make a lot of their snacks, or *borrelhapjes* (**bor**-relhahpyerss), when inviting people over for drinks: small portions of toast topped with various garnishes; vegetable dips; *zebras*—layers of rye bread alternating with cream-cheese, cut in tiny pieces, etc.

In restaurants fish is often served as a first course. Freshly caught, salt-cured herring—called "new herring" *(nieuwe haring* or *Hollandse nieuwe)*—is a treat not to be missed, as are the big Zeeland oysters and mussels.

I'd like a starter (appetizer).	**Ik wil graag een voorgerecht.**	ik √il ghraakh ern **voar**gherrekht
ansjovis	ahn**shoa**viss	anchovies
aspergepunten	ahs**pehr**zherpurntern	aspargus tips
bitterballen	**bitter**bahlern	small round breaded meatballs
champignons op toast	shahmpee**ñonss** op toast	button mushrooms on toast
gevulde eieren	gher**vuI**der **aiy**yerrern	stuffed eggs
garnalen	ghahr**naa**lern	prawns (shrimp)
-**cocktail**	-koktayl	...cocktail
-**kroketten**	-kroa**keh**tern	...croquettes
gevarieerde hors d'œuvre	ghervaa**ree**yayrder hordervr	assorted appetizers
haring	**haa**ring	herring
gerookte	gher**roak**ter	smoked
nieuwe	**nee**ºº√er	salt-cured
kaasbroodje	**kaas**broatyer	Welsh rarebit
kaassoufflé	**kaas**sooflay	cheese soufflé
kaviaar	**kaa**veeyaar	caviar
kievitseieren	**kee**veetsaiyyerrern	plover's eggs
krabcocktail	**krahp**koktayl	crabmeat cocktail
kreeft	krayft	lobster
kreeftecocktail	**krayf**terkoktayl	lobster cocktail
makreel	maa**krayl**	mackerel
gemarineerd	ghermaa**ree**nayrt	marinated
mosselen	**mos**serlern	mussels
oesters	**oos**terrss	oysters
paling	**paa**ling	eel
gerookte	gher**roak**ter	smoked
gesmoorde	gher**smoar**der	stewed

pasteitje	pahs**tai**yter	pastry shell with filling
schelvislever	s**kehl**vislayverr	haddock liver
(gevulde) tomaten	(gher**vul**der) toa**maa**tern	(stuffed) tomatoes
(gerookte) zalm	(gher**roak**ter) zahlm	(smoked) salmon

Hollandse nieuwe (hollahntser nee°°√er)	freshly caught, salt-cured herring served on toast, sometimes with chopped onions
Russisch ei (rurseess aiy)	hard-boiled eggs, halved and garnished with mayonnaise, herring, prawns, capers, anchovies and sometimes caviar; served on lettuce
zure haring (zewrer **haa**ring)	marinated herring, served on bread or toast

Salad dishes   *Salades*

A green or mixed salad (see page 49) is usually eaten with the main course. Other salads may be ordered as a first course or as part of a *koffietafel* (see page 34).

What salads do you have?	**Welke soorten salade hebt u?**	√**ehl**ker **soar**tern saa**laa**der hehpt ew
eiersalade (**aiy**errsaalaader)	hard-boiled eggs, asparagus, gherkins (pickles) and mayonnaise	
haringsalade (**haa**ringsaalaader)	herring, beetroot, apple, potato, gherkins (pickles) and mayonnaise	
huzarensalade (hew**zaa**rernsaalaader)	creamy mix of potato, apple, gherkins (pickles) and ham	
tonijnsalade (toa**naiy**nsaalaader)	creamy mix of tuna, potato and vegetables	

Egg dishes   *Eiergerechten*

boerenomelet	**boo**rernommerleht	omelet with diced vegetables and bacon
omelet	**om**mer**leht**	omelet
fines herbes	feen zehrb	with herbs
met champignons	meht shah**mpee**ñonss	with mushrooms
met ham	meht hahm	with ham
met kaas	meht kaass	with cheese
met kippelevertjes	meht **kip**perlayverrtyerss	with chicken livers
roerei	**roo**raiy	scrambled eggs
spiegeleieren met	**speegh**erlaiyyerrern	ham and eggs
ham	meht hahm	

Soups *Soepen*

Soups are an important part of Dutch cooking. They are either served as a hot dish with the traditional Dutch *koffie-tafel* (see page 34) or as a first course. Two types of soup can be found on menus: *heldere soep* (consommé or clear soup) and *gebonden soep* (cream).

aardappelsoep	aardahperlsoop	potato soup
aspergesoep	ahspehrzhersoop	asparagus soup
bisque de homard	beesk der omaar	lobster bisque
bloemkoolsoep	bloomkoalsoop	cauliflower soup
bouillon	boo**ee**yon	clear soup
met croutons	meht krootonss	with fried bread cubes
met groenten	meht ghroontern	with shredded vegetables
met kip	meht kip	with shredded chicken
Franse uiensoep	frahnser ur**ew**yernsoop	french onion soup
groentesoep (met balletjes)	ghroontersoop (meht bahlertyerss)	vegetable soup (with meat balls)
kerriesoep	kehreesoop	curry soup
kervelsoep	kehrverlsoop	chervil soup
kippesoep	kippersoop	chicken soup
koninginnesoep	koaninginnersoop	cream of chicken
kreeftesoep	krayftersoop	lobster bisque
oestersoep	oosterrsoop	oyster soup
ossestaartsoep	osserstaartsoop	oxtail soup
palingsoep	paalingsoop	cream of eel
preisoep	praiysoop	cream of leek
selderijsoep	sehlderraiysoop	celery soup
soep van de dag	soop vahn der dahkh	soup of the day
spinaziesoep	speenaazeesoop	spinach soup
tomatensoep	toamaaternsoop	tomato soup
vermicellisoep	vehrmersehleesoop	clear noodle soup
vissoep	vissoop	fish soup

and if you're very hungry try:

bruine bonesoep (brur**ew**ner boanernsoop)	red kidney-bean soup, a rich and thick soup; a small meal in itself
erwtensoep (met kluif) (ehrternsoop meht klur**ew**f)	Holland's famous thick pea soup with pieces of smoked sausage, cubes of pork fat and pig's knuckle; served with pumpernickel or brown bread

Fish and seafood   *Vis, schaal- en schelpdieren*

Sole is plentiful and served in a dozen classically French ways: with fruit, with prawns, with mushrooms, in a white sauce—even just poached or grilled on its own. Smoked eel is a Dutch delight you just shouldn't miss and local oysters and mussels are available from September to March.

I'd like some fish.	**Ik wil graag vis.**	ik vil ghraakh viss
What kind of seafood do you have?	**Wat voor schaal- en schelpdieren hebt u?**	vaht voar skhaal- ehn skhehlpdeerern hehpt ew

baars	baarss	perch
bokking	bokking	kipper
brasem	braaserm	bream
forel	foarehl	trout
garnalen	ghahrnaalern	prawns (shrimp)
haring	haaring	herring
heilbot	haiylbot	halibut
kabeljauw	kahberlyo^ow	cod
karper	kahrperr	carp
krab	krahp	crab
kreeft	krayft	lobster
langoest	lahngghoost	spiny lobster
maatjesharing	maatyershaaring	matie, maty
makreel	maakrayl	mackerel
mosselen	mosserlern	mussels
oesters	oosterrss	oysters
paling	paaling	eel
poon	poan	gurnard
rivierkreeft	reeveerkrayft	crayfish
sardines	sahrdeenerss	sardines
schar	skhahr	dab
schelvis	skhehlviss	haddock
schol	skhol	plaice
snoek	snook	pike
sprot	sprot	sprats
tarbot	tahrbot	turbot
tong	tong	sole
tongschar	tongskhahr	lemon sole
tonijn	toanaiyn	tuna
wijting	vaiyting	whiting
zalm	zahlm	salmon
zeehaan	zayhaan	(red) mullet
(kleine) zeekreeft	(klaiyner) zaykrayft	scampi
zeewolf	zayvolf	catfish

Fish are prepared in many different ways, you'll probably come across some of these:

gebakken	gherbahkern	fried
gebakken, in de oven	gherbahkern in der oavern	baked
gefrituurd	gherfreetewrt	deep fried
gegrild	gherghrillt	grilled (broiled)
gekookt	gherkoakt	boiled
gemarineerd	ghermaareenayrt	marinated
gepaneerd	gherpaanayrt	breaded
gepocheerd	gherposhayrt	poached
gerookt	gherroakt	smoked
geroosterd	gherroasterrt	grilled (broiled)
gesmoord	ghersmoart	braised
gestoofd	gherstoaft	stewed
gestoomd	gherstoamt	steamed
gevuld	ghervurlt	stuffed

Specialities worth trying:

forel à la meunière
(foarehl ah lah murnyehrer)
trout fried in butter and served with lemon and parsley

gerookte paling
(gherroakter paaling)
delicately smoked eel, served on toast when eaten for lunch or as a starter; as a main meal it will be served with potatoes and salad

mosselen
(mosserlern)
mussels served with a mustard sauce and chips (French fries)

paling in het groen
(paaling in heht ghroon)
eel stewed with white wine; served in a herb sauce flavoured with chervil, chives, taragon or dill (a Belgian speciality)

snoekbaars met mosterdsaus
(snookbaarss meht mosterrtso^ow^ss)
fried perch-pike with a mustard sauce. Boiled potatoes, vegetables or a salad generally accompanies this dish

stokvis
(stokviss)
stockfish; dried cod with rice, fried potatoes, onions and mustard sauce

zeetong doria
(zaytong doareeyaa)
rolled-up and poached fillets of sole, cucumber and *ravigote* sauce on a bed of rice

Meat *Vlees*

I'd like some...	**Ik wil graag...**	ik √il ghraakh... **hehbern**
	hebben.	
beef	**rundvlees**	**rurnt**vlayss
lamb	**lamsvlees**	**lahms**vlayss
pork	**varkensvlees**	**vahr**kensvlayss
veal	**kalfsvlees**	**kahlfs**vlayss
biefstuk	**beefsturk**	pan-fried beef
biefstuk van de haas	**beefsturk vahn der haass**	porterhouse steak
biefstuk tartaar	**beefsturk tahrtaar**	steak tartare
blinde vinken	**blinder vinkern**	slice of-veal rolled-up and stuffed
braadworst	**braat√orst**	frying sausage
contre-filet	**kontr-feeleh**	sirloin steak
Duitse biefstuk	**dur^{ew}tser beefsturk**	minced-beef steak
entrecôte	**ahntrerkoat**	rib or rib-eye steak
gehaktbal	**gherhahktbahl**	meat ball
Hollandse biefstuk	**hollahntser beefsturk**	loin of T-bone steak
kalfsborst	**kahlfsborst**	breast of veal
kalfshaas	**kahlfshaass**	tenderloin of veal
kalfskotelet	**kahlfskoaterleht**	veal cutlet
kalfsoester	**kahlfsoosterr**	thin fillet of veal
kalfstong	**kahlfstong**	veal tongue
karbonade	**kahrboanaader**	chop/cutlet
kotelet	**koaterleht**	chop/cutlet
krabbetje	**krahbertyer**	spare ribs
lamsbout	**lahmsbo^{ow}t**	leg of lamb
lamskotelet	**lahmskoaterleht**	lamb chop
lever	**layverr**	liver
niertjes	**neertyerss**	kidneys
ossehaas	**osserhaas**	fillet of beef
ossetong	**ossertong**	beef tongue
rookworst	**roak√orst**	smoked sausage
rosbief	**rosbeef**	roast beef
runderlap	**rurnderrlahp**	slice of beef
runderrollade	**rurnderrollaader**	roast roll of beef
saucijsjes	**soa**saiy**sherss**	sausages
speenvarken	**spaynvahrkern**	suck(l)ing-pig
spek	**spehk**	bacon
tournedos	**toornerdoa**	thick round fillet steak
varkenshaas	**vahrkernshaass**	pork tenderloin
varkenskarbonade	**vahrkernskahrboanaader**	pork chop
worst	**√orst**	sausage
zwezerik	**z√ayzerrik**	sweetbreads

baked	**in de oven gebakken**	in der oavern gherbahkern
boiled	**gekookt**	gherkoakt
braised	**gesmoord**	ghersmoart
breaded	**gepaneerd**	gherpaanayrt
fried	**gebakken**	gherbahkern
grilled (broiled)	**gegrild/geroosterd**	gherghrilt/gherroasterrt
minced	**gehakt**	gherhahkt
roasted	**gebraden**	gherbraadern
sautéed	**snel aangebraden**	snehl aangherbraadern
smoked	**gerookt**	gherroakt
steamed	**gestoomd**	gherstoamt
stewed	**gestoofd**	gherstoaft
underdone (rare)	**niet gaar/rood**	neet ghaar/roat
medium	**net gaar gebakken**	neht ghaar gherbahkern
well-done	**doorgebakken**	doargherbahkern

Typical Dutch food is very substantial and consists of dishes like potato and vegetable hash (*stamppot*—**stahm**pot) served with sausages and/or bacon. Here are some dishes you may come across, especially if you're invited to a Dutch home.

boerenkool met worst (boorern**koal** meht √orst)	curly kale and potatoes, served with smoked sausage *(rookworst)*; this is a typical winter dish
hete bliksem (hayter **blik**serm)	potatoes, bacon and apple, seasoned with salt and sugar (the name means ''hot lightning'')
hutspot met klapstuk (**hurt**spot meht **klahp**sturk)	mashed potatoes, carrots and onions mixed together, served with boiled beef *(klapstuk)*; a typical winter dish
jachtschotel (**yahkht**skhoaterl)	a meat casserole with onions and potatoes, often served with apple sauce
rolpens met rode kool (**rol**pehnss meht **roa**der koal)	minced meat and tripe roll, pickled, then sliced and fried, topped with apple and served with red cabbage
zuurkool (**zewr**koal)	sauerkraut; often served with bacon or tender roast partridge

Game and poultry *Wild en gevogelte*

Chicken, duck and turkey are served in Dutch restaurants all through the year. For game you'll have to go to specialized restaurants in hunting areas (mainly in the east and south Netherlands). The hunting season runs from August/September to January/February.

I'd like some game.	**Ik wil graag wild hebben.**	ik √il ghraakh √ilt **heh**bern
I prefer poultry.	**Ik heb liever gevogelte.**	ik hehp **lee**verr ghervoagherlter

braadhaantje	braat**haan**tyer	spring chicken
duif	dur^{ew}f	pigeon
eend	aynt	duck
fazant	fah**zahnt**	pheasant
gans	ghahnss	goose
haantje	**haan**tyer	cockerel
haas	haass	hare
hazepeper	**haa**zerpayperr	jugged hare
houtsnip	ho^{ow}tsnip	woodcock
kalkoen	kahl**koon**	turkey
kip	kip	chicken
gebraden kip	gher**braa**dern kip	roast chicken
kipfilet	kip**fee**lay	chicken breast
kippelevertjes	**kipp**erlayverrtyerss	chicken liver
konijn	koa**naiyn**	rabbit
korhoen	**kor**hoon	grouse
kuiken	kur^{ew}kern	spring chicken
kwartel	k√**ahr**terl	quail
parelhoen	**paar**erlhoon	guinea fowl
patrijs	paa**traiyss**	partridge
reebout/reerug	**ray**bo^{ew}t/**ray**rurkh	venison
smient	smeent	widgeon
taling	**taa**ling	teal
watersnip	**√aa**terrsnip	snipe
wilde eend	**√il**der aynt	wild duck
wild zwijn	√ilt z√**aiyn**	wild boar

With game you'll usually have a choice of side dishes:

Brussels sprouts	**spruitjes**	**sprur**^{ew}tyerss
chestnut purée	**kastanjepuree**	kah**stahn**yerpewray
cranberry sauce	**vossebessen**	**voss**erbehsern
mashed potatoes	**aardappelpuree**	**aar**dahperlpewray

Vegetables *Groenten*

What vegetables do you recommend?	**Welke groente kunt u aanbevelen?**	√ehlker ghroonter kurnt ew aanbervaylern
I prefer a mixed salad.	**Ik heb liever gemengde sla.**	ik hehp leeverr ghermehngder slaa
andijvie	ahndaiyvee	endive (Am. chicory)
artisjokken	ahrteeshokkern	artichoke
asperge(punten)	ahspehrzher(purntern)	asparagus (tips)
bieten	beetern	beetroot
bloemkool	bloomkoal	cauliflower
boerenkool	boorernkoal	kale
bonen	boanern	beans
witte bonen	√itter boanern	white beans
bruine bonen	brur^{ew}ner boanern	kidney beans
broccoli	brokkoalee	broccoli
Brussels lof	brurserlss lof	chicory (Am. endive)
champignons	shahmpeeñonss	button mushrooms
doperwtjes	dopehrrtyerss	peas
kapucijners	kahpewsaiynerrss	marrowfat peas
knolselderij	knolsehlderraiy	celeriac
komkommer	komkommerr	cucumber
kool	koal	cabbage
rode kool	roader koal	red cabbage
zuurkool	zewrkoal	sauerkraut
linzen	linzern	lentils
maïs	mah^{ee}ss	sweet corn
maïskolven	mah^{ee}skolvern	corn on the cob
paprika's	paapreekaass	sweet peppers
peultjes	purltyerss	sugar peas
postelein	posterlaiyn	purslane
prei	praiy	leeks
prinsessenbonen	prinsehsernboanern	French (green) beans
radijs	raadaiyss	radishes
selderij	sehlderraiy	celery
sla	slaa	green salad
snijbonen	snaiyboanern	sliced French beans
sperziebonen	spehrzeeboanern	French (green) beans
spinazie	speenaazee	spinach
spruitjes	sprur^{ew}tyerss	Brussels sprouts
tomaten	toamaatern	tomatoes
tuinbonen	tur^{ew}nboanern	broad beans
uien	ur^{ew}yern	onions
venkel	vehnkerl	fennel
waterkers	√aaterrkehrss	watercress
worteltjes	√orterltyerss	carrots

Potatoes, rice and pasta *Aardappelen, rijst en meelspijzen*

| I'd like some... | **Ik wil graag...** | ik √il ghraakh... |
| | **hebben.** | hehbern |

aardappelen	aardahperlern	potatoes
gebakken	gherbahkern	fried
gekookt	gherkoakt	boiled
in de schil gekookt	in der skhil gherkoakt	in their jackets
nieuwe	nee^{oo}ver	new
aardappelpuree	aardahperlpewray	mashed potatoes
patates frites	paataht freet	chips (French fries)
rijst	raiyst	rice

macaronischotel	creamed macaroni with ham, cheese and
(mahkahroanee-	tomato sauce
skhoaterl)	

Sauces *Sauzen*

The Dutch consume huge quantities of gravy (*saus*—so^{ow}ss or *jus*—zhew) and mayonnaise with their food. In more sophisticated restaurants you'll be served mainly French sauces.

botersaus	a sauce made from butter, flour and stock;
(boaterrso^{ow}s)	often served with fish
gesmolten boter	melted butter, often served with asparagus
(ghersmoltern boaterr)	and fish
Hollandse saus	also called *sauce hollandaise;* butter, flour,
(hollantser so^{ow}ss)	egg yolks and cream
jagersaus	rich sauce with wine, mushrooms, onions,
(yaagherrso^{ow}ss)	shallots and herbs
kaassaus	butter, flour, milk or stock and grated cheese
(kaasso^{ow}ss)	
kappertjessaus	butter, flour, stock and capers; flavoured with
(kahperrtyersso^{ow}ss)	vinegar
mosterdsaus	a white milk sauce flavoured with mustard
(mosterrtso^{ow}ss)	
ravigotesaus	tarragon, chervil, chives, with stock and vine-
(rahveeghotteso^{ow}ss)	gar; served hot or cold
witte wijnsaus	butter, flour, stock, white wine and cream
(√itter √aiynso^{ow}ss)	

... and some of the herbs (*kruiden*—**krur^{ew}dern**):

Dutch	Pronunciation	English
anijs	ahnaiys	aniseed
basilicum	baazeeleekurm	basil
bieslook	beesloak	chives
bonenkruid	boanernkrur^{ew}t	savoury
dille	diller	dill
dragon	draaghon	tarragon
kaneel	kaanayl	cinnamon
kappertjes	kahperrtyerss	capers
kerrie	kehree	curry seasoning
kervel	kehrverl	chervil
knoflook	knofloak	garlic
kruidnagel	krur^{ew}tnaagerl	cloves
kummel	kurmerl	caraway
laurier	lo^{ow}reer	bay leaf
mierikswortel	meeriks√orterl	horseradish
nootmuskaat	noatmurskaat	nutmeg
peterselie	payterrsaylee	parsley
rozemarijn	roazermaaraiyn	rosemary
saffraan	sahfraan	saffron
tijm	taiym	thyme

Cheese   *Kaas*

Cheese is served either at breakfast, with a cold lunch or with aperitifs and rarely at the end of a meal. Young, fresh cheeses are called *jonge kaas,* the older ones *belegen kaas.*

Edammer kaas
(aydahmerr kaass)
a firm mild-flavoured cheese; sealed in red wax (it comes from Edam)

Friese nagelkaas
(freeser naagherlkaass)
made from skimmed milk and cloves (it comes from Friesland)

Goudse kaas
(gho^{ow}tser kaass)
a renowned Dutch cheese, similar to *Edammer kaas* (from Gouda)

Kernhemmer
(kehrnhehmerr kaass)
a Dutch cheese of the soft dessert type; mellow in taste (from Kernhem)

komijnekaas
(koamaiynerkaass)
cumin cheese; well-known names are *Delftse kaas* and *Leidse kaas*

Limburgse kaas
(limburrghserkaass)
a creamy cheese with a spicy taste (from Limburg)

witte meikaas
(√itter maiykaass)
a creamy cheese with a high fat content; made from the first spring milk

Fruit and nuts *Vruchten en noten*

| Do you have fresh fruit? | **Hebt u vers fruit?** | hehpt ew vehrss frur^{ew}t |
| I'd like a fruit salad (of fresh fruit). | **Ik wil graag een vruchtensalade (van verse vruchten).** | ik vil ghraakh ern vrurkhternsaalaader (vahn vehrser vrurkhtern) |

aalbessen	aalbehsern	redcurrants
aardbeien	aartbaiyyern	strawberries
abrikozen	aabreekoazern	apricots
amandelen	aamahnderlern	almonds
ananas	ahnaanahss	pineapple
appel	ahperl	apple
banaan	baanaan	banana
bosbessen	bosbehsern	blueberries/ bilberries
bramen	braamern	blackberries
citroen	seetroon	lemon
dadels	daaderlss	dates
druiven	drur^{ew}vern	grapes
blauwe/witte	blo^{ow}er/vitter	black/green
frambozen	frahmboazern	raspberries
grapefruit	''grapefruit''	grapefruit
groene pruimen	ghrooner prur^{ew}mern	greengages
hazelnoten	haazerlnoatern	hazelnuts
kastanjes	kahstahnyerss	chestnuts
kersen	kehrsern	cherries
zwarte kersen	zvahrter kehrsern	black cherries
kokosnoot	koakosnoat	coconut
kruisbessen	krur^{ew}sbehsern	gooseberries
mandarijn	mahndaaraiyn	tangerine
meloen	merloon	melon
noten	noatern	nuts
peer	payr	pear
perzik	pehrzik	peach
pompelmoes	pomperlmooss	grapefruit
pruimen	prur^{ew}mern	plums
pruimedanten	prur^{ew}merdahntern	prunes
rabarber	raabahrberr	rhubarb
rozijnen	roazaiynern	raisins
sinaasappel	seenaasahperl	orange
studentenhaver	stewdehnternhaaverr	almonds and raisins
vijgen	vaiyghern	figs
walnoten	vahlnoatern	walnuts
watermeloen	vaaterrmerloon	watermelon
zwarte bessen	zvahrter behsern	blackcurrrants

Desserts *Nagerechten*

I'd like a dessert, please.	**Ik wil graag een na-gerecht, alstublieft.**	ik vil ghraakh ern naa-gherrekht ahlstewbleeft
Just a small portion.	**Slechts een kleine portie.**	slehkhts ern klaiyner porsee
Something light, please.	**Iets lichts, graag.**	eets likhts ghraakh
With/Without…	**Met/Zonder…**	meht/zonderr
sugar	**suiker**	sur^{ew}ker
whipped cream	**slagroom**	slahghroam

appeltaart	ahperltaart	apple tart
caramelpudding	kaaraamehlpurding	creme caramel
chocolademousse	shoakoalaadermooss	chocolate mousse
citroenmousse	seetroonmooss	lemon mousse
flensjes	flehnsyerss	thin pancakes
met ananas	meht ahnaanahss	with pineapple
met appel	meht ahperl	with apple
met rozijnen	meht roazaiynern	with raisins
fruit naar keuze	frur^{ew}t naar kurzer	a choice of fruit
gember met slag-room	ghehmberr meht slahghroam	pieces of fresh ginger with whipped cream
ijs	aiyss	ice cream
aardbeien	aartbaiyyern	strawberry
chocolade	shoakoalaader	chocolate
pistache	peestahsh	pistachio
vanille	vaaneeyer	vanilla
ijstaart	aiystaart	ice-cream cake
pannekoeken	pahnerkookern	pancakes
rijstebrijpudding	raiysterbraiypurding	rice pudding
schuimomelet	skhur^{ew}mommerleht	fluffy dessert omelet
sorbet	sorbeht	sorbet (sherbet)
vla	vlaa	custard
yoghurt	''yoghurt''	yoghurt

broodschoteltje (broatskhoaterltyer)	kind of bread pudding with apples, currants or raisins
chipolatapudding (sheepoalaatahpurding)	pudding with biscuits, eggs and liqueur
dame blanche (dahm blahnsh)	vanilla ice cream with hot chocolate sauce
Haagse bluf (haaghser blurf)	dessert of whipped egg whites, served with redcurrant sauce

Indonesian dishes *Indonesische gerechten*

As a result of many centuries of colonial presence in Indonesia (then called the Dutch East Indies), the Dutch developed a taste for spicy foods, and now consider Indonesian food part of Dutch cuisine.

The most famous Indonesian speciality is *rijsttafel* (**raiyst-taaferl**) a real banquet of a meal. It consists of white rice served with an amazing number of small and very tasty dishes: stewed vegetables, delicately prepared beef and chicken, meat on skewers with peanut sauce, fruit and spices, to name only a few. Other dishes worth trying are:

Bami goreng (baamee ghoarehng)	fried *mie* (noodles) and vegetables with diced pork, prawns and shredded omelet
Nasi goreng (nahsee ghoarehng)	fried rice with onions, meat, chicken, prawns, ham and varied spices, usually topped with a fried egg
Nasi rames (nahsee rahmehss)	a mini *rijsttafel*
Babi pangang (baabee pahngghahng)	grilled pork in a sweet-and-sour sauce

The above dishes are often accompanied by *kroepoek* (**kroopook**), golden-brown crisp prawn crackers. On the table you will also find *seroendeng* (ser**roon**derng), a mixture of peanuts, ground coconut and spices, which is sprinkled over Indonesian dishes as a form of condiment. Among the exotic spices, that come with the dishes, are the *sambals* (**sahm-bahls**), peppery-hot pastes which should be used in moderation. The red one is called *sambal oelek* and the slightly milder, brown versions *sambal badjak, sambal brandal* and *sambal manis*.

As for the many side dishes, here are just a few:

Atjar tjampoer (ahtyahr tyahmpoor)	sweet-and-sour shredded vegetables; side dish to *rijsttafel*
Gado gado (gahdoa gahdoa)	a variety of vegetables covered with peanut sauce

Pisang goreng
(peesahng ghoarehng)
fried banana, usually served with *rijsttafel*

Roedjak manis
(roodyahk maaniss)
apples, cucumber and oranges in a soya sauce

Sajoer kerrie
(saayoor kehree)
spicy cabbage soup; side dish to *rijsttafel*

Sajoer lodeh
(saayoor lodder)
kind of soup with vegetables, meat or shrimps

Sateh babi
(sahtay baabee)
grilled cubes of pork on skewers; usually dipped in a spicy peanut sauce

Belgian specialities *Belgische specialiteiten*

ballekessoep
(bahlerkerssoop)
a soup made from beef or chicken stock and onions, turnips, leek and carrots; served with tiny meatballs

hochepot
(hoshpot)
a casserole of beef, pork, mutton, carrots, cabbage, leek, onions, potatoes and spices; garnished with fried sausages

Vlaamse bloedworst
(vlaamser bloot√orst)
black pudding (blood sausage) served with apples; Flemish speciality

Vlaamse karbonade
(ylaamser kahrboa-naader)
slices of beef and onions braised in broth that may contain beer; Flemish speciality

Vlaamse kool
(vlaamser koal)
green cabbage prepared with apples and gooseberry jelly; Flemish speciality

Vlaamse hazepeper
(vlaamser haazer-payperr)
jugged hare stewed with onions and plums; Flemish speciality

waterzooi
(√aaterrzoa^ee)
chicken poached in white wine, with shredded vegetables, cream and egg yolk added

waterzooi met vis
(√aaterrzoa^ee meht viss)
a delicious fish soup

Two somewhat special brands of Belgian beer you might like to try are *Kriekenlambiek* (**kree**kernlahmbeek), a strong Brussels bitter beer flavoured with morello cherries, and *trappistenbier* (trah**pi**sternbeer), a malt beer brewed originally by Trappist monks.

Drinks   *Dranken*

Bars and cafés open at all times of the day, but generally from mid-morning till 1 a.m., or an hour later on Fridays and Saturdays. If you want a beer or a *borreltje* (**bo**rrerltyer)— an aperitif or, more specifically, a jenever—in an authentic Dutch atmosphere, the best places are *bruine cafés,* so called because they are panelled in dark wood and stained by centuries of pipe smoke.

Aperitifs and beer   *Aperitief en bier*

For an aperitif the Dutch have simple tastes—beer and jenever are by far the most popular drinks. The two best-known Dutch beers are *Heineken* and *Amstel*. There is also a dark, sweetish stout called *oud bruin*—o^{ow}t brur^{ew}n (old brown). Belgian beers are renowned (see page 55.) Jenever is a juniper-flavoured spirit, somewhat similar to gin, though not as strong. There are several kinds. *Jonge* (young) jenever is crystal-clear; as it matures it takes on a yellowish tinge, and is known as *oude* (old) jenever. Whatever you ask for, it will be served in a small glass, filled to the brim—it's a real tour de force to get it to your lips without spilling any (especially after a few). Jenever can be referred to as *klare* (undiluted); it is sometimes served with angostura or other bitters, in which case it becomes a *bittertje,* but never with tonic or orange juice. You might prefer a sweetened version: *bessenjenever,* flavoured with blackcurrant, or *citroenjenever,* with lemon.

I'd like a/an...	**Ik wil graag...**	ik vil ghraakh
aperitif	**een aperitief**	ern ahpayree**teef**
beer	**en biertje/een pils**	ern **beer**tyer/ern pilss
dark beer	**een donker bier**	ern **don**kerr beer
light beer	**een licht bier**	ern likht beer
draught (tap) beer	**een bier van het vat**	ern beer vahn heht vaht
port	**port**	port
sherry	**sherry**	**sheh**ree
vermouth	**vermouth**	**vehr**moot

For a wider selection of drinks, see page 58.

I'd like a... of beer.	**Ik wil graag... bier.**	ik vil ghraakh... beer
bottle	**een fles**	ern flehss
glass	**een glas**	ern ghlahss
a small one	**een glaasje**	ern **ghlaa**syer
a large one	**een groot glas**	ern ghroat ghlahss
Waiter! Another beer, please.	**Ober! Nog een bier, alstublieft.**	oaberr nokh ern beer ahlstew**bleeft**

Wine *Wijn*

All wine is imported; there is a comprehensive range of French and German wines on most wine lists. But Italian, Greek and Spanish wines are also becoming popular. For economy's sake ask for open or house wine *(open wijn)*.

May I have the wine list, please?	**Kan ik de wijnkaart krijgen, alstublieft?**	kahn ik der vaiynkaart kraiyghern ahlstew**bleeft**
I'd like... of white wine.	**Ik wil graag... witte wijn.**	ik vil ghraakh... vitter vaiyn
a carafe	**een karaf**	ern kaa**rahf**
a bottle	**een fles**	ern flehss
half a bottle	**een halve fles**	ern **hahl**ver flehss
a glass	**een glas**	ern ghlahss
I'd like another bottle of red wine, please.	**Ik wil graag nog een fles rode wijn.**	ik vil ghraakh nokh ern flehss roader vaiyn
Where does the wine come from?	**Waar komt de wijn vandaan?**	vaar komt der vaiyn vahn**daan**
A bottle of champagne, please.	**Een fles champagne, alstublieft.**	ern flehss shahm**pahn**yer ahlstew**bleeft**

red	**rood**	roat
white	**wit**	vit
rosé	**rosé**	roa**zay**
dry	**droog**	droakh
light	**licht**	likht
full-bodied	**vol**	vol
sparkling	**mousserend**	moo**sayr**ernt
very dry	**brut**	brewt
sweet	**zoet**	zoot

Other alcoholic drinks   *Andere alcoholische dranken*

I'd like a...	**Ik wil graag ...**	ik √il ghraakh
brandy	**een brandewijn**	ern brahnder√aiyn
gin and tonic	**een gin-tonic**	ern zhin tonik
liqueur	**een likeur**	ern leekurr
(double) whisky	**een (dubbele) whisky**	ern (durberler) √iskee
neat (straight)	**puur**	pewr
on the rocks	**met ijsblokjes**	meht aiysblokyerss
with (soda) water	**met (soda) water**	meht (soadaa) √aaterr

Some typical Dutch drinks you may come across:

advokaat	ahtvoakaat	egg liqueur, served with a small spoon
berenburg	bayrernburrkh	Frisian gin
bessenjenever	behsernyernayverr	blackcurrant gin
bisschopswijn	bisskhops√aiyn	mulled claret (warm)
boerenjongens	boorernyongernss	Dutch brandy with raisins
boerenmeisjes	boorernmaiysherss	Dutch brandy with apricots
citroenjenever	seetroonyernayverr	lemon gin
jenever	yernayverr	Dutch gin
jonge jenever	yonger yernayverr	"young" Dutch gin
oude jenever	o^{ow}der yernayverr	"old" Dutch gin
klare	klaarer	jenever
oranjebitter	oarahñerbitterr	orange-flavoured bitters

...and some Dutch liqueurs worth trying:

I'd like to try a glass of..., please.	**Ik wil graag een glas... proberen, alstublieft.**	ik √il ghraakh ern ghlahss... proabayrern ahlstew**bleeft**
Curaçao	kewraaso^{ow}	orange-flavoured
half om half	hahlf om hahlf	sweet strong
parfait'amour	pahrfeh taamoor	highly perfumed, amethyst-coloured

> **PROOST!**
> (proast)
> CHEERS!

Nonalcoholic drinks *Alcoholvrije dranken*

I'd like a/an...	**Ik wil graag...**	ik √il ghraakh
buttermilk	**karnemelk**	kahrnermehlk
fruit juice	**vruchtesap**	vrurkhtersahp
apple juice	**appelsap**	ahperlsahp
grapefruit juice	**grapefruitsap**	"grapefruit"sahp
grape juice	**druivesap**	drur^{ew}versahp
lemon juice	**citroensap**	seetroonsahp
orange juice	**sinaasappelsap**	seenaasahperlsahp
tomato juice	**tomatesap**	toamaatersahp
ginger ale	**gemberbier**	ghehmberrbeer
iced tea	**ijsthee**	aiystay
lemonade	**limonade**	leemoanaader
(glass of) milk	**een (glas) melk**	ern (ghlahss) mehlk
milkshake	**milkshake**	"milkshake"
mineral water	**mineraalwater**	meenerraal√aaterr
fizzy (carbonated)	**met koolzuur**	meht koalzewr
still	**zonder koolzuur**	zonderr koalzewr
soft drink	**een frisdrank**	ern frisdrahnk

Hot drinks *Warme dranken*

Coffee is the national drink and you'll frequently see the announcement *Koffie is klaar* (Coffee is ready). It is usually served black, but you'll be offered cream, *koffiemelk,* a thick evaporated Dutch variety, which should be used sparingly if you want the taste of the coffee to come through. If you are looking for something a little different, then try a *citroenkwast,* a hot lemon squash.

I'd like a/an...	**Ik wil graag...**	ik √il ghraakh
hot chocolate	**een warme choco-lademelk**	ern √ahrmer shoakoa-laadermehlk
coffee	**een koffie**	ern koffee
a pot of	**een potje**	ern potyer
decaffeinated	**cafeïnevrije**	kahfayeenervraiyyer
with cream	**met room**	meht roam
with whipped cream	**met slagroom**	meht slahghroam
espresso	**een espresso**	ern ehsprehsoa
herb tea	**een kruidenthee**	ern krur^{ew}derntay
tea	**een thee**	ern tay
a cup of	**een kopje**	ern kopyer
with lemon/milk	**met citroen/melk**	meht seetroon/mehlk

Complaints *Klachten*

There's a . . . missing.	Er ontbreekt een . . .	ehr ontbraykt ern
plate/glass	**bord/glas**	bort/ghlahss
I don't have a knife/fork/spoon.	**Ik heb geen mes/vork/lepel.**	ik hehp ghayn mehss/vork/**lay**perl
That's not what I ordered.	**Dit heb ik niet besteld.**	dit hehp ik neet ber**stehlt**
I asked for . . .	**Ik heb om . . . gevraagd.**	ik hehp om . . . gher**vraakht**
There must be a mistake.	**Er moet een vergissing zijn.**	ehr moot ern verr**ghissing** zaiyn
May I change this?	**Kunt u mij hiervoor iets anders brengen?**	kurnt ew maiy **heer**voar eets **ahn**derrss **breh**ngern
I asked for a small portion (for the child).	**Ik vroeg een kleine portie (voor het kind).**	ik vrookh ern **klai**yner **por**see (voar heht kint)
The meat is . . .	**Het vlees is . . .**	heht vlayss iss
overdone	**te gaar**	ter ghaar
underdone	**niet gaar**	neet ghaar
too rare	**te rood**	ter roat
too tough	**te taai**	ter taa[ee]
This is too . . .	**Dit is te . . .**	dit iss ter
bitter/salty/sweet	**bitter/zout/zoet**	**bitt**err/zo[ow]t/zoot
I don't like this.	**Ik houd hier niet van.**	ik ho[ow]t heer neet vahn
The food is cold.	**Het eten is koud.**	heht **ay**tern iss ko[ow]t
This isn't fresh.	**Dit is niet vers.**	dit iss neet vehrss
What's taking so long?	**Waarom duurt het zo lang?**	[√]aarom dewrt heht zoa lahng
Have you forgotten our drinks?	**Hebt u onze drankjes vergeten?**	hehpt ew **on**zer **drahnk**yerss verrgh**ay**tern
The wine doesn't taste right.	**De wijn smaakt niet goed.**	der [√]aiyn smaakt neet ghoot
This isn't clean.	**Dit is niet schoon.**	dit iss neet skhoan
Would you call the head waiter, please?	**Wilt u de gerant roepen, alstublieft?**	[√]ilt ew der zhay**rahng** **roo**pern ahlstew**bleeft**

The bill (check) *De rekening*

B.T.W. en bediening inbegrepen. These words simplify your life as a tourist in Holland. They mean: Value Added Tax (sales tax) and service charge included. Anything extra for the waiter is optional.

Credit cards are accepted in an increasing number of restaurants.

I'd like to pay.	**Ik wil graag betalen.**	ik vil ghraakh bertaalern
We'd like to pay separately.	**Wij willen graag apart betalen.**	vaiy villern ghraakh ahpahrt bertaalern
I think there's a mistake in this bill.	**Ik geloof dat er een vergissing is in deze rekening.**	ik gherloaf daht ehr ern verrghissing iss in dayzer raykerning
What's this amount for?	**Waarvoor is dit bedrag?**	vaarvoar iss dit berdrahkh
Is the cover charge included?	**Is het couvert inbegrepen?**	iss heht koovehr inberghraypern
Is everything included?	**Is alles inbegrepen?**	iss ahlerss inberghraypern
Do you accept traveller's cheques?	**Neemt u reischeques aan?**	naymt ew raiysshehks aan
Can I pay with this credit card?	**Kan ik met deze credit card betalen?**	kahn ik meht dayzer "credit card" bertaalern
Please round it up to...	**Wilt u het afronden tot...**	vilt ew heht ahfrondern tot
Keep the change.	**U kunt het wisselgeld houden.**	ew kurnt heht visserlghehlt hoowdern
That was delicious.	**Het was heerlijk.**	heht vahss hayrlaiyk
We enjoyed it, thank you.	**Wij hebben genoten, dank u.**	vaiy hehbern ghernoatern dahnk ew

---

BEDIENING INBEGREPEN
SERVICE INCLUDED

TIPPING, see inside back-cover

Snacks   *Snacks*

Broodjeswinkels (sandwich shops) are fast on service, appear to be permanently open and always display a price list prominently. Sandwiches take the form of a soft bread roll stuffed with five or six slices of ham, cheese, spoonfuls of prawns, creamed salad—not easy to handle, but delicious. Maybe you should also try herrings at a street stall (see page 34). Another excellent place to go for a snack is a *pannekoekhuisje* (pancake house) which may serve more than 50 different sorts of pancakes. Children are specially fond of *poffertjes,* a small version served with icing sugar.

I'll have one of those.	**Ik wil die daar hebben.**	ik √il dee daar hehbern
Can I have two of these, please.	**Kan ik twee van deze hebben, alstublieft.**	kahn ik t√ay vahn dayzer hehbern ahlstewbleeft
to the left/right above/below	**links/rechts boven/onder**	links/rehkhts boavern/onderr
It's to take away.	**Het is om mee te nemen.**	heht iss om may ter naymern
I'd like a/an/some...	**Ik wil graag...**	ik √il ghraakh
(grilled) chicken	**een (gegrilde) kip**	ern (gherghrilder) kip
frankfurter	**een knakworst**	ern knahk√orst
meat croquettes	**vleeskroketten**	vlayskroakehtern
pancake	**een pannekoek**	ern pahnerkook
roll	**een broodje**	ern broatyer
with ham	**met ham**	meht hahm

A *broodje* may also be stuffed with *kaas* (cheese), *paling* (smoked eel), *rookvlees* (smoked beef)—you can even have a *broodje gezond* which is a health-food roll with lettuce, cucumber and tomato. A *broodje halfom* is stuffed with liver and salted meat. Other specialities are:

een zakje patat (ern **zahk**yer paa**taht**)	a portion of chips (French fries), with mayonnaise *(met mayonaise)* or without *(zonder)*
loempia (**loom**peeyaa)	spring roll with vegetables and bean sprouts
uitsmijter (ur^{ew}tsmaiyterr)	two slices of bread with ham, roast beef or cheese, topped with fried eggs

Pastries and cakes *Gebak en taarten*

Can you help me?	**Kunt u mij helpen?**	kurnt ew maiy **hehl**pern
What kind of pastries do you have?	**Wat hebt u voor gebak?**	√aht hehpt ew voar gher**bahk**
What do you recommend?	**Wat kunt u aanbevelen?**	√aht kurnt ew **aan**bervaylern
I'd like a...	**Ik wil graag...**	ik √il ghraakh
bun	**een broodje**	ern **broa**tyer
pastry	**een gebakje**	ern gher**bahk**yer
piece of cake	**een stuk taart**	ern sturk taart
tart	**een taartje**	ern **taart**yer
It's to take away.	**Het is om mee te nemen.**	heht iss om may ter **nay**mern
How much is that?	**Hoeveel is dat?**	**hoo**vayl iss daht

moorkop (**moarkop**)	chocolate coated puff pastry with whipped cream filling
poffertjes (**poffertyerss**)	kind of small round pancake with icing sugar and a knob of butter
profiterole (**profeeterrol**)	pyramid of small puffs filled with whipped cream or custard
tompoes (**tompooss**)	flaky pastry filled with custard and topped with pink icing
vlaai (Limburgse) [vlaa^{ee} (**limburrghser**)]	dough base topped with all kinds of fruit or rice

Some biscuits (cookies) and other good things:

appelbeignets	ahperlbehñayss	apple fritters
appelgebak	ahperlgherbahk	apple pastry
bitterkoekjes	bitterrkookyerss	almond biscuits
boterkoek	boaterrkook	shortbread
kaneelbeschuitjes	kaanaylberskhur^{ew}tyerss	cinnamon biscuits
koffiebroodjes	koffeebroatyerss	sweet buns
kwarktaart	k√ahrktaart	cheese cake
gemberkoek	ghemberrkook	ginger cake
speculaas	spaykew**laas**	spiced biscuits
stroopwafels	stroap√aaferlss	biscuits filled with honey
wafels (Belgische)	√aaferlss (**behl**gheeser)	waffles (Belgian)

Picnic *Picknick*

Here's a basic list of food and drinks that might come in useful for a light meal or when shopping for a picnic.

I'd like a/an/some...	Ik wil graag...	ik vil ghraakh
apples	**appels**	ahperlss
bananas	**bananen**	baanaanern
beer	**bier**	beer
biscuits (Br.)	**beschuitjes/koekjes**	berskhur^{ew}tyerss/kookyerss
bread	**een brood**	ern broat
butter	**boter**	boaterr
cheese	**kaas**	kaass
chocolate bar	**een reep chocolade**	ern rayp shoakoalaader
chips (Am.)	**chips**	"chips"
(instant) coffee	**(instant) koffie**	(instahnt) koffee
cold cuts	**vleeswaren**	vlaysvaarern
cookies	**beschuitjes/koekjes**	berskhur^{ew}tyerss/kookyerss
crisps	**chips**	"chips"
cucumber	**een komkommer**	ern komkommerr
eggs	**eieren**	aiyyerrern
frankfurters	**knakworstjes**	knahkvorstyerss
gherkins (pickles)	**augurken**	o^{ow}ghurrkern
grapefruit	**pompelmoes**	pomperlmooss
ham	**ham**	hahm
ice-cream	**ijs**	aiyss
lemons	**citroenen**	seetroonern
liver sausage	**leverworst**	layverrvorst
milk	**melk**	mehlk
mustard	**mosterd**	mosterrt
olives	**olijven**	oalaiyvern
oranges	**sinaasappels**	seenaasahperlss
peanuts	**pinda's**	pindaass
pepper	**peper**	payperr
rolls	**broodjes**	broatyerss
salami	**salami**	saalaamee
salt	**zout**	zo^{ow}t
sandwich	**een sandwich**	ern "sandwich"
sausage	**een worst**	ern vorst
spices	**specerijen**	spayserraiyern
sugar	**suiker**	sur^{ew}kerr
sweets	**snoep**	snoop
tea	**thee**	tay
tea bags	**theezakjes**	tayzahkyerss
tomatoes	**tomaten**	toamaatern
yoghurt	**yoghurt**	"yoghurt"

Travelling around

Plane *Vliegtuig*

In Holland and Belgium you are more likely to get around by car or train than by air. However, in some Dutch tourist resorts, panoramic flights are operated all year round.

When's the next flight to Amsterdam?	**Wanneer gaat het volgende vliegtuig naar Amsterdam?**	√ahnayr ghaat heht volghender vleeghtur^{ew}kh naar ahmsterrdahm
Is there a... to Maastricht?	**Is er een... naar Maastricht?**	iss ehr ern... naar maastrikht
connection	**verbinding**	verrbinding
direct flight	**rechtstreekse vlucht**	rehkhtstraykser vlurkht
I'd like a...	**Ik wil graag een...**	ik √il ghraakh ern
ticket to Brussels	**ticket naar Brussel**	"ticket" naar brurserl
single (one-way)	**enkele reis**	ehnkerler raiyss
return (round-trip)	**retour**	rertoor
aisle seat	**plaats aan het gangpad**	plaats aan heht ghahngpaht
window seat	**plaats bij het raam**	plaats baiy heht raam
What time...?	**Hoe laat...?**	hoo laat
do we take off	**vertrekken wij**	verrtrehkern √aiy
do we arrive	**komen wij aan**	koamern √aiy aan
should I check in	**moet ik inchecken**	moot ik inshehkern
Is there a bus to the airport?	**Gaat er een bus naar de luchthaven?**	ghaat ehr ern burss naar der lurkhthaavern
What's the flight number?	**Wat is het vlucht-nummer?**	√aht iss heht vlurkhtnurmerr
I'd like to... my reservation.	**Ik wil graag mijn reservering...**	ik √il ghraakh maiyn rayzehrvayring
cancel	**annuleren**	ahnewlayrern
change	**veranderen**	verrahnderrern
confirm	**bevestigen**	bervehsterghern

AANKOMST	**VERTREK**
ARRIVAL	DEPARTURE

Train *Trein*

Trains run frequently between major cities and are generally punctual. Inter city and long distance trains have comfortable first class coaches and more than adequate second class ones, while local trains only have second class.

Crossing Holland or Belgium by train is a matter of a few hours travel, so there's no need for accommodation or restaurant facilities. However, refreshments are available on certain lines. Seat reservations cannot be made for domestic journeys in Holland, but if you're going abroad, then a reservation also covers the domestic leg of the journey.

EuroCity (EC) (urroasittee)	International express train stopping only at major cities. Supplement may be requested.
D-trein (day-traiyn)	International intermediate- to long-distance train.
Intercity (IC) (interrsittee)	Fast and frequently running train stopping only at a few stations.
Stoptrein (stoptraiyn)	Dutch local train stopping at all stations.
Direct (deerehkt)	Belgian long-distance train stopping only at main stations.
Omnibus (omneeburss)	Belgian local train stopping at all stations.
Boottrein (boattraiyn)	Boat train connecting with the ferry crossing to England.

International trains may have:

Slaapwagen (slaap√aaghern)	Sleeping car with single-, double- or triple-berth compartments and washing facilities.
Ligrijtuig (likhraiytur^{ew}kh)	Couchette car. An ordinary compartment in which the seats fold into four or six berths with blankets and pillows.
Restauratiewagen (rehstoaraatsee-√aaghern)	Dining car.

To the railway station *Naar het station*

Where's the railway station?	**Waar is het station?**	√aar iss heht stahsyon
Taxi!	**Taxi!**	tahksee
Take me to the..., please.	**Brengt u mij naar..., alstublieft.**	brehngt ew maiy naar... ahlstewbleeft
What's the fare?	**Hoeveel is dat?**	hoovayl iss daht

INGANG	ENTRANCE
UITGANG	EXIT
NAAR DE PERRONS	TO THE PLATFORMS
INFORMATIE	INFORMATION

Where's the...? *Waar is...?*

Where is/are (the)...?	**Waar is/zijn...?**	√aar iss/zaiyn
bar	**de bar**	der ''bar''
booking office	**het reserverings- bureau**	heht rayzehrvayrings- bewroa
currency exchange office	**het wisselkantoor**	heht √isserlkahntoar
hotel reservation	**de hotelbemiddeling**	der hoatehlbermidderling
information office	**het inlichtingenbureau**	heht inlikhtingernbewroa
left-luggage office (baggage check)	**het bagagedepot**	heht baaghaazherdaypoa
lost property (lost and found) office	**het bureau voor gevonden voor- werpen**	heht bewroa voar ghervondern voar- √ehrpern
luggage lockers	**de bagagekluizen**	der baaghaazherklur[ew]zern
newsstand	**de kiosk**	der keeyosk
platform 2	**perron 2**	pehron 2
reservations office	**het reserverings- bureau**	heht rayzehrvayringsbewroa
restaurant	**het restaurant**	heht rehstoarahnt
snack bar	**de snackbar**	der ''snackbar''
ticket office	**het loket**	heht loakeht
track 7	**spoor 7**	spoar 7
waiting room	**de wachtkamer**	der √ahkhtkaamerr
Where are the toilets?	**Waar zijn de toiletten?**	√aar zaiyn der t√aalehtern

TAXI, see page 21

Inquiries *Inlichtingen*

In Holland and Belgium the sign 🛈 indicates an information office.

When is the... train to The Hague?	**Wanneer gaat de... trein naar Den Haag?**	√ahnayr ghaat der... traiyn naar dehn haakh
first	**eerste**	ayrster
last	**laatste**	laatster
next	**volgende**	volghernder
What time does the train to Breda leave?	**Hoe laat vertrekt de trein naar Breda?**	hoo laat verrtrehkt der traiyn naar braydaa
What's the fare to Haarlem?	**Hoeveel kost een kaartje naar Haarlem?**	hoovayl kost ern kaartyer naar haarlehm
Is it a through train?	**Is het een doorgaande trein?**	iss heht ern doarghaander traiyn
Is there a connection to...?	**Is er aansluiting naar...?**	iss ehr aanslur^{ew}ting naar
Do I have to change trains?	**Moet ik overstappen?**	moot ik oaverrstahpern
Is there enough time to change?	**Is er genoeg tijd om over te stappen?**	iss ehr ghernookh taiyt om oaverr ter stahpern
Will the train leave on time?	**Vertrekt de trein op tijd?**	verrtrehkt der traiyn op taiyt
What time does the train arrive in Rotterdam?	**Hoe laat komt de trein in Rotterdam aan?**	hoo laat komt der traiyn in rotterrdahm aan
Is there a dining car/sleeping car on the train?	**Is er een restauratie-wagen/slaapwagen in de trein?**	iss ehr ern rehstoaraatsee-√aaghern/slaap√aaghern in der traiyn
Does the train stop in Antwerp?	**Stopt de trein in Antwerpen?**	stopt der traiyn in ahnt√ehrpern
Which platform does the train to Brussels leave from?	**Van welk perron vertrekt de trein naar Brussel?**	vahn √ehlk pehron verrtrehkt der traiyn naar brurserl
Which platform does the train from Gouda arrive at?	**Op welk perron komt de trein uit Gouda aan?**	op √ehlk pehron komt der traiyn ur^{ew}t gho^{ow}daa aan
I'd like a timetable.	**Ik wil graag een spoorboekje.**	ik √il ghraakh ern spoarbookyer

Het is een doorgaande trein.	It's a through train.
U moet overstappen in...	You have to change at...
Stapt u in... over en neemt u dan een stoptrein.	Change at... and get a local train.
Perron 2 is...	Platform 2 is...
daar/boven	over there/upstairs
links/rechts	on the left/on the right
Er is om 8 uur een trein naar...	There's a train to... at 8 a.m.
Uw trein vertrekt van spoor 7.	Your train will leave from track 7.
De trein heeft... minuten vertraging.	The train is running... minutes late.
Eerste klas vooraan/in het midden/achteraan.	First class at the front/in the middle/at the rear.

Tickets *Kaartjes*

I'd like a ticket to Leiden.	**Ik wil graag een kaartje naar Leiden.**	ik √il ghraakh ern kaartyer naar laiydern
single (one-way)	**enkele reis**	ehnkerler raiyss
return (round-trip)	**retour**	rertoor
first/second class	**eerste/tweede klas**	ayrster/t√ayder klahss
half price	**halve prijs**	hahlver praiyss
supplement	**toeslag**	tooslahkh
reduced fare	**gereduceerd tarief**	gherraydewsayrt taareef

Reservation *Reservering*

I'd like to reserve a...	**Ik wil graag... reserveren.**	ik √il ghraakh rayzehr-vayrern
berth in the sleeping car	**een couchette in de slaapwagen**	ern kooshehter in der slaap√aaghern
couchette	**een couchette**	ern kooshehter
upper	**boven**	boavern
middle	**in het midden**	in heht middern
lower	**onder**	onderr
seat (by the window)	**een plaats (bij het raam)**	ern plaats (baiy heht raam)

All aboard *Instappen*

Is this the right platform for the train to Paris?	Is dit het goede perron voor de trein naar Parijs?	iss dit heht ghooder pehron voar der traiyn naar paaraiyss
Is this the train to Antwerp?	Is dit de trein naar Antwerpen?	iss dit der traiyn naar ahnt√ehrpern
Is the train from Groningen late?	Is de trein uit Groningen te laat?	iss der traiyn ur^{ew}t ghroaningern ter laat
Excuse me. Could I get past?	Pardon. Mag ik even passeren?	pahrdon. mahhk ik ayvern pahsayrern
Is this seat taken?	Is deze plaats bezet?	iss dayzer plaats berzeht

ROKEN SMOKING	**NIET-ROKEN** NO SMOKING

I think that's my seat.	Ik geloof dat dit mijn plaats is.	ik gherloaf daht dit maiyn plaats iss
Would you let me know before we get to Liège?	Kunt u mij waarschuwen als wij in Luik aankomen?	kurnt ew maiy √aarskhew√ern ahlss √aiy in lur^{ew}k aankoamern
What station is this?	Welk station is dit?	√ehlk stahsyon iss dit
How long does the train stop here?	Hoelang stopt de trein hier?	hoolahng stopt der traiyn heer
When do we arrive in Utrecht?	Hoe laat komen wij in Utrecht aan?	hoo laat koamern √aiy in ewtrehkht aan

Sleeping *Slaapwagen*

Where's the...?	Waar is...?	√aar iss
couchette car sleeping car	het ligrijtuig de slaapwagen	heht likhraiytur^{ew}kh der slaap√aaghern
Are there any free compartments in the sleeping car?	Zijn er nog coupés in de slaapwagen vrij?	zaiyn ehr nokh koopayss in der slaap√aaghern vraiy
I'd like a single/ double compartment.	Ik wil graag een éénpersoons-/tweepersoonscompartiment.	ik √il ghraakh ern aynpehrsoans-/t√aypehrsoanskompahrteemehnt

| Would you make up our berths? | **Wilt u onze cou-chettes klaarmaken?** | √ilt ew **onzer** kooshehterss **klaarmaakern** |
| Would you wake me at 7 o'clock? | **Wilt u mij om 7 uur wekken?** | √ilt ew maiy om 7 ewr vehkern |

Eating *In de restauratiewagen*

On some trains an attendant comes around with snacks, coffee, tea and soft drinks.

Where's the...?	**Waar is...?**	√aar iss
buffet car	**het buffetrijtuig**	heht bewfehtraiytur^ew kh
dining car	**de restauratiewagen**	der rehstoaraatsee√aaghern

Baggage and porters *Bagage en kruiers*

Porter!	**Kruier!**	krur^ew yerr
Can you help me carry my luggage?	**Kunt u mij helpen mijn bagage te dragen?**	kurnt ew maiy hehlpern maiyn baaghaazher ter draaghern
Where are the...?	**Waar zijn...?**	√aar zaiyn
luggage trolleys (carts)	**de bagagewagentjes**	der baaghaazher√aaghern-tyerss
luggage lockers	**de bagagekluizen**	der baaghaazherklur^ew zern
Where's the left-luggage office (baggage check)?	**Waar is het bagage-depot?**	√aar iss heht baaghaazher-daypoa
I'd like to... my luggage.	**Ik wil mijn bagage graag...**	ik √il maiyn baaghaazher ghraakh
leave	**achterlaten**	ahkhterlaatern
register (check)	**inschrijven**	inskhraiyvern
I'd like to take out luggage insurance.	**Ik wil graag een bagageverzekering afsluiten.**	ik √il ghraakh ern baaghaazherverrzaykerring ahfslur^ew tern

---

INSCHRIJVEN BAGAGE
REGISTERING LUGGAGE (CHECKING BAGGAGE)

PORTERS, see also page 18

Coach (long-distance bus) *Bus*

Where's the coach terminal?	**Waar is het bus-station?**	√aar iss heht bursstah-syon
When's the next coach to...?	**Hoe laat gaat de vol-gende bus naar...?**	hoo laat ghaat der volghernder burss naar
Does this coach stop at...?	**Stopt deze bus in...?**	stopt dayzer burss in
How long does the journey (trip) take?	**Hoelang duurt de rit?**	hoolahng dewrt der rit

Note: Most of the phrases on the previous pages can be used or adapted for travelling on local transport.

Bus—Tram (streetcar) *Bus—Tram*

Holland, for the purposes of public transport, is divided into some 2,000 zones. Fares are therefore calculated in zones by a system of "strip tickets" *(strippenkaart),* valid throughout the country. Tickets valid for one hour with transfer and some multi-ride tickets are sold by drivers in both Holland and Belgium. Other tickets and passes are available at railway and underground stations and sometimes from ticket machines.

I'd like a day ticket (24-hour pass).	**Ik wil graag een dag-kaart.**	ik √il ghraakh ern dahkk-kaart
Which tram (street-car) goes to the town centre?	**Welke tram rijdt naar het stadscentrum?**	√ehlker trehm raijt naar heht stahtssehntrurm
When is the... tram to the Rokin?	**Wanneer gaat de... tram naar het Rokin?**	√ahnayr ghaat der... trehm naar heht roakin
first/last/next	**eerste/laatste/volgende**	ayrster/laatster/volghernder
Where can I get a bus to Volendam?	**Waar kan ik een bus naar Volendam nemen?**	√aar kahn ik ern burss naar voalerndahm naymern
Which bus do I take to...?	**Welke bus moet ik nemen naar...?**	√ehlker burss moot ik naymern naar
Where's the bus stop?	**Waar is de bushalte?**	√aar iss der burshahlter

How much is the fare to...?	**Hoeveel kost het naar...?**	hoovayl kost heht naar
How long is the ticket valid?	**Hoelang is het kaartje geldig?**	hoolahng iss heht kaartyer ghehldikh
Do I have to change?	**Moet ik overstappen?**	moot ik oaverrstahpern
Will you tell me when to get off?	**Wilt u mij zeggen wanneer ik moet uitstappen?**	√ilt ew maiy zehghern √ahnayr ik moot ur^{ew}tstahpern
I want to get off at the Royal Palace.	**Ik wil bij het Koninklijk Paleis uitstappen.**	ik √il baiy heht koaninklerk paalaiyss ur^{ew}tstahpern

| **BUSHALTE** | BUS STOP |
| **STOPT OP VERZOEK** | REQUEST STOP |

Underground (subway) *Metro*

In Holland you use "strip tickets" (see buses), while in Belgium there is a flat fare, irrespective of the distance travelled. Large maps of the system are displayed at stations.

Where's the underground station?	**Waar is het metrostation?**	√aar iss heht maytroastahsyon
Does this train go to...?	**Gaat deze trein naar...?**	ghaat dayzer traiyn naar
Where do I change for...?	**Waar moet ik overstappen als ik naar ... wil?**	√aar moot ik oaverrstahpern ahlss ik naar... √il
Which line should I take to...?	**Welke lijn moet ik nemen naar...?**	√ehlker laiyn moot ik naymern naar

Boat services *Boot*

Ferries still have a real function in Holland. Driving on secondary roads involves some river and canal crossings.

| When does the next boat for... leave? | **Wanneer vertrekt de volgende boot naar...?** | √ahnayr verrtrehkt der volghernder boat naar |

How long does the crossing take?	**Hoelang duurt de overtocht?**	hoolahng dewrt der oaverr-tokht
I'd like to take a...	**Ik wil graag... maken.**	ik √il ghraakh... maakern
canal tour	**een rondvaart door de grachten**	ern rontvaart doar der grahkhtern
cruise	**een "cruise"**	ern "cruise"
boat trip	**een boottocht**	ern boattokht
tour of the harbour	**een rondvaart door de haven**	ern rontvaart doar der haavern
boat	**de boot**	der boat
cabin	**de cabine**	der kaabeener
single	**éénpersoons-**	aynpehrsoans-
double	**tweepersoons-**	t√aiypehrsoans-
car ferry	**de veerboot**	der vayrboat
deck	**het dek**	heht dehk
gangway	**de loopplank**	der loapplahnk
hydrofoil	**de draagvleugelboot**	der draakhvlurgherlboat
life belt	**de reddingsboei**	der rehdingsboo⁰⁰
life boat	**de reddingsboot**	der rehdingsboat
life jacket	**het reddingsvest**	heht rehdingsvehst
pier	**de pier**	der peer
port	**de haven**	der haavern
ship	**het schip**	heht skhip
steamer	**de stoomboot**	der stoamboat

Other means of transport   *Andere vervoermiddelen*

Bicycles and mopeds are extremely popular in Holland which is crisscrossed with a network of cycle tracks and trails. Bicycles can be hired at many railway stations. Moped drivers must wear crash helmets.

I'd like to hire a...	**Ik wil graag... huren.**	ik √il ghraakh... hewrern
bicycle	**een fiets**	ern feets
moped	**een bromfiets**	ern bromfeets
motorbike	**een motorfiets**	ern moaterrfeets
scooter	**een scooter**	ern "scooter"

Or perhaps you prefer:

to hike	**trekken**	trehkkern
to hitchhike	**liften**	liftern
to walk	**wandelen**	√ahnderlern

Car *Auto*

In Holland and Belgium roads are good and motorways (expressways) are free. Seat-belts *(veiligheidsgordels)* are obligatory.

Where's the nearest filling station?	**Waar is het dichtst- bijzijnde benzine- station?**	√aar iss heht dikhstbaiyzaiyn- der behnzeener stahsyon
Fill it up, please.	**Vol, alstublieft.**	vol ahlstewbleeft
Give me... litres of petrol (gasoline).	**Geeft u mij... liter benzine.**	ghayft ew maiy... leeterr behnzeener
super (premium)/ regular/unleaded/ diesel	**super/ normaal/loodvrij/ diesel**	sewperr/ normaal/loatvraiy/ deeserl
Would you check the... please?	**Wilt u... controleren, alstublieft?**	√ilt ew... kontroaleyrern ahlstewbleeft
battery	**de accu**	der ahkew
brake fluid	**de remvloeistof**	der rehmvloo⁰⁰stof
oil/water	**de olie/het water**	der oalee/heht √aaterr
Would you check the tyre pressure?	**Wilt u de banden- spanning contro- leren?**	√ilt ew der bahndernspahning kontroaleyrern
1.6 front 1.8 rear	**vóór 1,6 achter 1,8**	voar ayn komma zehss ahkhterr ayn komma ahkht
Please check the spare tyre, too.	**Controleert u ook het reservewiel, alstublieft.**	kontroaleyrt ew oak heht rerserhvverveel ahlstewbleeft
Can you mend this puncture (fix this flat)?	**Kunt u deze lekke band repareren?**	kurnt ew dayzer lehker bahnt raypaarayrern
Would you change the... please?	**Wilt u... verwis- selen, alstublieft?**	√ilt ew... vehr√isserlern ahlstewbleeft
bulb	**de gloeilamp**	der ghloo⁰⁰lahmp
fan belt	**de ventilatorriem**	der vehnteelaatorreem
spark(ing) plugs	**de bougies**	der boozheess
tyre	**de band**	der bahnt
wipers	**de ruitenwissers**	der rur⁰ᵂtern√isserrss
Would you clean the windscreen (wind- shield)?	**Kunt u de voorruit schoonmaken?**	kurnt ew der voarrur⁰ᵂt skhoanmaakern

CAR HIRE, see page 20

Asking the way   *De weg vragen*

Can you tell me the way to...?	**Kunt u mij de weg wijzen naar...?**	kurnt ew maiy der √ehkh √aiyzern naar
In which direction is...?	**In welke richting is...?**	in √ehlker rikhting iss
How do I get to this place/this address?	**Hoe kom ik naar deze plaats/dit adres?**	hoo kom ik naar dayzer plaats/dit aadrehss
Am I on the right road for...?	**Ben ik op de goede weg naar...?**	behn ik op der ghooder √ehkh naar
How far is it to... from here?	**Hoever is het van hier naar...?**	hoovehr iss heht vahn heer naar
How long does it take by car/on foot?	**Hoelang is het met de auto/te voet?**	hoolahng iss heht meht der oᵒʷtoa/ter voot
Can I... to the centre of town?	**Kan ik naar het centrum van de stad...?**	kahn ik naar heht sehntrurm vahn der staht
drive/walk	**rijden/lopen**	raiydern/loapern
Where is...?	**Waar is...?**	√aar iss
Can you show me on the map where I am?	**Kunt u mij op de kaart laten zien waar ik ben?**	kurnt ew maiy op der kaart laatern zeen √aar ik behn

Landmarks   *Oriëntatiepunten*

bridge	**de brug**	der brurkh
dyke	**de dijk**	der daiyk
dunes	**de duinen**	der durᵉʷnern
farm	**de boerderij**	der boorderraiy
field	**het veld**	heht vehlt
gable(stone)	**de gevel(spits)**	der ghayverl(spits)
garden	**de tuin**	der turᵉʷn
hill	**de heuvel**	der hurverl
mill	**de molen**	der moalern
motorway (expressway)	**de autosnelweg**	der oᵒʷtoasnehl√ehkh
path	**het pad**	heht paht
pond	**de vijver**	der vaiyverr
river	**de rivier**	der reeveer
sea	**de zee**	der zay
valley	**het dal**	heht dahl
village	**het dorp**	heht dorp
wall	**de muur**	der mewr
wood	**het bos**	heht boss

🖙	🖘
U bent op de verkeerde weg.	You're on the wrong road.
U moet rechtdoor rijden.	Go straight ahead.
Het is daarginds links/rechts.	It's down there on the left/right.
tegenover/achter...	opposite/behind...
naast/na...	next to/after...
noord/zuid/oost/west	north/south/east/west
U moet verder gaan tot het eerste/tweede kruispunt.	Carry on to the first/second crossroads (intersection).
U moet bij de stoplichten links afslaan.	Turn left at the traffic lights.
U moet bij de volgende hoek rechts afslaan.	Turn right at the next corner.
Neem de... weg.	Take the ... road.
Het is een straat met een-richtingsverkeer.	It's a one-way street.
U moet teruggaan naar...	You have to go back to...
Volg de borden naar Brussel.	Follow signs for Brussels.

Parking *Parkeren*

In town centres most street parking is metered. In blue zones a parking disc, available from filling stations, must be prominently displayed.

Where can I park?	**Waar kan ik parkeren?**	√aar kahn ik pahrkayrern
Is there a car park (parking lot) nearby?	**Is er een parkeer-plaats in de buurt?**	iss ehr ern pahrkayrplaats in der bewrt
May I park here?	**Mag ik hier parkeren?**	mahkh ik heer pahrkayrern
How long can I park here?	**Hoelang kan ik hier parkeren?**	hoolahng kahn ik heer pahrkayrern
What's the charge per hour?	**Hoeveel kost het per uur?**	hoovayl kost heht perr ewr
Do you have some change for the parking meter?	**Hebt u wisselgeld voor de parkeer-meter?**	hehpt ew √isserlghehlt voar der pahrkayrmayterr

Breakdown—Road assistance *Motorpech—Wegenwacht*

Where's the nearest garage?	**Waar is de dichtst-bijzijnde garage?**	√aar iss der dikhtst-baiyzaiynder ghaaraazher
My car has broken down.	**Ik heb autopech.**	ik hehp o^{oo}toapehkh
May I use your phone?	**Mag ik uw telefoon even gebruiken?**	mahkh ik ew^{oo} taylayfoan ayvern gherbrur^{ew}kern
I've had a break-down at...	**Ik sta met autopech bij...**	ik staa meht o^{oo}toapehkh baiy
Can you send a mechanic?	**Kunt u een monteur sturen?**	kurnt ew ern monturr stewrern
My car won't start.	**Mijn auto wil niet starten.**	maiyn o^{ew}toa √il neet stahrtern
The battery is dead.	**De accu is leeg.**	der ahkew iss laykh
I've run out of petrol (gasoline).	**Ik heb geen benzine meer.**	ik hehp ghayn behnzeener mayr
I have a flat tyre.	**Ik heb een lekke band.**	ik hehp ern lehker bahnt
The engine is over-heating.	**De motor kookt.**	der moaterr koakt
There's something wrong with the...	**Er is iets mis met...**	ehr iss eets miss meht
brakes	**de remmen**	der rehmern
carburettor	**de carburator**	der kahrbewraator
exhaust (tail) pipe	**de uitlaatpijp**	der ur^{ew}tlaatpaiyp
radiator	**de radiator**	der raadeeyaator
wheel	**het wiel**	heht √eel
Can you send a breakdown van (tow truck)?	**Kunt u een takel-wagen sturen?**	kurnt ew ern taakerl-√aaghern stewrern
How long will you be?	**Hoelang duurt het?**	hoolahng dewrt heht
Can you give me an estimate of the cost?	**Kunt u mij een opgave van de kosten geven?**	kurnt ew maiy ern opghaaver vahn der kostern ghayvern

Accident—Police *Ongeval—Politie*

There's been an accident. It's about 2 km. from...	**Er is een ongeluk gebeurd. Het is ongeveer 2 km van...**	ehr iss ern ongherlurk gherburrt. heht iss onghervayr 2 km vahn

Please call the police.	**Roep de politie, alstublieft.**	roop der poaleetsee ahlstewbleeft
Where's there a telephone?	**Waar is een telefoon?**	√aar iss ern taylerfoan
Call... quickly.	**Roep snel...**	roop snehl
an ambulance	**een ziekenauto**	ern zeekerno^{ow}toa
a doctor	**een dokter**	ern dokterr
There are people injured.	**Er zijn gewonden.**	ehr zaiyn gher√ondern
Here's my driving licence.	**Hier is mijn rijbewijs.**	heer iss maiyn raiyber√aiyss
What's your name and address?	**Wat is uw naam en adres?**	√aht iss ew^{oo} naam ehn aadrehss
What's your insurance company?	**Wat is uw verzekeringsmaatschappij?**	√aht iss ew^{oo} verrzaykerringsmaatskhahpaiy

Road signs *Verkeersborden*

BEPERKTE DOORRIJHOOGTE	Height limit
DOORGAAND VERKEER GESTREMD	No through road
EENRICHTINGSVERKEER	One-way traffic
EINDE INHAALVERBOD	End of no-pass zone
FIETSERS	(Watch out for) cyclists
FILE	Traffic jam
INHAALVERBOD	No overtaking (passing)
LANGZAAM RIJDEN	Slow down
LICHTEN	Switch on headlights
LOSSE STEENSLAG	Loose gravel
OMLEIDING	Diversion (detour)
PARKEERVERBOD	No parking
PAS OP	Caution
SLECHT WEGDEK	Bad road surface
STOPLICHTEN OP 100 M	Traffic lights in 100 meters
TEGENLIGGERS	Oncoming traffic
UITRIT VRACHTAUTO'S	Lorry (truck) exit
VERKEER OVER EEN RIJBAAN	Single-lane traffic
VOETGANGERS	Pedestrians
WERK IN UITVOERING	Roadworks ahead (men working)
WIELRIJDERS	Cyclists
ZACHTE BERM	Soft shoulders

Sightseeing

Where's the tourist office?	**Waar is het verkeers-bureau?** *	√aar iss heht verr**kayrs**-bewroa
What are the main sights?	**Wat zijn de belang-rijkste bezienswaar-digheden?**	√aht zaiyn der ber**lahng**-raiykster berzeens√aar-derghhaydern
We're here for...	**Wij blijven hier...**	√aiy **blaiy**vern heer
only a few hours	**maar een paar uur**	maar ern paar ewr
a day	**een dag**	ern dahkh
a week	**een week**	ern wayk
Can you recommend a sightseeing tour/ an excursion?	**Kunt u een sight-seeing toer/een ex-cursie aanbevelen?**	kurnt ew ern ''sightseeing'' toor/ern ehks**kurr**see **aan**bervaylern
Where do we leave from?	**Van waar vertrekken wij?**	vahn √aar verr**trehk**ern √aiy
Will the bus pick us up at the hotel?	**Haalt de bus ons af van het hotel?**	haalt der burss onss ahf vahn heht hoa**tehl**
How much does the tour cost?	**Hoeveel kost de toer?**	hoo**vayl** kost der toor
What time does the tour start?	**Hoe laat begint de toer?**	hoo laat ber**ghint** der toor
Is lunch included?	**Is de lunch inbe-grepen?**	iss der ''lunch'' inber-**ghray**pern
What time do we get back?	**Hoe laat komen wij terug?**	hoo laat **koa**mern √aiy ter**rurkh**
Do we have free time in...?	**Hebben wij vrije tijd in...?**	**heh**bern √aiy **vraiy**er taiyt in
I'd like to see...	**Ik wil graag... zien.**	ik √il ghraakh... zeen
Can we visit...?	**Kunnen we... bezoeken?**	**kur**nern √aiy... ber**zoo**kern
Is there an English-speaking guide?	**Is er een Engels-sprekende gids?**	iss ehr ern **ehn**gerls-spraykernder ghits
I'd like to hire a private guide for...	**Ik wil graag een privé-gids huren voor...**	ik √il ghraakh ern pree**vay**-ghits **hew**rern voar
half a day	**een halve dag**	ern **hahl**ver dahkh
a day	**een dag**	ern dahkh

---

* In Holland simply called VVV (vay vay vay).

Where is/are the...?	Waar is/zijn...?	√aar iss/zaiyn
abbey	de abdij	der ahpdaiy
art museum	het museum voor beeldende kunst	heht mewzayyurm voar bayldernder kurnst
botanical gardens	de botanische tuinen	der botaaneeser tur^ew nern
business district	de zakenwijk	der zaakern√aiyk
canal	de gracht	der ghrahkt
castle	het kasteel	heht kahstayl
cathedral	de kathedraal	der kahterdraal
cave	de grot	der ghrot
cemetery	het kerkhof	heht kehrkhof
chapel	de kapel	der kaapehl
church	de kerk	der kehrk
city centre	het (stads)centrum	heht (stahts)sehntrurm
concert hall	het concertgebouw	heht konsehrtgherboow
convent	het klooster	heht kloasterr
court house	het gerechtshof	heht gherrehkhtshof
cut-flower auction hall	de bloemenveiling	der bloomernvaiyling
docks	de dokhavens	der dokhaavernss
downtown area	het (stads)centrum	heht (stahts)sehntrurm
embankment	de kade	der kaader
exhibition	de tentoonstelling	der tehntoanstehling
factory	de fabriek	der faabreek
fair	de jaarmarkt	der yaarmahrkt
flea market	de vlooienmarkt	der vloa^ee ernmahrkt
flower market	de bloemenmarkt	der bloomernmahrkt
fortress	de vesting	der vehsting
fountain	de fontein	der fontaiyn
harbour	de haven	der haavern
library	de bibliotheek	der beebleeyoatayk
market	de markt	der mahrkt
memorial	het gedenkteken	heht gherdehnktaykern
monastery	het klooster	heht kloasterr
monument	het monument	heht moanewmehnt
museum	het museum	heht mewzayyurm
old town	de oude stad	der oowder staht
opera house	de opera	der oaperraa
open-air museum	het openlucht museum	heht oapernlurkht mewzayyurm
palace	het paleis	heht paalaiyss
park	het park	heht pahrk
parliament building	het parlements-gebouw	heht pahrlermehnts-gherboow
planetarium	het planetarium	heht plaanertaareeyurm

ruins	de ruïnes	der rew√eenerss
shopping area	de winkelwijk	der √inkerl√aiyk
square	het plein	heht plaiyn
stadium	het stadion	heht staadeeyon
statue	het standbeeld	heht stahntbaylt
stock exchange	de beurs	der burrss
theatre	de schouwburg	der skho^{ow}burrkh
tomb	het graf	heht ghrahf
tower	de toren	der toarern
town hall	het stadhuis	heht stahthur^{ew}ss
university	de universiteit	der ewneevehrseetaiyt
windmill	de windmolen	der √intmoalern
zoo	de dierentuin	der deererntur^{ew}n

Admission *Toegang*

Is... open on Sundays?	Is... open op zondag?	iss... oapern op zondahkh
What are the opening hours?	Wat zijn de openingstijden?	√aht zaiyn der oaperningstaiydern
When does it close?	Wanneer gaat het dicht?	√ahnayr ghaat heht dikht
How much is the entrance fee?	Hoeveel is de toegangsprijs?	hoovayl iss der tooghahngspraiyss
2 adults and 1 child.	2 volwassenen en 1 kind.	2 vol√ahsernern ehn 1 kint
Is there any reduction for (the)...?	Is er reductie voor...?	iss ehr rerdurksee voar
children	kinderen	kinderrern
disabled	invaliden	invaaleedern
groups	groepen	ghroopern
senior citizens	gepensioneerden	gherpehnsyoanayrdern
students	studenten	stewdehntern
Do you have a guide-book (in English)?	Hebt u een gids (in het Engels)?	hehpt ew ern ghits (in heht ehngerlss)
Can I buy a catalogue?	Kan ik een catalogus kopen?	kahn ik ern kaataaloaghurss koapern

---

VRIJE TOEGANG ADMISSION FREE
VERBODEN TE FOTOGRAFEREN NO CAMERAS ALLOWED

NUMBERS, see page 147

Who—What—When? *Wie—Wat—Wanneer?*

What's that building?	**Wat is dat voor gebouw?**	√aht iss daht voar gherbo^{ow}
Who built it?	**Wie heeft het gebouwd?**	√ee hayft heht gherbo^{ew}t
When was it built?	**Wanneer is het gebouwd?**	√ahnayr iss heht gherbo^{ew}t
Who was the...?	**Wie was...?**	√ee wahss
architect	**de architect**	der ahrkheetehkt
artist	**de kunstenaar**	der kurnsternaar
painter	**de schilder**	der skhilderr
sculptor	**de beeldhouwer**	der bayltho^{ow}err
Who painted that picture?	**Wie heeft dat schilderij gemaakt?**	√ee hayft daht skhilderraiy ghermaakt
When did he live?	**Wanneer leefde hij?**	√ahnayr layfder haiy
Where's the house where... lived?	**Waar is het huis waar... woonde?**	√aar iss heht hur^{ew}ss √aar... √oander
We're interested in ...	**Wij hebben belangstelling voor...**	√aiy hehbern berlahngstehling voar
agriculture	**landbouw**	lahntbo^{ow}
antiques	**antiek**	ahnteek
art	**kunst**	kurnst
botany	**botanie**	boataanee
ceramics	**keramiek**	kayraameek
coins	**munten**	murntern
fine arts	**beeldende kunst**	bayldernder kurnst
furniture	**meubels**	murberlss
geology	**geologie**	ghayoaloaghee
handicrafts	**kunstnijverheid**	kurnstnaiyverrhaiyt
history	**geschiedenis**	gherskheederniss
horticulture	**tuinbouw**	tur^{ew}nbo^{ow}
maritime history	**maritieme geschiedenis**	maáreeteemer gherskheederniss
medicine	**geneeskunde**	ghernayskurnder
ornithology	**vogelkunde**	voagherlkurnder
painting	**schilderkunst**	skhilderrkurnst
pottery	**pottenbakken**	potternbahkern
religion	**godsdienst**	ghotsdeenst
sculpture	**beeldhouwkunst**	bayltho^{ew}kurnst
zoology	**dierkunde**	deerkurnder
Where's the... department?	**Waar is de... afdeling?**	√aar iss der... ahfdayling

It's ...	Het is...	heht iss
amazing	**verbazingwekkend**	verbaazing√ehkernt
awful	**afschuwelijk**	ahfskhew√erlerk
beautiful	**mooi**	moa^{ew}
fantastic	**fantastisch**	fahntahsteess
gloomy	**somber**	somberr
impressive	**indrukwekkend**	indrurk√ehkernt
interesting	**interessant**	interrehsahnt
magnificent	**prachtig**	prahkhterkh
pretty	**aardig**	aarderkh
strange	**vreemd**	vraymt
superb	**groots**	ghroats
terrifying	**vreselijk**	vrayserlerk
tremendous	**enorm**	aynorm
ugly	**lelijk**	laylerk

Religious services *Kerkdiensten*

Most churches and cathedrals are open for the public to visit except, of course, when a service is being conducted.

Services are sometimes conducted in English in major towns. Ask the local tourist office for further details.

Is there a... near here?	**Is er een... in de buurt?**	iss ehr ern... in der bewrt
Catholic church	**katholieke kerk**	kahtoaleeker kehrk
Protestant church	**protestantse kerk**	proatehstahntser kehrk
mosque	**moskee**	moskay
synagogue	**synagoge**	seenaaghoagher
What time is...?	**Hoe laat is...?**	hoo laat iss
mass	**de mis**	der miss
the service	**de dienst**	der deenst
Where can I find a... who speaks English?	**Waar kan ik een... vinden die Engels spreekt?**	√aar kahn ik ern... vindern dee ehngherlss spraykt
priest/minister/ rabbi	**priester/dominee/ rabbi**	preesterr/doameenay/ rahbee
I'd like to visit the church.	**Ik wil graag de kerk bezichtigen.**	ik √il ghraakh der kehrk ber-zikhterghern
Is it allowed to take pictures?	**Is fotograferen toegestaan?**	iss foatoaghraafayrern toogherstaan

In the countryside *Op het platteland*

Is there a scenic route to the bulb-fields?	**Is er een schilder-achtige weg naar de bollenvelden?**	iss ehr ern **skhilderr**-ahkhtergher wehkh naar der **bollernvehldern**
Is this area above/below sea level?	**Is dit gebied boven/onder de zeespiegel?**	iss dit gherbeet boavern/onderr der zayspeegherl
What kind of animal/bird is that?	**Wat voor een dier/vogel is dat?**	√aht voar ern deer/voagherl iss daht

and if you are a keen gardener you may want to say:

I'd like to visit a nursery.	**Ik wil graag een kwekerij bezoeken.**	ik √il ghraakh ern k√aykerraiy berzookern
What are you growing there?	**Wat kweekt u daar?**	√aht k√aykt ew daar
When do you... it?	**Wanneer... u het?**	√ahnayr... ew heht
plant/sow/pick	**plant/zaait/plukt**	plahnt/zaa^{ee}t/plurkt
Is it an evergreen?	**Is het een groen-blijvende plant?**	iss heht ern **ghroon**-blaiyvernder plahnt
Does it need sun/shade?	**Heeft het zon/schaduw nodig?**	hayft heht zon/skhaadew noadikh
How often does this plant need watering?	**Hoe dikwijls heeft deze plant water nodig?**	hoo dik√erlss hayft **dayzer** plahnt √aaterr noadikh
Is this flower biennial/perennial?	**Is deze bloem twee-jarig/overblijvend?**	iss dayzer bloom t√ay-yaarikh/oaverrblaiyvernt
When does it flower?	**Wanneer is de bloei?**	√ahnayr iss der bloo^{ee}
I'd like a/some...	**Ik wil graag...**	ik √il ghraakh...
bulbs	**bloembollen**	bloombollern
bunch of flowers	**een boeket bloemen**	ern bookeht bloomern
carnations	**anjers**	ahnyerrss
crocuses	**krokussen**	kroakursern
daffodils	**narcissen**	nahrsissern
house plant	**een kamerplant**	ern kaamerrplahnt
hyacinths	**hyacinthen**	heeyaasintern
lilies	**lelies**	layleess
tulips	**tulpen**	turlpern
roses	**rozen**	roazern
seed	**zaad**	zaat
shrub	**een heester**	ern haysterr
tree	**een boom**	ern boam

Relaxing

Cinema (movies) — Theatre *Bioscoop — Theater*

You can find out what's on from newspapers and, in larger places, from weekly/monthly tourist publications.

All films are shown in the original language with Dutch subtitles. Advance booking is essential for theatres and the opera.

What's on at the cinema tonight?	**Wat draait er vanavond in de bioscoop?**	√aht draa^{ee}t ehr vahnaa-vont in der beeyoskoap
What's playing at the... Theatre?	**Wat wordt er in het... theater gespeeld?**	√aht √ort ehr in heht... tayaaterr gherspaylt
What sort of play is it?	**Wat is het voor een stuk?**	√aht iss heht voar ern sturk
Who's it by?	**Van wie is het?**	vahn √ee iss heht
Can you recommend a...?	**Kunt u... aan-bevelen?**	kurnt ew... aanber-vaylern
good film	**een goede film**	ern ghooder film
comedy	**een blijspel**	ern blaiyspehl
musical	**een musical**	ern "musical"
Where's that new film directed by... being shown?	**Waar draait die nieuwe film gere-gisseerd door...?**	√aar draa^{ee}t dee nee^{oo}er film gherraygheesayrt doar
Who's in it?	**Wie spelen er in?**	√ee spaylern ehr in
Who's playing the lead?	**Wie speelt de hoofdrol?**	√ee spaylt der **hoaf**trol
Who's the director?	**Wie is de regisseur?**	√ee iss der raygheesurr
At which theatre is that new play by... being performed?	**In welk theater wordt het nieuwe stuk van... gespeeld?**	in √ehlk tayaaterr √ort heht nee^{oo}er sturk vahn... gherspaylt
What time does it...?	**Hoe laat... het?**	hoo laat... heht
begin	**begint**	berghint
finish	**eindigt**	aiyndikht

Are there any seats for tonight?	**Zijn er nog plaatsen voor vanavond?**	zaiyn ehr nokh **plaat**sern voar vah**naa**vont
How much are the seats?	**Hoe duur zijn de plaatsen?**	hoo dewr zaiyn der **plaat**sern
I'd like to reserve 2 seats for the show on Friday evening.	**Ik wil graag 2 plaatsen reserveren voor de vrijdagavond-voorstelling.**	ik √il ghraakh 2 **plaat**sern rayzehr**vay**rern voar der **vraiy**dahk**haa**vont-**voor**stehling
Can I have a ticket for the matinée on Tuesday?	**Kan ik een kaartje krijgen voor de matinee op dinsdag?**	kahn ik ern **kaar**tyer **kraiy**ghern voar der mah**tee**nay op **dins**dahkh
I'd like a seat in the stalls (orchestra).	**Ik wil graag een plaats in de zaal.**	ik √il ghraakh ern plaats in der zaal
Not too far back.	**Niet te ver naar achteren.**	neet ter vehr naar **ahkh**terrern
Somewhere in the middle.	**Ergens in het midden.**	**ehr**ghernss in heht **mid**dern
How much are the seats in the circle (mezzanine)?	**Hoe duur zijn de plaatsen op het balkon?**	hoo dewr zaiyn der **plaat**sern op heht bahl**kon**
May I have a programme, please?	**Mag ik een programma, alstublieft?**	mahkh ik ern proagh**rah**maa ahlstew**bleeft**
Where's the cloakroom?	**Waar is de garderobe?**	√aar iss der ghahr**derro**ber

---

Het spijt mij, alles is uitverkocht.	I'm sorry, we're sold out.
Er zijn alleen nog een paar plaatsen over op het balkon.	There are only a few seats left in the circle (mezzanine).
Mag ik uw kaartje zien, alstublieft?	May I see your ticket, please?
Dit is uw plaats.	This is your seat.

---

* It's customary to tip usherettes *(l'ouvreuse)* in most Belgian theatres.

DAYS OF THE WEEK, see page 151

Opera—Ballet—Concert *Opera—Ballet—Concert*

Can you recommend a(n)...?	**Kunt u... aanbevelen?**	kurnt ew... **aan**bervaylern
ballet	**een ballet**	ern bah**leht**
concert	**een concert**	ern kon**sehrt**
opera	**een opera**	ern **oa**perraa
operetta	**een operette**	ern oaper**reh**ter

| Where's the opera house/ the concert hall? | **Waar is de opera/ het concertgebouw?** | √aar iss der **oa**perraa/heht kon**sehrt**gherboo**ow** |

| What's on at the opera tonight? | **Welke opera is er vanavond?** | √**ehl**ker **oa**perraa iss ehr vah**naa**vont |

| Who's singing/ dancing? | **Wie zingt/danst er?** | √ee zingt/dahnst ehr |

| Which orchestra is playing? | **Welk orkest speelt er?** | √**ehlk** or**kehst** spaylt ehr |

| What are they playing? | **Wat spelen zij?** | √aht **spay**lern zaiy |

| Who's the conductor/ soloist? | **Wie is de dirigent/ solist?** | √ee iss der deeree**ghehnt**/ soa**list** |

Nightclubs *Nachtclubs*

| Can you recommend a good nightclub? | **Kunt u een goede nachtclub aanbevelen?** | kurnt ew ern **ghoo**der **nahkht**klurp **aan**bervaylern |

| Is there a floor show? | **Is er een floorshow?** | iss ehr ern "floorshow" |

| What time does the show start? | **Hoe laat begint de voorstelling?** | hoo laat ber**ghint** der **voar**stehling |

| Is evening dress required? | **Is avondkleding noodzakelijk?** | iss **aa**vontklayding noatzaa**ker**lerk |

Discos *Discotheken*

| Where can we go dancing? | **Waar kunnen we gaan dansen?** | √aar **kur**nern √aiy ghaan **dahn**sern |

| Is there a discotheque in town? | **Is er een discotheek in de stad?** | iss ehr ern disko**atayk** in der staht |

| Would you like to dance? | **Wilt u dansen?** | √ilt ew **dahn**sern |

Sports   *Sport*

Football (soccer), skating, ice-hockey, cycling and horse racing are among the most popular sports in Belgium and Holland.

Are there any sports events going on?	**Wat zijn er voor sport-gebeurtenissen?**	√aht zaiyn ehr voar **sport**gherburternissern

basketball	**basketbal**	baaskertbahl
boxing	**boksen**	boksern
canoeing	**kanoën**	kaanoaern
cycling	**fietsen**	feetsern
football (soccer)	**voetbal**	vootbahl
horse racing	**paardenrennen**	paardernrehnern
(horse-back) riding	**paardrijden**	paartraiydern
motor racing	**autoracen**	o^{ow}toarayssern
sailing	**zeilen**	zaiylern
skating	**schaatsenrijden**	skhaatsernraiydern
swimming	**zwemmen**	z√ehmern
tennis	**tennis**	tehniss
volleyball	**volleybal**	volleebahl

Is there a football (soccer) match anywhere this Saturday?	**Is er ergens een voetbalwedstrijd aanstaande zaterdag?**	iss ehr **ehrghernss** ern vootbahl√ehtstraiyt **aanstaander** zaaterrdahkh
Which teams are playing?	**Welke teams spelen er?**	√ehlker "teams" spaylern ehr
Can you get me a ticket?	**Kunt u een kaartje voor mij krijgen?**	kurnt ew ern kaartyer voar maiy **kraiy**ghern
I'd like to see a...	**Ik wil graag... zien.**	ik √il ghraakh... zeen
boxing match	**een bokswedstrijd**	ern boks√ehtstraiyt
ice-hockey match	**een ijshockey-wedstrijd**	ern aiyshokkee√ehtstraiyt
Are there any skating races?	**Zijn er schaatswedstrijden?**	zaiyn ehr skhaats√ehtstraiydern
What's the admission charge?	**Wat is de toegangsprijs?**	√aht iss der **tooghahngs**praiyss
Where's the race course (track)?	**Waar is de renbaan?**	√aar iss der **rehn**baan

And if you want to take a more active part:

Where's the nearest golf course?	**Waar is het dichtstbijzijnde golfterrein?**	√aar iss heht dikhtst-baiy**zaiy**nder **gholf**tehraiyn
Can we hire (rent) clubs?	**Kunnen wij golf-clubs huren?**	kurnern √aiy **gholf**klurpss hewrern
Where are the tennis courts?	**Waar zijn de tennis-banen?**	√aar zaiyn der **tehnis**-baanern
Can I hire (rent) rackets?	**Kan ik rackets huren?**	kahn ik **rehkert**ss hewrern
What's the charge per...?	**Wat kost het per...?**	√aht kost heht pehr
day/round/hour	**dag/ronde/uur**	dahkh/**ronder**/ewr
Do I have to sign up beforehand?	**Moet ik van tevoren reserveren?**	moot ik vahn tervoarern rayzehr**vayr**ern
Can I take lessons?	**Kan ik les nemen?**	kahn ik lehss **naymer**n
Where can I hire a bike?	**Waar kan ik een fiets huren?**	√aar kahn ik ern feets hewrern
Is there any good fishing/hunting around here?	**Kun je hier ergens goed vissen/jagen?**	kurn yer heer **ehrghernss** ghoot **vissern**/**yaagher**n
Do I need a permit?	**Heb ik een vergun-ning nodig?**	hehp ik ern verr**ghur**ning **noa**derkh
Where can I get one?	**Waar kan ik die krijgen?**	√aar kahn ik dee **kraiygher**n
Can one swim in the lake?	**Kan men in het meer zwemmen?**	kahn mehn in heht mayr z√ehmern
Is there a swimming pool here?	**Is hier een zwem-bad?**	iss heer ern z√ehmbaht
Is it an open-air or indoor pool?	**Is het een buitenbad of binnenbad?**	iss heht ern bur^ew ternbaht off binnernbaht
Is it heated?	**Is het verwarmd?**	iss heht verr√ahrmt
Is there a skating rink near here?	**Is er hier in de buurt een ijsbaan?**	iss ehr heer in der bew rt ern aiysbaan
I'd like to skate.	**Ik wil graag schaatsen.**	ik √il ghraakh skhaatsern
I want to hire some skates.	**Ik wil graag schaatsen huren.**	ik √il ghraakh skhaatsern hewrern

On the beach *Op het strand*

Is there a sandy beach?	**Is er een zand-strand?**	iss ehr ern **zahn**tstrahnt
Is it safe for swimming?	**Kan men hier veilig zwemmen?**	kahn mehn heer **vai**ylikh z√ehmern
Is there a lifeguard?	**Is er een reddings-brigade?**	iss ehr ern **reh**dings-breehhaader
There are some big waves.	**Er zijn grote golven.**	ehr zaiyn **ghroa**ter **ghol**vern
Are there any dangerous currents?	**Zijn er gevaarlijke stromingen?**	zaiyn ehr gher**vaar**laiyker **stroa**mingern
Is it safe here for children?	**Is het hier veilig voor kinderen?**	iss heht heer **vaiy**lerkh voar **kin**derrern
What time is high tide/low tide?	**Wanneer is het vloed/eb?**	√ah**nayr** iss heht **vloot/ehp**
What's the temperature of the water?	**Welke temperatuur heeft het water?**	**√ehl**ker tehmperraa**tewr** hayft heht **√aa**terr
I want to hire a/an/some...	**Ik wil graag... huren.**	ik wil ghraakh... **hew**rern
air matress	**een luchtbed**	ern **lurkht**beht
bathing hut (cabana)	**een badhokje**	ern **baht**hokyer
deck chair	**een ligstoel**	ern **likh**stool
skin diving equipment	**een duikuitrusting**	ern **dur**ᵉʷ**kur**ᵉʷ**trursting**
sunshade (umbrella)	**een parasol**	ern **paa**raasol
water skis	**waterski's**	**√aa**terrskeess
windsurfer	**een surfplank**	ern **surrf**plahnk
Where can I rent a...?	**Waar kan ik... huren?**	√aar kahn ik... **hew**rern
canoe	**een kano**	ern **kaa**noa
motorboat	**een motorboot**	ern **moa**terrboat
rowing boat	**een roeiboot**	ern **roo**ᵉᵉboat
sailing boat	**een zeilboot**	ern **zaiyl**boat
What's the charge per hour?	**Wat kost het per uur?**	√aht kost heht pehr ewr

PRIVESTRAND	PRIVATE BEACH
VERBODEN TE ZWEMMEN	NO SWIMMING

Making friends

Introductions *Kennismaking*

May I introduce...?	**Mag ik u... voorstellen?**	mahkh ik ew **voar**stehlern
John, this is...	**John, dit is...**	john dit iss
My name is...	**Mijn naam is...**	maiyn naam iss
Pleased to meet you!	**Prettig kennis te maken!**	**preh**tikh **keh**niss ter **maa**kern
What's your name?	**Hoe heet u?**	hoo hayt ew
How are you?	**Hoe maakt u het?**	hoo maakt ew heht
Fine, thanks. And you?	**Uitstekend, dank u. En u?**	ur^{ew}tstaykernt dahnk ew. ehn ew

Follow up *En daarna*

How long have you been here?	**Hoelang bent u hier al?**	hoo**lahng** behnt ew heer ahl
We've been here a week.	**Wij zijn hier al een week.**	√aiy zaiyn heer ahl ern √ayk
We're on a 3-day visit.	**Wij zijn op een 3-daags bezoek.**	√aiy zaiyn op ern 3-daakhss ber**zook**
I'm on a business trip.	**Ik ben op zakenreis.**	ik behn op **zaa**kernrayss
Is this your first visit?	**Bent u hier voor de eerste keer?**	behnt ew heer voar der **ayr**ster kayr
No, we came here last year.	**Nee, wij kwamen hier vorig jaar ook.**	nay √aiy k√**aa**mern heer **vo**rikh yaar oak
Do you like it here?	**Bevalt het u hier?**	ber**vahlt** heht ew heer
Yes, I like it very much.	**Ja, het bevalt mij heel goed.**	yaa heht ber**vahlt** maiy hayl ghoot
I like the scenery a lot.	**Ik vind het landschap erg mooi.**	ik vint heht **lahnts**khahp ehrkh moo^{ee}
What do you think of the country/people?	**Hoe vindt u het land/de mensen?**	hoo`vint ew heht lahnt/der **mehn**sern
Where do you come from?	**Waar komt u vandaan?**	√aar komt ew vahn**daan**

I'm from...	Ik kom uit...	ik kom ur^{ew}t
What nationality are you?	Welke nationaliteit hebt u?	√ehlker naasyoanaaleetaiyt hehpt ew
I'm...	Ik ben...	ik behn
American	Amerikaan(se)	aamayreekaan(ser)
British	Brit(se)	brit(ser)
Canadian	Canadees (Canadese)	kahnaadays (kahnaadaysser)
English	Engels(e)	ehngerls(er)
Irish	Ier(se)	eer(ser)
Where are you staying?	Waar logeert u?	√aar loazhayrt ew
Are you on your own?	Bent u alleen?	behnt ew ahlayn
I'm with my...	Ik ben met...	ik behn meht
wife	mijn vrouw	maiyn vro^{ow}
husband	mijn man	maiyn mahn
family	mijn gezin	maiyn gherzin
children	mijn kinderen	maiyn kinderrern
parents	mijn ouders	maiyn o^{ow}derrss
boyfriend/girlfriend	mijn vriend/vriendin	maiyn vreent/vreendin

father/mother	de vader/moeder	der vaaderr/mooderr
son/daughter	de zoon/dochter	der zoan/dokhterr
brother/sister	de broer/zuster	der broor/zursterr
uncle/aunt	de oom/tante	der oam/tahnter
nephew	de neef	der nayf
niece	de nicht	der nikht
cousin	de neef/nicht	der nayf/nikht

Are you married/ single?	Bent u getrouwd/ ongetrouwd?	behnt ew ghertro^{ow}t/ onghertro^{ow}t
Do you have children?	Hebt u kinderen?	hehpt ew kinderrern
What do you do?	Wat is uw beroep?	√aht iss ew berroop
I'm a student.	Ik ben student.	ik behn stewdehnt
What are you studying?	Wat studeert u?	√aht stewdayrt ew
Do you travel a lot?	Reist u veel?	raiyst ew vayl
Do you play cards/ chess?	Speelt u kaart/ schaak?	spaylt ew kaart/skhaak

COUNTRIES, see page 146

The weather   *Het weer*

What a lovely day!	**Wat een prachtige dag!**	√aht ern **prahkhtergher** dahkh
What awful weather!	**Wat een afschuwelijk weer!**	√aht ern ahfskhew√erlerk √ayr
Isn't it cold/ hot today?	**Wat een kou/hitte vandaag!**	√aht ern ko^ew/**hitter** vahndaakh
Is it usually as warm as this?	**Is het altijd zo warm hier?**	iss heht ahltaiyt zoa √ahrm heer
Do you think it's going to... tomorrow?	**Denkt u dat het morgen...?**	dehnkt ew daht heht morghern
be a nice day	**een mooie dag is**	ern **moa**^ee^er dahkh iss
rain	**regent**	rayghernt
snow	**sneeuwt**	snay^oo^t
What's the weather forecast?	**Wat is de weersvoorspelling?**	√aht iss der √ayrsvoorspehling

cloud	**de wolk**	der √olk
fog	**de mist**	der mist
frost	**de vorst**	der vorst
hail	**de hagel**	der **haagherl**
ice	**het ijs**	heht aiyss
lightning	**de bliksem**	der **blikserm**
moon	**de maan**	der maan
rain	**de regen**	der **rayghern**
sky	**de hemel**	der **haymerl**
snow	**de sneeuw**	der snay^oo^
star	**de ster**	der stehr
sun	**de zon**	der zon
thunder	**de donder**	der donderr
thunderstorm	**het onweer**	heht on√ayr
wind	**de wind**	der √int

Invitations   *Uitnodigingen*

Would you like to have dinner with us on...?	**Wilt u met ons dineren op...?**	√ilt ew meht onss deenayrern op
May I invite you to lunch?	**Mag ik u uitnodigen voor de lunch?**	mahkh ik ew ur^ew^tnoaderghern voar der "lunch"

DAYS OF THE WEEK, see page 151

Can you come round for a drink this evening?	**Kunt u vanavond een glaasje bij ons komen drinken?**	kurnt ew vahnaavont ern ghlaasyer baiy onss koamern drinkern
There's a party. Are you coming?	**Er is een feestje. Kunt u ook komen?**	ehr iss ern faystyer. kurnt ew oak koamern
That's very kind of you.	**Dat is erg vriendelijk van u.**	daht iss ehrkh vreenderlerk vahn ew
Great. I'd love to come.	**Geweldig. Ik kom graag.**	gher√ehldikh. ik kom ghraakh
What time shall we come?	**Hoe laat zullen wij komen?**	hoo laat zurlern √aiy koamern
May I bring a friend?	**Mag ik een vriend meenemen?**	mahkh ik ern vreent maynaymern
I'm afraid we have to leave now.	**Helaas moeten wij nu weggaan.**	haylaass mootern √aiy new √ehkhghaan
Next time you must come to visit us.	**De volgende keer moet u bij ons komen.**	der volghernder kayr moot ew baiy onss koamern
Thanks for the evening. It was great.	**Hartelijk bedankt voor de avond. Het was geweldig.**	hahrterlerk berdahnkt voar der aavont. heht √ahss gher√ehlderkh

Dating *Afspraakjes*

Do you mind if I smoke?	**Stoort het u als ik rook?**	stoart heht ew ahlss ik roak
Would you like a cigarette?	**Wilt u een sigaret?**	√ilt ew ern seeghaareht
Do you have a light, please?	**Hebt u een vuurtje, alstublieft?**	hehpt ew ern vewrtyer ahlstew bleeft
Why are you laughing?	**Waarom lacht u?**	√aarom lahkht ew
Is my Dutch that bad?	**Is mijn Nederlands zo slecht?**	iss maiyn nayderrlahnts zoa slehkht
Do you mind if I sit here?	**Mag ik hier gaan zitten?**	mahkh ik heer ghaan zittern
Would you like a drink?	**Wilt u wat drinken?**	√ilt ew √aht drinkern
Are you waiting for someone?	**Wacht u op iemand?**	√ahkht ew op eemahnt

Are you free this evening?	**Bent u vanavond vrij?**	behnt ew vahn**aa**vont vraiy
Would you like to go out with me tonight?	**Hebt u zin om vanavond met mij uit te gaan?**	hehpt ew zin om vahn**aa**vont meht maiy ur**ew**t ter ghaan
I know a good discotheque.	**Ik weet een goede discotheek.**	ik √ayt ern **gh**ooder disko**tayk**
Shall we go to the cinema (movies)?	**Zullen we naar de bioscoop gaan?**	zurlern wer naar der beeyoskoap ghaan
Would you like to...?	**Hebt u zin om...?**	hehpt ew zin om
go dancing	**te gaan dansen**	ter ghaan **dahns**ern
go for a drive	**een autorit te maken**	ern o**ow**toarit ter **maak**ern
Where shall we meet?	**Waar zullen we elkaar ontmoeten?**	√aar zurlern √er ehlkaar ontm**oo**tern
I'll pick you up at your hotel.	**Ik kom u in uw hotel afhalen.**	ik kom ew in ew**oo** hoat**ehl** **ahf**haalern
I'll call for you at 8.	**Ik kom u om 8 uur afhalen.**	ik kom ew om 8 ewr **ahf**haalern
May I take you home?	**Mag ik u naar huis brengen?**	mahkh ik ew naar hur**ew**ss **breh**ngern
Can I see you again tomorrow?	**Zie ik u morgen weer?**	zee ik ew **morgh**ern √ayr
I hope we'll meet again.	**Ik hoop dat wij elkaar weer zullen ontmoeten.**	ik hoap daht wer ehl**kaar** √ayr zurlern ontm**oo**tern

...and you might answer:

I'd love to, thank you.	**Graag, dank u.**	ghraakh dahnk ew
Thank you, but I'm busy.	**Dank u, maar ik heb het te druk.**	dahnk ew maar ik hehp heht ter drurk
No, I'm not interested, thank you.	**Nee, ik heb geen interesse, dank u.**	nay ik hehp gayn inter**reh**ser dahnk ew
Leave me alone, please!	**Laat mij met rust, alstublieft!**	laat maiy meht rurst ahlstew**bleeft**
Thank you, it's been a wonderful evening.	**Dank u, het was een heerlijke avond.**	dahnk ew heht √ahss ern **hay**rlerker aavont
I've enjoyed myself.	**Ik heb genoten.**	ik hehp gher**noa**tern

Shopping Guide

This shopping guide is designed to help you find what you want with ease, accuracy and speed. It features:

1. A list of all major shops, stores and services (p. 98).

2. Some general expressions required when shopping to allow you to be specific and selective (p. 100).

3. Full details of the shops and services most likely to concern you. Here you'll find advice, alphabetical lists of items and conversion charts listed under the headings below.

		page
Bookshop/ Stationer's	books, magazines, newspapers, stationery	104
Camping and sports equipment	useful items for camping and other leisure activities	106
Chemist's (drugstore)	medicine, first-aid, cosmetics, toilet articles	107
Clothing	clothes and accessories, shoes	111
Electrical appliances	radios, cassette recorders, shavers	118
Grocer's	some general expressions, weights, measures and packaging	119
Household articles	useful items for the house: tools, crockery, cutlery	120
Jeweller's/ Watchmaker's	jewellery, watches, watch repairs	121
Optician	glasses, lenses, binoculars	123
Photography	cameras, films, developing, accessories	124
Tobacconist's	smoker's supplies	126
Miscellaneous	souvenirs, records, cassettes, toys	127

LAUNDRY, see page 29/HAIRDRESSER, see page 30

Winkelen

Shops, stores and services   *Winkels en diensten*

Shops are usually open Monday to Friday from 8.30/9 a.m. to 5.30/6 p.m. and on Saturdays generally till 5 p.m. Some smaller businesses close for lunch, but department stores are open continuously. However, the latter are often closed on Monday mornings. In Holland most towns shops stay open until 9 p.m. on Thursdays or Fridays.

Where's the nearest...	**Waar is de/het dichtstbijzijnde...?**	√aar iss der/heht dikhtstbaiyzaiynder
antique shop	**de antiekwinkel**	der ahnteek√inkerl
art gallery	**de kunstgalerij**	der kurnstghahlerraiy
baker's	**de bakker**	der bahkerr
bank	**de bank**	der bahnk
barber's	**de herenkapper**	der hayrernkahperr
beauty salon	**de schoonheidssalon**	der skhoanhaiytssaloan
bookshop	**de boekhandel**	der bookhanderl
butcher's	**de slagerij**	der slaagherraiy
cake shop	**de banketbakkerij**	der bahnkehtbahkerraiy
camera shop	**de fotozaak**	der foatoazaak
candy store	**de snoepwinkel**	der snoep√inkerl
cheese shop	**de kaaswinkel**	der kaas√inkerl
chemist's	**de apotheek**	der ahpoatayk
china shop	**de porseleinwinkel**	der porserlaiyn√inkerl
currency exchange office	**het wisselkantoor**	heht √isserlkahntoar
dairy	**de melkwinkel**	der mehlk√inkerl
delicatessen	**de delicatessenzaak**	der dayleekaatehsernzaak
dentist	**de tandarts**	der tahntahrts
department store	**het warenhuis**	heht √aarernhur^{ew}ss
doctor	**de dokter**	der dokterr
drugstore	**de apotheek**	der ahpoatayk
dry cleaner's	**de stomerij**	der stoamerraiy
electrical goods shop	**de elektriciteits-zaak**	der aylehktreeseetaiyts-zaak
fishmonger's	**de vishandel**	der visshahnderl
florist's	**de bloemist**	der bloomist
furrier's	**de bontzaak**	der bontzaak
greengrocer's	**de groenteman**	der ghroontermahn
grocer's	**de kruidenier**	der krur^{ew}derneer
hairdresser's (ladies/men)	**de kapper (dames-/heren-)**	der kahperr (daamers-/hayrern-)
hardware store	**de ijzerhandel**	der aiyzerrhahnderl
health food shop	**de reformwinkel**	der rerform√inkerl

hospital	het ziekenhuis	heht zeekernhur^{ew}ss
ironmonger's	de ijzerhandel	der aiyzerrhahnderl
jeweller's	de juwelier	der yew√erleer
launderette	de wasserette	der √ahsserrehter
laundry	de wasserij	der √ahsserraiy
library	de bibliotheek	der beebleeoatayk
liquor store	de slijterij	der slaiyterraiy
lost property (lost and found) office	het bureau voor gevonden voorwerpen	heht bewroa voar ghervondern voar-√ehrpern
market	de markt	der mahrkt
newsstand	de krantenkiosk	der krahnternkeeyosk
optician	de opticiën	der opteesyehn
pastry shop	de banketbakkerij	der bahnkehtbahkerraiy
pharmacy	de apotheek	der ahpoatayk
photographer	de fotograaf	der foatoaghraaf
police station	het politiebureau	heht poaleetseebewroa
post office	het postkantoor	heht postkahntoar
second-hand shop	de tweedehandswinkel	der t√ayderhahnts√inkerl
shoemaker's (repairs)	de schoenmaker	der skhoonmaakerr
shoe shop	de schoenenwinkel	der skhoonernvinkerl
shopping centre	het winkelcentrum	heht √inkerlsehntrurm
souvenir shop	de souvenirwinkel	der sooverneer√inkerl
sporting goods shop	de sportzaak	der sportzaak
stationer's	de kantoorboekhandel	der kahntoarbookhahnderl
supermarket	de supermarkt	der sewperrmahrkt
sweet shop	de snoepwinkel	der snoop√inkerl
tailor's	de kleermaker	der klayrmaakerr
telegraph office	het postkantoor	heht postkahntoar
tobacconist's	de sigarenwinkel	der seeghaarern√inkerl
toy shop	de speelgoedwinkel	der spaylghoot√inkerl
travel agency	het reisbureau	heht raiysbewroa
vegetable store	de groentewinkel	der ghroonter√inkerl
veterinarian	de dierenarts	der deerernahrts
watchmaker's	de horlogemaker	der horloazhermaakerr
wine merchant	de wijnhandel	der √aiynhahnderl

INGANG	ENTRANCE
UITGANG	EXIT
NOODUITGANG	EMERGENCY EXIT

General expressions *Algemene uitdrukkingen*

Where? *Waar?*

Where's there a good...?	**Waar is een goede...?**	√aar iss ern ghooder
Where can I find a...?	**Waar kan ik een... vinden?**	√aar kahn ik ern... vindern
Where's the main shopping area?	**Waar is de winkel-buurt?**	√aar iss der √inkerlbewrt
Is it far from here?	**Is het ver hier vandaan?**	iss heht vehr heer vahndaan
How do I get there?	**Hoe kom ik daar?**	hoo kom ik daar

> **UITVERKOOP** SALE

Service *Bediening*

Can you help me?	**Kunt u mij helpen?**	kurnt ew maiy hehlpern
I'm just looking.	**Ik kijk alleen even rond.**	ik kaiyk ahlayn ayvern ront
Do you sell...?	**Verkoopt u...?**	vehrkoapt ew
I'd like to buy...	**Ik wil graag... kopen.**	ik √il ghraakh... koapern
I'd like...	**Ik wil graag...**	ik √il ghraakh
Can you show me...?	**Kunt u mij... laten zien?**	kurnt ew maiy... laatern zeen
this/that	**dit/dat**	dit/daht
the one in the window	**die in de etalage**	dee in der aytaalaazher
the one in the display case	**die in de vitrine**	dee in der veetreener
Do you have any...?	**Hebt u...?**	hehpt ew
Where is the ...?	**Waar is...?**	√aar iss
...department	**de...-afdeling**	der...-ahfdayling
escalator	**de roltrap**	der roltrahp
lift (elevator)	**de lift**	der lift
Where do I pay?	**Waar moet ik betalen?**	√aar moot ik bertaalern

Defining the article   *Omschrijving van het artikel*

| I'd like a... one. | **Ik wil graag een...** | ik √il ghraakh ern... |
| | **hebben.** | hehbern |

big	**grote**	ghroater
cheap	**goedkope**	ghootkoaper
dark	**donkere**	donkerrer
good	**goede**	ghooder
heavy	**zware**	z√aarer
large	**grote**	ghroater
light	**lichte**	likhter
oval	**ovale**	oavaaler
rectangular	**rechthoekige**	rehkhthookergher
round	**ronde**	ronder
small	**kleine**	klaiyner
square	**vierkante**	veerkahnter
sturdy	**stevige**	stayvergher

| It is too... | **Het is te...** | heht iss ter... |
| big/small. | **groot/klein.** | ghroat/klaiyn |

| I don't want anything | **Het mag niet te** | heht mahkh neet ter dewr |
| too expensive. | **duur zijn.** | zaiyn |

Preference   *Ik heb liever...*

| Can you show me | **Kunt u mij nog wat** | kurnt ew maiy nokh √aht |
| some others? | **laten zien?** | laatern zeen |

| Don't you have | **Hebt u niet iets...?** | hehpt ew neet eets |
| anything ...? | | |

| cheaper/better | **goedkopers/beters** | ghootkoaperrss/bayterrss |
| larger/smaller | **groters/kleiners** | ghroaterrss/klaiynerrss |

How much?   *Hoeveel?*

How much is this?	**Hoeveel kost dit?**	hoovayl kost dit
How much are they?	**Hoeveel kosten ze?**	hoovayl kostern zer
I don't understand.	**Ik begrijp het niet.**	ik beghraiyp heht neet
Please write it down.	**Schrijft u het als-**	skhraiyft ew heht ahls-
	tublieft even op.	tewbleeft ayvern op
I don't want to	**Ik wil niet meer dan**	ik √il neet mayr dahn
spend more than...	**...gulden uitgeven.**	...ghurldern ur^{ew}tghayvern
guilders.		

COLOURS, see page 112

Decision   *Beslissing*

It's not quite what I want.	**Dat is niet precies wat ik zoek.**	daht iss neet prerseess √aht ik zook
No, I don't like it.	**Nee, het bevalt mij niet.**	nay heht bervahlt maiy neet
I'll take it.	**Ik neem dit.**	ik naym dit

Ordering—Delivery   *Bestellen—Bezorgen*

Can you order it for me?	**Kunt u het voor mij bestellen?**	kurnt ew heht voar maiy berstehlern
How long will it take?	**Hoe lang duurt het?**	hoo lahng dewrt heht
I'll take it with me.	**Ik neem het mee.**	ik naym heht may
Deliver it to the... Hotel.	**Stuurt u het naar het... hotel.**	stewrt ew heht naar heht... hoatehl
Please send it to this address.	**Stuurt u het alstublieft naar dit adres.**	stewrt ew heht ahlstewbleeft naar dit aadrehss
Will I have any difficulty with customs?	**Krijg ik geen moeilijkheden met de douane?**	kraiykh ik ghayn moo°°lerkhaydern meht der doo√aaner

Paying   *Betalen*

How much is it?	**Hoeveel is het?**	hoovayl iss heht
Can I pay by traveller's cheque?	**Kan ik met reischeques betalen?**	kahn ik meht raiysshehks bertaalern
Do you accept dollars/pounds?	**Neemt u dollars/ponden aan?**	naymt ew dollahrss/pondern aan
Do you accept credit cards?	**Neemt u credit cards aan?**	naymt ew "credit cards" aan
Do I have to pay VAT (sales tax)?	**Moet ik B.T.W. betalen?**	moot ik bay-tay-√ay bertaalern
Could I have a receipt, please?	**Mag ik een kwitantie hebben, alstublieft?**	mahkh ik ern k√eetahnsee hehbern ahlstewbleeft
I think there's a mistake in the bill.	**Ik geloof dat er een fout in de rekening is.**	ik gherloaf daht ehr ern fo°ʷt in der raykerning iss

Anything else? *Nog iets anders?*

No, thanks, that's all.	**Nee, dank u, dat is alles.**	nay dahnk ew daht iss **ahlerss**
Yes, I'd like...	**Ja, ik wil graag...**	yaa ik √il ghraakh
May I have a bag, please?	**Hebt u een tas, alstublieft?**	hehpt ew ern tahss ahlstew**bleeft**
Could you wrap it up for me, please?	**Kunt u het voor mij inpakken, alstublieft?**	kurnt ew heht voar maiy inpahkern ahlstew**bleeft**

Dissatisfied? *Niet tevreden*

Can you exchange this, please?	**Kan ik dit ruilen, alstublieft?**	kahn ik dit rur**ew**lern ahlstew**bleeft**
I want to return this.	**Ik wil dit teruggeven.**	ik √il dit terrurkh**ghay**vern
I'd like a refund. Here's the receipt.	**Ik wil graag mijn geld terug. Hier is de kwitantie.**	ik √il ghraakh maiyn ghehlt terrurkh. heer iss der k√eetahnsee

---

Kan ik u helpen?	Can I help you?
Wat wilt u hebben?	What would you like?
Welke... wilt u hebben?	What... would you like?
kleur/vorm/kwaliteit	colour/shape/quality
Het spijt mij, maar dat hebben we niet.	I'm sorry, we don't have any.
Dat hebben wij niet in voorraad.	We're out of stock.
Zullen wij het voor u bestellen?	Shall we order it for you?
Wilt u het meenemen of zullen wij het u toesturen?	Will you take it with you or shall we send it?
Nog iets?	Anything else?
Dat is dan... gulden, alstublieft.	That's... guilders, please.
De kassa is daar.	The cash desk is over there.

Bookshop—Stationer's *Boekhandel—Kantoorboekhandel*

In Holland, bookshops and stationers' are usually separate shops, although the latter will often sell paperbacks. Newspapers and magazines in English and other languages are sold in kiosks and in many bookshops as well as in hotels.

Where's the nearest ...?	**Waar is de dichtst-bijzijnde...?**	√aar iss der dikhst-baiy**zaiy**nder
bookshop	**boekhandel**	**book**hahnderl
stationer's	**kantoorboekhandel**	kahntoar**book**hahnderl
newsstand	**krantenkiosk**	**krahn**ternkeeyosk
Where can I buy an English-language newspaper?	**Waar kan ik een Engelse krant kopen?**	√aar kahn ik ern **ehng**erlser krahnt **koa**pern
Where's the guide-book section?	**Waar staan de reis-gidsen?**	√aar staan der **raiys**ghitsern
Where are the English books?	**Waar staan de Engelse boeken?**	√aar staan der **ehng**erlser **book**ern
Do you have any of ...'s books in English?	**Hebt u een boek van ...in het Engels?**	hehpt ew ern book vahn ...in heht **ehng**erlss
Do you have second-hand books?	**Hebt u tweedehands boeken?**	hehpt ew t√ayder**hahnts book**ern
I'd like to buy a/an/some...	**Ik wil graag... kopen.**	ik √il ghraakh... **koa**pern
address book	**een adresboekje**	ern aa**drehs**bookyer
adhesive tape	**plakband**	**plahk**bahnt
ball-point pen	**een ballpoint**	ern ''ballpoint''
blotting paper	**vloeipapier**	vloo**ee**paapeer
book	**een boek**	ern book
calendar	**een kalender**	ern kaa**lehn**derr
carbon paper	**carbonpapier**	kahr**bon**paapier
coloured pencils	**kleurpotloden**	klurr**pot**loadern
crayons	**tekenstiften**	**tay**kernstiftern
diary	**een agenda**	ern aa**gehn**daa
dictionary	**een woordenboek**	ern √oar**den**book
Dutch-English	**Nederlands-Engels**	nayderr**lahnts-ehng**erlss
drawing paper	**tekenpapier**	**tay**kernpaapeer
drawing pins	**punaises**	pew**neh**serss
envelopes	**enveloppen**	ehnve**lop**pern
eraser	**een gummetje**	ern **ghur**mertyer
exercise book	**een schrift**	ern skhrift

felt-tip pen	**een viltstift**	ern **viltstift**
fountain pen	**een vulpen**	ern **vurlpehn**
glue	**lijm**	laiym
grammar book	**een grammatica**	ern **ghrahmaateekaa**
guidebook	**een reisgids**	ern **raiysghits**
ink	**inkt**	inkt
(adhesive) labels	**(zelfklevende)**	**(zehlfklayvernder)**
	etiketten	ayteekehtern
magazine	**een tijdschrift**	ern **taiytskhrift**
map	**een landkaart**	ern **lahntkaart**
street map	**plattegrond**	plaht**erghront**
road map of...	**wegenkaart van...**	√ay**ghernkaart vahn**
mechanical pencil	**een vulpotlood**	ern **vurlpotloat**
newspaper	**een krant**	ern **krahnt**
American	**Amerikaanse**	aamayree**kaanser**
English	**Engelse**	**ehng**erlser
notebook	**een notitieboekje**	ern noa**teetseebookyer**
note paper	**briefpapier**	**breef**paapeer
paintbox	**een verfdoos**	ern **vehrfdoass**
paper	**papier**	**paapeer**
paperback	**een pocketboek**	ern **pokkertbook**
paperclips	**paperclips**	"paperclips"
paper napkins	**papieren servetten**	paapeerern sehr**vehtern**
pen	**een pen**	ern **pehn**
pencil	**een potlood**	ern **potloat**
pencil sharpener	**een puntenslijper**	ern **purnternslaiyperr**
phrase book	**een taalgids**	ern **taalghits**
picture book	**een prentenboek**	ern **prehnternbook**
playing cards	**speelkaarten**	spayl**kaartern**
pocket calculator	**een zakreken-**	ern **zahkraykern-**
	machientje	maasheentyer
postcard	**een briefkaart**	ern **breefkaart**
propelling pencil	**een vulpotlood**	ern **vurlpotloat**
refill (for a pen)	**een vulling (voor**	ern **vurling (voar ern pehn)**
	een pen)	
rubber	**een gummetje**	ern **ghurmertyer**
rubber bands	**elastiekjes**	aylah**steekyerss**
ruler	**een lineaal**	ern **leeneeyaal**
staples	**nietjes**	**neetyerss**
string	**touw**	to^ow
thumbtacks	**punaises**	pew**nehserss**
travel guide	**een reisgids**	ern **raiysghits**
typewriter ribbon	**een schrijfmachinelint**	ern **skhraiyfmaasheenerlint**
typing paper	**schrijfmachinepapier**	**skhraiyfmaasheenerpaapier**
wrapping paper	**pakpapier**	**pahkpaapier**
writing pad	**een blocnote**	ern **bloknoat**

Camping and sports equipment *Kampeer- en sportuitrusting*

I'd like a/an/some...	**Ik wil graag... hebben.**	ik √il ghraakh... **heh**bern
I'd like to hire a(n)/some...	**Ik wil graag... huren.**	ik √il ghraakh... **hew**rern
air bed (mattress)	**een luchtbed**	ern **lurkht**beht
backpack	**een rugzak**	ern **rurgh**zahk
butane gas	**butagas**	bew**taa**ghahss
campbed	**een veldbed**	ern **vehlt**beht
(folding) chair	**een (klap)stoel**	ern **(klahp)**stool
charcoal	**houtskool**	hoᵒʷtskoal
compass	**een kompas**	ern kom**pahss**
cool box	**een koelbox**	ern **kool**box
deck chair	**een ligstoel**	ern **likh**stool
fire lighters	**aansteekblokjes**	**aan**staykblokyerss
fishing tackle	**visgerei**	**vis**gherraiy
flashlight	**een zaklantaarn**	ern **zahk**lahntaarn
groundsheet	**een grondzeil**	ern **ghront**zaiyl
hammock	**een hangmat**	ern **hahng**maht
ice pack	**een koelelement**	ern **kool**aylermehnt
insect spray (killer)	**insektenspray**	in**sehk**ternspray
kerosene	**petroleum**	pay**troa**layyurm
lamp	**een lamp**	ern **lahmp**
lantern	**een lantaarn**	ern **lahn**taarn
mallet	**een (houten) hamer**	ern **(hoᵉʷ**tern) **haa**merr
matches	**lucifers**	**lew**seefehrss
(foam rubber) mattress	**een (schuimrubber) matras**	ern **(skhur**ᵉʷmrurberr) **mah**trahss
mosquito net	**een muskietennet**	ern **mur**skeeternneht
paraffin	**petroleum**	pay**troa**layyurm
picnic basket	**een picknickmand**	ern **pik**nikmahnt
pump	**een pomp**	ern **pomp**
rope	**een touw**	ern toᵒʷ
rucksack	**een rugzak**	ern **rurgh**zahk
skiing equipment	**een ski-uitrusting**	ern **skee**-urᵉʷtrursting
skin-diving equipment	**een duikuitrusting**	ern durᵉʷk-urᵉʷtrursting
sleeping bag	**een slaapzak**	ern **slaap**zahk
(folding) table	**een (vouw)tafel**	ern **(voᵒʷ√)**taaferl
tent	**een tent**	ern **tehnt**
tent pegs	**haringen**	**haa**ringern
tent pole	**een tentstok**	ern **tehnt**stok
torch	**een zaklantaarn**	ern **zahk**lahntaarn
windsurfer	**een surfplank**	ern **surrf**plahnk
water flask	**een veldfles**	ern **vehlt**flehss

CAMPING, see page 32

Chemist's (drugstore) *Apotheek*

Chemists in Holland usually carry most of the goods you'll find in Britain or the U.S.A. The sign denoting a chemist's is *Apotheek* (ahpoa**tayk**). In the window of an *apotheek,* you'll see a notice telling you where the nearest all-night chemist's is located.

For perfume, cosmetics and toilet articles you'll have to go to a *drogisterij* (droaghister**raiy**)—drugstore, or non-dispensing chemist's.

This section is divided into two parts:

1. Medicine, first aid, etc.
2. Toilet articles, cosmetics, etc.

General *Algemeen*

Where's the nearest (all-night) chemist's?	**Waar is de dichtst-bijzijnde (dienst-doende) apotheek?**	√aar iss der dikhtstbaiy-zaiynder (**deenst**doonder) ahpoa**tayk**
What time does the chemist's open/close?	**Hoe laat gaat de apotheek open/dicht?**	hoo laat ghaat der ahpoa**tayk** o**a**pern/dikht

1 – Pharmaceutical *Medicijnen*

I'd like something for ...	**Ik wil graag iets tegen...**	ik √il ghraakh eets **tay**ghern
a cold	**een verkoudheid**	ern verrko^{ow}thaiyt
a cough	**hoest**	hoost
hayfever	**hooikoorts**	hoa^{ee}koarts
a headache	**hoofdpijn**	**hoaft**paiyn
insect bites	**insektenbeten**	in**sehk**ternbaytern
sunburn	**zonnebrand**	**zonner**brahnt
travel sickness	**reisziekte**	**raiys**zeekter
an upset stomach	**indigestie**	in**dee**ghehstee
Can you prepare this prescription for me?	**Kunt u dit recept voor mij klaarmaken?**	kurnt ew dit rer**sehpt** voar maiy **klaar**maakern
Can I get it without a prescription?	**Kan ik het zonder recept krijgen?**	kahn ik heht **zonder**r rer**sehpt kraiy**ghern
Shall I wait?	**Kan ik erop wachten?**	kahn ik ehrop √**ahkh**tern

DOCTOR, see page 137

Winkelen

Can I have a/an/ some...?	**Mag ik... van u hebben?**	mahhk ik... vahn ew hehbern
absorbent cotton	**watten**	√ahtern
analgesic	**een pijnstillend middel**	ern paiynstillernt midderl
antiseptic cream	**antiseptische crème**	ahnteesehpteesser krehm
aspirin	**aspirine**	ahspeereener
bandage	**verband**	verrbahnt
elastic bandage	**elastisch verband**	aylahsteess verrbahnt
Band-Aids	**pleisters**	plaiysterrss
...capsules	**...capsules**	...kahpsewlerss
condoms	**condooms**	kondoamss
contraceptives	**voorbehoeds- middelen**	voarberhootsmidderlern
corn plasters	**likdoornpleisters**	likdoarnplaiysterrss
cotton wool	**watten**	√ahtern
cough drops	**hoestpastilles**	hoostpahsteeyerss
cough syrup	**hoestsiroop**	hoostseeroap
disinfectant	**een ontsmettings- middel**	ern ontsmehtingsmidderl
ear drops	**oordruppels**	oardrurperlss
Elastoplast	**pleisters**	plaiysterrss
eye drops	**oogdruppels**	oaghdrurperlss
first-aid kit	**een verbandtrommel**	ern verrbahnttrommerl
gauze	**verbandgaas**	verrbahntghaass
insect repellent	**een insektenwerend middel**	ern insehktern√ayrernt midderl
iodine	**jodium**	yoadeeyurm
laxative	**laxeermiddel**	lahksayrmidderl
mouthwash	**mondwater**	mont√aaterr
nose drops	**neusdruppels**	nursdrurperlss
...ointment	**...zalf**	...zahlf
sanitary towels (napkins)	**maandverband**	maantverrbahnt
suppositories	**zetpillen**	zehtpillern
...tablets	**...tabletten**	...tahblehtern
tampons	**tampons**	tahmponss
thermometer	**een thermometer**	ern tehrmoamayterr
throat lozenges	**keelpastilles**	kaylpahsteeyerss
vitamin pills	**vitaminepillen**	veetahmeenerpillern

	VERGIF	POISON
	ALLEEN VOOR UITWENDIG GEBRUIK	FOR EXTERNAL USE ONLY

Winkelen

2—Toiletry *Toiletartikelen*

I'd like a/an/ some...	Ik wil graag...	ik vil ghraakh
after-shave lotion	een aftershave lotion	ern "aftershave lotion"
astringent	een adstringens	ern ahtstringernss
bath salts	badzout	bahtzo^{ou}t
blusher	rouge	roozher
bubble bath	badschuim	bathskhur^{ew}m
cosmetics	cosmetica	kosmayteekaa
cream	een crème	ern krehm
cleansing cream	reinigingscrème	raynighingskrehm
foundation cream	basiscrème	baaserskrehm
moisturizing cream	vochtinbrengende crème	vokhtinbrehngernder krehm
night cream	nachtcrème	nahkhtkrehm
cuticle remover	een nagelriem remover	ern naagherlreem "remover"
deodorant	een deodorant	ern dayoadoarahnt
emery board	kartonnen nagel- vijlen	kahrtonnern naagherl- vaiylern
eyebrow pencil	een wenkbrauw- potlood	ern vehnkbro^{ow}potloat
eyeliner	een oogpotlood	ern oaghpotloat
eye shadow	een oogschaduw	ern oaghskhaadew^{oo}
face powder	poeder	pooderr
foot cream	een voetcrème	ern vootkrehm
handcream	een handcrème	ern hahntkrehm
lipsalve	lippenpommade	lippernpommaaderr
lipstick	een lippenstift	ern lippernstift
make-up remover pads	make-up remover watten	"make-up remover" vahtern
mascara	mascara	mahskaaraa
nail brush	een nagelborsteltje	ern naagherlborsterltyer
nail clippers	een nagelschaartje	ern naagherlskhaartyer
nail file	een nagelvijl	ern naagherlvaiyl
nail polish	nagellak	naagherllahk
nail polish remover	nagellak remover	naagherllahk "remover"
nail scissors	een nagelschaartje	ern naagherlskhaartyer
perfume	parfum	pahrfurm
powder	poeder	pooderr
powder puff	een poederdons	ern pooderrdonss
razor	een scheermes	ern skhayrmehss
razor blades	scheermesjes	skhayrmehsherss
safety pins	veiligheidsspelden	vaiylighhaiytsspehldern

shaving brush	**een scheerkwast**	ern skhayrk√ahst
shaving cream	**een scheercrème**	ern skhayrkrehm
shower gel	**doucheschuim**	dooshskhur^{ew}m
soap	**zeep**	zayp
sponge	**een spons**	ern sponss
sun-tan cream	**een zonnebrand-crème**	ern zonnerbrahntkrehm
sun-tan oil	**zonnebrandolie**	zonnerbrahntoalee
talcum powder	**talkpoeder**	tahlkpooderr
tissues	**papieren zakdoeken**	paapeerern zahkdoekern
toilet paper	**toiletpapier**	t√aalehtpaapeer
toilet water	**eau de toilette**	oa der t√ahleht
toothbrush	**een tandenborstel**	ern tahndernborsterl
toothpaste	**tandpasta**	tahntpahstaa
towel	**een handdoek**	ern hahndook
tweezers	**een pincet**	ern pinseht

For your hair   *Voor uw haar*

bobby pins	**schuifspeldjes**	skur^{ew}fspehldyerss
colour shampoo	**kleurshampoo**	klurrshahmpoa
comb	**een kam**	ern kahm
curlers	**haarrollers**	haarrollerrss
dry shampoo	**droogshampoo**	droaghshahmpoa
hairbrush	**een haarborstel**	ern haarborsterl
hair dye	**haarverf**	haarvehrf
hair (styling) gel	**haargel**	haarzhehl
hairgrips	**schuifspeldjes**	skhur^{ew}fspehldyerss
hair lotion	**haarwater**	haar√aaterr
hairpins	**haarspelden**	haarspehldern
hair slide	**een haarspeld**	ern haarspehlt
hair spray	**haarlak**	haarlahk
setting lotion	**een haarversteviger**	ern haarverrstayvergherr
shampoo	**shampoo**	shahmpoa
for dry/greasy (oily) hair	**voor droog/vet haar**	voar droakh/veht haar
wig	**een pruik**	ern prur^{ew}k

For the baby   *Voor de baby*

baby food	**babyvoeding**	baybeevooding
dummy (pacifier)	**een fopspeen**	ern fopspayn
feeding bottle	**een zuigfles**	ern zur^{ew}ghflehss
nappies (diapers)	**luiers**	lur^{ew}yerrss

Winkelen

Clothing *Kleding*

If you want to buy something specific, prepare yourself in advance. Look at the list of clothing on page 115. Get some idea of the colour, material and size you want. They're all listed on the next few pages.

General *Algemeen*

I'd like...	**Ik wil graag...**	ik √il ghraakh
I'd like... for a boy/ a 10-year-old girl.	**Ik wil graag... voor een jongen/een meisje van 10 jaar.**	ik √il ghraak... voar ern yongern/ern maiysher vahn 10 yaar
I'd like something like this.	**Ik wil graag iets dergelijks hebben.**	ik √il ghraakh eets dehrgherlerks hehbern
I like the one in the window.	**Die in de etalage bevalt mij.**	dee in der aytaalaazher bervahlt maiy
How much is that per metre?	**Hoeveel kost het per meter?**	hoovayl kost heht pehr mayterr

1 centimetre (cm.) =	0.39 in.	1 inch = 2.54 cm.
1 metre (m.)	= 39.37 in.	1 foot = 30.5 cm.
10 metres	= 32.81 ft.	1 yard = 0.91 m.

Colour *Kleur*

I'd like something in...	**Ik wil iets in het... hebben.**	ik √il eets in heht... hehbern
I'd like a darker/ lighter shade.	**Ik wil het iets donkerder/lichter hebben.**	ik √il heht eets donkerrderr/likhterr hehbern
I'd like something to match this.	**Ik wil iets dat hierbij past.**	ik √il eets daht heerbaiy pahst
I don't like the colour/pattern.	**De kleur/Het patroon bevalt mij niet.**	der klurr/heht paatroan bervahlt maiy neet

beige	beige	baiyzher
black	zwart	zvahrt
blue	blauw	blo^{ow}
brown	bruin	brur^{ew}n
golden	goud	gho^{ow}t
green	groen	ghroon
grey	grijs	ghraiyss
mauve	mauve	moaver
orange	oranje	oarahñer
pink	rose	rozer
purple	paars	paarss
red	rood	roat
scarlet	scharlakenrood	skhahrlaakernroat
silver	zilver	zilverr
turquoise	turkoois	turrkoo^{ee}ss
white	wit	$\sqrt{i}$t
yellow	geel	ghayl
light ...	licht...	likht
dark ...	donker...	donkerr

zonder patroon

(zonderr paatroan)

gestippeld

(ghersti-pperlt)

gestreept

(gherstraypt)

geruit

(gherrur^{ew}t)

met een patroon

(meht ayn paatroan)

Fabric *Stof*

Do you have anything in...?	Hebt u iets in...?	hehpt ew eets in
Is that...?	Is dat...?	iss daht
handmade	handwerk	hahntwehrk
imported	geïmporteerd	gherimportayrt
made in Holland	in Holland gemaakt	in hollahnt ghermaakt
I'd like something thinner.	Ik wil graag iets dunners.	ik $\sqrt{i}$l ghraakh eets durnerrss
Do you have anything of better quality?	Hebt u een betere kwaliteit?	hehpt ew ern bayterrer k$\sqrt{a}$aleetaiyt

What kind of fabric is it?	Welke stof is het?	√ehlker stof iss heht

cambric	batist	baatist
camelhair	kameelhaar	kaamaylhaar
chiffon	chiffon	sheefon
corduroy	ribfluweel	ripflew√ayl
cotton	katoen	kaatoon
crepe	crêpe	krehp
denim	denim	daynim
felt	vilt	vilt
flannel	flanel	flaanehl
gabardine	gabardine	ghaabahrdeener
lace	kant	kahnt
linen	linnen	linnern
poplin	popeline	poaperleener
satin	satijn	saataiyn
silk	zijde	zaiyder
towelling	badstof	bahtstof
velvet	fluweel	flew√ayl
velveteen	katoenfluweel	kaatoonflew√ayl
wool	wol	√ol
worsted	kamgaren	kahmgaarern

Is it...?	Is het...?	iss heht
pure cotton/wool	zuiver katoen/wol	zur°w verr kaatoon/√ol
synthetic	synthetisch	sintayteess
colourfast	kleurecht	klurrehkht
crease resistant (wrinkle-free)	kreukvrij	krurkvraiy
Is it hand washable/ machine washable?	Kan het met de hand/ in de machine gewassen worden?	kahn heht meht der hahnt/ in der maasheener gher√ahssern √ordern
Will it shrink?	Krimpt het?	krimpt heht

Size *Maat*

I take size 38.	Ik heb maat 38.	ik hehp maat 38
Could you measure me?	Kunt u mijn maat nemen?	kurnt ew maiyn maat naymern
I don't know the Dutch sizes.	Ik ken de Neder- landse maten niet.	ik kehn der nayderrlahntser maatern neet

Sizes can vary somewhat from one manufacturer to another, so be sure to try on shoes and clothing before you buy.

Women *Dames*

Dresses/Suits						
American	8	10	12	14	16	18
British	10	12	14	16	18	20
Continental	36	38	40	42	44	46

Stockings							Shoes			
American	8	8½	9	9½	10	10½	5½	6½	7½	8½
British							4	5	6	7
Continental	1		2		3		37	38	39	40

Men *Heren*

Suits/Overcoats							Shirts			
American	36	38	40	42	44	46	15	16	17	18
British										
Continental	46	48	50	52	54	56	38	40	42	44

Shoes								
American	6	7	7½	8	8½	9	10	11
British	5	6	7	8	9	10	11	12
Continental	38	39	40	41	42	43	44	45

A good fit? *Past het?*

Can I try it on?	**Kan ik het aanpassen?**	kahn ik heht **aan**pahssern
Where's the changing room?	**Waar is de paskamer?**	√aar iss der **pahs**kaamerr
Is there a mirror?	**Is er een spiegel?**	iss ehr ern **spee**gherl
It doesn't fit.	**Het past niet.**	heht pahst neet
It's too...	**Het is te...**	heht iss ter
short/long	**kort/lang**	kort/lahng
tight/loose	**nauw/wijd**	no^{ow}/√aiyt

NUMBERS, see page 147

| How long will it take to alter? | **Hoe lang duurt het om het te vermaken?** | hoo lahng dewrt heht om heht ter verrmaakern |
| It fits very well. | **Het past uitstekend.** | heht pahst ur^{ew}tstaykernt |

Clothes and accessories *Kleren en accessoires*

I'd like some... clothes.	**Ik wil graag... kleding.**	ik vil ghraakh... **klay**ding
children's/men's/ women's	**kinder-/heren-/ dames-**	kinderr-/hayrern-/ daamerss-
I'd like a/an/some...	**Ik wil graag... hebben.**	ik vil ghraakh... **heh**bern

anorak	**een jekker**	ern yehkerr
bathing cap	**een badmuts**	ern bahtmurts
bathrobe	**een badjas**	ern bahtyahss
blouse	**een blouse**	ern blooss
bow tie	**een vlinderdas**	ern vlinderrdahss
bra	**een beha**	ern bayhaa
braces	**bretels**	brertehlss
cap	**een pet**	ern peht
cardigan	**een gebreid vest**	ern gherbraiyt vehst
(fur) coat	**een (bont)jas**	ern (bont)yahss
dress	**een jurk**	ern yurrk
with long sleeves	**met lange mouwen**	meht lahnger mo^{ow}ern
with short sleeves	**met korte mouwen**	meht korter mo^{ow}ern
sleeveless	**zonder mouwen**	zonderr mo^{ow}ern
dressing gown	**een kamerjas**	ern kaamerryahss
evening dress (woman's)	**een avondjurk**	ern aavontyurrk
girdle	**een step-in**	ern "step-in"
gloves	**handschoenen**	hahntskhoonern
handbag	**een handtas**	ern hahnttahss
handkerchief	**een zakdoek**	ern zahkdook
hat	**een hoed**	ern hoot
jacket	**een jasje**	ern yahsyer
jeans	**een spijkerbroek**	ern spaiykerrbrook
jumper (Br.)	**een trui**	ern trur^{ew}
kneesocks	**kniekousen**	kneeko^{ow}sern
knitwear	**breigoed**	braiyghoot
nightdress (-gown)	**een nachtjapon**	ern nahkhtyaapon
overalls	**een overal**	ern oaverrahl
pair of ...	**een paar...**	ern paar
panties	**een slipje**	ern slipyer
pants (Am.)	**een lange broek**	ern lahnger brook

panty girdle	een step-in broekje	ern "step-in" brookyer
panty hose	een panty	ern "panty"
parka	een jekker	ern yehkerr
pullover	een pullover	ern "pullover"
crew-neck	met ronde hals	meht ronder hahlss
polo (turtle)-neck	met col	meht kol
V-neck	met V-hals	meht vayhahlss
pyjamas	een pyjama	ern peeyaamaa
raincoat	een regenjas	ern rayghernyahss
scarf	een sjaal	ern shaal
shirt	een overhemd	ern oaverrhehmt
shorts	een short	ern "short"
skirt	een rok	ern rok
slip	een onderjurk	ern onderryurrk
socks	sokken	sokkern
sportswear	sportkleding	sportklayding
stockings	kousen	ko^{ow}sern
suit (man's)	een kostuum	ern kostewm
suit (woman's)	een mantelpak	ern mahnterlpahk
suspenders (Am.)	bretels	brertehlss
sweater	een trui	ern trur^{ew}
sweatshirt	een sweatshirt	ern "sweatshirt"
swimming trunks	een zwembroek	ern zvehmbrook
swimsuit	een badpak	ern bahtpahk
T-shirt	een T-shirt	ern "T-shirt"
tie	een stropdas	ern stropdahss
tights	een maillot	ern mighoa
tracksuit	een trainingspak	ern trayningspahk
trousers	een lange broek	ern lahnger brook
umbrella	een paraplu	ern paaraaplew
underpants	een onderbroek	ern onderrbrook
undershirt	een hemd	ern hehmt
underwear	onderkleding	onderrklayding
vest (Am.)	een vest	ern vehst
vest (Br.)	een hemd	ern hehmt
waistcoat	een vest	ern vehst

belt	een ceintuur	ern sehntewr
buckle	een gesp	ern ghehsp
button	een knoop	ern knoap
collar	een kraag	ern kraakh
pocket	een zak	ern zahk
press stud (snap fastener)	een drukknoop	ern drurkknoap
zip (zipper)	een ritssluiting	ern ritsslur^{ew}ting

Shoes *Schoenen*

I'd like a pair of...	**Ik wil graag een paar... hebben.**	ik √il ghraakh ern paar... hehbern
boots	**laarzen**	laarzern
lined/unlined	**gevoerd/ongevoerd**	ghervoort/onghervoort
plimsolls (sneakers)	**gymnastiekschoenen**	ghimnahsteekskhoonern
sandals	**sandalen**	sahndaalern
shoes	**schoenen**	skhoonern
flat	**platte**	plahter
with a heel	**met een hak**	meht ern hahk
with leather soles	**met leren zolen**	meht layrern zoalern
with rubber soles	**met rubber zolen**	meht rurberr zoalern
slippers	**pantoffels**	pahntofferlss
These are too...	**Deze zijn te...**	dayzer zaiyn ter
narrow/wide	**nauw/wijd**	no^{ow}/√aiyt
big/small	**groot/klein**	ghroat/klaiyn
Do you have a larger/smaller size?	**Hebt u een grotere/ kleinere maat?**	hehpt ew ern groaterrer/ klaiynerrer maat
Do you have the same in black?	**Hebt u dezelfde in het zwart?**	hehpt ew derzehlfder in heht z√ahrt
cloth	**linnen**	linnern
leather	**leer**	layr
rubber	**rubber**	rurberr
suede	**suède**	swehder
Is it real leather?	**Is het echt leer?**	iss heht ekht layr
I need some...	**Ik heb... nodig.**	ik hehp... noadikh
insoles	**binnenzolen**	binnernzoalern
shoe polish	**schoenpoets**	skhoonpoots
shoelaces	**schoenveters**	skhoonvayterrss

Shoes worn out? Here's the way to get them mended again:

Can you repair these shoes?	**Kunt u deze schoenen repareren?**	kurnt ew dayzer skhoonern raypaarayrern
Can you stitch this?	**Kunt u dit stikken?**	kurnt ew dit stikkern
I want new soles and heels.	**Ik wil graag nieuwe zolen en hakken.**	ik √il ghraakh nee^{oo}√er zoalern ehn hahkern
When will they be ready?	**Wanneer zijn ze klaar?**	√ahnayr zaiyn zer klaar

COLOURS, see page 112

Electrical appliances *Elektrische apparaten*

220-volt, 50-cycle A.C. is standard everywhere.

Do you have a/an... for this?	**Hebt u... hiervoor?**	hehpt ew... **heer**voar
adaptor	**een verloopstekker**	ern verr**loop**stehkerr
battery	**een batterij**	ern bahter**raiy**
This is broken. Can you repair it?	**Dit is kapot. Kunt u het repareren?**	dit iss kaapot. kurnt ew heht raypaa**ray**rern
When will it be ready?	**Wanneer is het klaar?**	√ah**nayr** iss heht klaar
Can you show me how it works?	**Kunt u uitleggen hoe het werkt?**	kurnt ew ur^{ew}t**leh**ghern hoo heht √ehrkt
How do I switch it on?	**Hoe doe ik het aan?**	hoo doo ik heht aan
I'd like to hire a video cassette.	**Ik wil graag een videocassette huren.**	ik √il ghraakh ern veedeeyoa**kah**sehter **hew**rern
I'd like a/an/some...	**Ik wil graag...**	ik √il ghraakh
amplifier	**een versterker**	ern verr**stehr**kerr
bulb	**een gloeilamp**	ern ghloo^{ee}lahmp
cassette recorder	**een cassetterecorder**	ern kah**seh**ter''recorder''
CD-player	**een CD-speler**	ern say**day**-spaylerr
clock-radio	**een radiowekker**	ern raadeeyoa√ehkerr
electric toothbrush	**een elektrische tandenborstel**	ern ay**lehk**treeser **tahn**dernborsterl
extension lead (cord)	**een verlengsnoer**	ern verr**lehng**snoor
hair dryer	**een haardroger**	ern **haar**droagherr
headphones	**een koptelefoon**	ern **kop**taylerfoan
(travelling) iron	**een (reis)strijkijzer**	ern (raiys)**straiy**kaiyzerr
lamp	**een lamp**	ern lahmp
plug	**een stekker**	ern **stehk**err
portable...	**een draagbare...**	ern **draagh**baarer
radio	**een radio**	ern **raa**deeyoa
record player	**een platenspeler**	ern **plaa**ternspaylerr
(cordless) shaver	**een (snoerloos) scheerapparaat**	ern (**snoor**loas) skhayrahpaaraat
speakers	**luidsprekers**	lur^{ew}t**spray**kerrss
(colour) television	**een (kleuren)tele-visie**	ern (**klur**rern)taylerveezee
transformer	**een transformator**	ern trahns**for**maator
video recorder	**een videorecorder**	ern vee**dee**yoa''recorder''

Grocer's *Kruidenier*

I'd like some bread, please.	Ik wil graag een brood, alstublieft.	ik √il ghraakh ern broat ahlstewbleeft
current bread	krentenbrood	krehnternbroat
rye bread	roggebrood	rogherbroat
white bread	wit brood	√it broat
whole-meal bread	volkoren brood	volkoarern broat
What sort of cheese do you have?	Welke kaassoorten hebt u?	√ehlker kaassoortern hehbt ew
A piece of that one, please.	Een stuk daarvan, alstublieft.	ern sturk daarvahn ahlstewbleeft
I'll have one of those, please.	Ik wil die daar hebben, alstublieft.	ik √il dee daar hehbern ahlstewbleeft
May I help myself?	Mag ik mijzelf bedienen?	mahkh ik maiyzehlf berdeenern
I'd like...	Ik wil graag...	ik √il ghraakh
a kilo of apples	een kilo appels	ern keeloa ahperlss
half a kilo of tomatoes	een pond/halve kilo tomaten	ern pont/hahlver keeloa toamaatern
250 grams of butter	250 gram boter	250 ghrahm boaterr
a litre of milk	een liter melk	ern leeterr mehlk
4 slices of ham	4 plakken ham	4 plahkern hahm
a packet of tea	een pakje thee	ern pahkyer tay
a jar of jam	een pot jam	ern pot zhehm
a tin (can) of peaches	een blik perziken	ern blik pehrzikern
a tube of mustard	een tube mosterd	ern tewber mosterrt
a box of chocolates	een doos chocolade	ern doas shoakoalaader

---

Weights and measures

1 kilogram or kilo (kg.) = 1000 grams (g.)

| 100 g. = 3.5 oz. | ½ kg. = 1.1 lbs. |
| 200 g. = 7.0 oz. | 1 kg. = 2.2 lbs. |

1 oz. = 28.35 g.
1 lb. = 453.60 g.

---

1 litre (l.) = 0.88 imp. quarts = 1.06 U.S. quarts

| 1 imp. quart = 1.14 l. | 1 U.S. quart = 0.95 l. |
| 1 imp. gallon = 4.55 l. | 1 U.S. gallon = 3.8 l. |

FOOD, see also page 64

Household articles   *Huishoudelijke artikelen*

Could you give me a/an/some...?	**Kunt u mij... geven?**	kurnt ew maiy... **ghay**vern
bottle opener	**een flesopener**	ern **fleh**soapernerr
bucket	**een emmer**	ern **eh**merr
candles	**kaarsen**	**kaar**sern
clothes pegs (pins)	**wasknijpers**	√ahsknaiyperrss
corkscrew	**een kurketrekker**	ern **kurr**kertrehkerr
dish detergent	**afwasmiddel**	ahf√ahsmidderl
frying pan	**een koekepan**	ern **koo**kerpahn
matches	**lucifers**	**lew**seefehrss
paper towel	**een huishoudrol**	ern hur^{ew}sho^{ow}trol
plastic bags	**plastic zakken**	**pleh**stik **zah**kern
saucepan	**een pan**	ern pahn
tin (can) opener	**een blikopener**	ern **blik**oapernerr
tea towel	**een theedoek**	ern **tay**dook
vacuum flask	**een thermosfles**	ern **tehr**mosflehss
washing powder	**waspoeder**	√ahs**poo**derr
washing-up liquid	**afwasmiddel**	ahf√ahsmidderl

... and some more useful items:

hammer	**een hamer**	ern **haa**merr
nails	**spijkers**	**spaiy**kerss
penknife (pocketknife)	**een zakmes**	ern **zahk**mehss
pliers	**een nijptang**	ern **naiyp**tahng
scissors	**een schaar**	ern skhaar
screws	**schroeven**	**skhroo**vern
screwdriver	**een schroevedraaier**	ern **skhroo**verdraa^{ee}err
spanner	**een moersleutel**	ern **moors**lurterl
tools	**gereedschap**	gher**ayt**skhahp

Crockery—Cutlery (flatware)   *Serviesgoed—Bestek*

cups	**kopjes**	**kop**yerss
forks	**vorken**	**vor**kern
knives	**messen**	**meh**sern
mugs	**mokken**	**mo**kern
plates	**borden**	**bor**dern
saucers	**schoteltjes**	**skhoa**terltyerss
spoons	**lepels**	**lay**perlss
teaspoons	**theelepeltjes**	**tay**layperltyerss
tumblers	**bekerglazen**	**bay**kerrghlaazern
(made of) plastic/ stainless steel	**(van) plastic/ roestvrij staal**	(vahn) **pleh**stik/ **roost**vraiy staal

Jeweller's—Watchmaker's *Juwelier—Horlogemaker*

Could I see that, please?	**Mag ik dat even zien, alstublieft?**	mahkh ik daht ayvern zeen ahlstewbleeft
Do you have anything in gold?	**Hebt u iets in goud?**	hehpt ew eets in gho^{ow}t
How many carats is this?	**Hoeveel karaats is dit?**	hoovayl kaaraats iss dit
Is this real silver?	**Is dit echt zilver?**	iss dit ehkht zilverr
Can you repair this watch?	**Kunt u dit horloge repareren?**	kurnt ew dit horloazher raypaarayrern
I'd like a/an/some ...	**Ik wil graag... hebben.**	ik √il ghraakh... hehbern

alarm clock	**een wekker**	ern √ehkerr
bangle	**een armband**	ern ahrmbahnt
battery	**een batterij**	ern bahterraiy
bracelet	**een armband**	ern ahrmbahnt
chain bracelet	**schakelarmband**	ern skhaakerlahrmbahnt
charm bracelet	**bedelarmband**	ern bayderlahrmbahnt
brooch	**een broche**	ern brosh
chain	**een ketting**	ern kehting
charm	**een gelukshangertje**	ern gherlurkshahngerrtyer
clock	**een klok**	ern klok
cross	**een kruis**	ern krur^{ew}ss
cuff links	**manchetknopen**	mahnshehtknoapern
cutlery	**bestek**	berstehk
earrings	**oorbellen**	oarbehlern
flatware (Am.)	**bestek**	berstehk
gem	**een edelsteen**	ern ayderlstayn
jewel box	**een bijouteriekistje**	ern beezhooterreekisher
music box	**een muziekdoos**	ern mewzeekdoass
necklace	**een halsketting**	ern hahlskehting
pendant	**een hanger**	ern hahngerr
pin	**een speld**	ern spehlt
pocket watch	**een zakhorloge**	ern zahkhorloazher
powder compact	**een poederdoos**	ern pooderrdoass
ring	**een ring**	ern ring
diamond ring	**een diamantring**	ern deeyaamahntring
engagement ring	**een verlovingsring**	ern verrloavingsring
signet ring	**een zegelring**	ern zaygherlring
wedding ring	**een trouwring**	ern tro^{ow}ring
rosary	**een rozenkrans**	ern roazernkrahnss
silverware	**zilverwerk**	zilverr√ehrk
tie clip	**een dasclip**	ern dahsklip

tie pin	een dasspeld	ern dahsspehlt
watch	een horloge	ern horloazher
digital	digitaal	deegheetaal
with a second hand	met secondewijzer	meht serkonder√aiyzerr
waterproof	waterdicht	√aaterrdikht
watchstrap	een horlogebandje	ern horloazherbahntyer
wristwatch	een polshorloge	ern polshorloazher
What kind of stone is it?	Wat is het voor een steen?	√aht iss heht voar ern stayn

amber	barnsteen	bahrnstayn
amethyst	amethist	aamertist
diamond	diamant	deeyaamahnt
emerald	smaragd	smaarahkht
moonstone	maansteen	maanstayn
pearl	parel	paarerl
ruby	robijn	roabaiyn
sapphire	saffier	sahfeer
tigereye	tijgeroog	taiygherroakh
topaz	topaas	toapaass
turquoise	turkoois	turrkoa°°ss

| What's it made of? | Waar is het van gemaakt? | √aar iss heht vahn ghermaakt |

alabaster	albast	ahlbahst
brass	geel koper	ghayl koaperr
bronze	brons	bronss
chromium	chroom	ghroam
copper	koper	koaperr
coral	koraal	koaraal
crystal	kristal	kristahl
enamel	email	aymigh
glass	glas	ghlahss
cut glass	geslepen glas	gherslaypern ghlahss
gold	goud	gho°°t
gold plated	verguld	verrghurlt
jade	jade	yaader
mother-of-pearl	paarlemoer	paarlermoor
pewter	tin	tin
platinum	platina	plaateenaa
silver	zilver	zilverr
silver plated	verzilverd	verrzilverrt

Optician *Opticien*

I've broken my glasses.	**Mijn bril is gebroken.**	maiyn bril iss gherbroakern
Can you repair them for me?	**Kunt u het voor mij repareren?**	kurnt ew heht voar maiy raypaarayrern
When will they be ready?	**Wanneer is het klaar?**	√ahnayr iss heht klaar
Can you change the lenses?	**Kunt u de glazen verwisselen?**	kurnt ew der ghlaazern verr√isserlern
I'd like tinted lenses.	**Ik wil graag gekleurde glazen.**	ik √il ghraakh gherklurrder ghlaazern
The frame is broken.	**Het montuur is gebroken.**	heht montewr iss gherbroakern
I'd like a glasses case.	**Ik wil graag een brille-koker.**	ik √il ghraakh ern briller-koakerr
I'd like to have my eyesight checked.	**Ik wil graag mijn gezichtsscherpte laten controleren.**	ik √il ghraakh maiyn gherzikhtsskhehrpter laatern kontroalayrern
I'm short-sighted/ long-sighted.	**Ik ben bijziend/ verziend.**	ik behn baiyzeent/vehrzeent
I'd like some contact lenses.	**Ik wil graag contact-lenzen.**	ik √il ghraakh kontahkt-lehnzern
I've lost one of my contact lenses.	**Ik heb een van mijn contactlenzen verloren.**	ik hehp ayn vahn maiyn kontahktlehnzern verrloarern
Could you give me another one?	**Kunt u mij een andere bezorgen?**	kurnt ew maiy ern ahnderer berzorghern
I have hard/soft lenses.	**Ik heb harde/zachte lenzen.**	ik hehp hahrder/zahkhter lehnzern
Do you have any contact-lens fluid?	**Hebt u vloeistof voor contactlenzen?**	hehpt ew vloo^{ee}stof voar kontahktlehnzern
I'd like to buy a pair of sunglasses.	**Ik wil graag een zonnebril kopen.**	ik √il ghraakh ern zonnerbril koapern
May I look in a mirror?	**Mag ik even in de spiegel kijken?**	mahkh ik ayvern in der speegherl kaiykern
I'd like...	**Ik wil graag...**	ik √il ghraakh
a magnifying glass	**een vergrootglas**	ern verrghroatghlahss
a pair of binoculars	**een verrekijker**	ern vehrerkaiykerr

Photography   *Fotografie*

I'd like a(n) . . . camera.	**Ik wil graag een . . . fototoestel.**	ik √il ghraakh ern . . . foatoatoostehl
automatic	**automatisch**	oᵒʷtoamaateess
inexpensive	**goedkoop**	ghootkoap
simple	**eenvoudig**	aynvoᵒʷdikh
Can you show me some video cameras, please?	**Kunt u mij video-camera's laten zien, alstublieft?**	kurnt ew maiy veedeeyoa-kaamerraas laatern zeen ahlstewbleeft
I'd like to have some passport photos taken.	**Ik wil graag pasfoto's laten maken.**	ik √il ghraakh pahsfoatoass laatern maakern

Film   *Film*

I'd like a film for this camera.	**Ik wil graag een film voor dit toestel.**	ik √il ghraakh ern film voar dit toostehl
black and white	**zwart-wit**	z√ahrt-√it
colour	**kleuren**	klurrern
colour negative	**kleurennegatief**	klurrernnayghaateef
cartridge	**een cassette**	ern kahsehter
disc film	**een disc**	ern disk
roll film	**een rolfilm**	ern rolfilm
slide film	**een diafilm**	ern deeyaafilm
video cassette	**een videocassette**	ern veedeeyoakahsehter
24/36 exposures	**vierentwintig/zesendertig opnamen**	veerehnt√interkh/zehsehn-dehrterkh opnaamern
this size	**dit formaat**	dit formaat
this ASA/DIN number	**dit ASA/DIN nummer**	dit aa-ehs-aa/din nurmerr
artificial light type	**voor kunstlicht**	voar kurnstlikht
daylight type	**voor daglicht**	voar dahghlikht
fast (high-speed)	**snel**	snehl
fine grain	**fijnkorrelig**	faiynkorrerlerkh

Processing   *Ontwikkelen*

Does the price include processing?	**Is het ontwikkelen bij de prijs inbegrepen?**	iss heht ont√ikkerlern baiy der praiys inbergraypern

How much do you charge for processing?	**Hoeveel kost het ontwikkelen?**	hoovayl kost heht ontvikkerlern
I'd like ... prints of each negative.	**Ik wil graag ... afdrukken van elk negatief.**	ik vil ghraakh ...ahfdrurkern vahn ehlk nayghaateef
with a mat finish	**mat**	maht
with a glossy finish	**glanzend**	ghlahnzernt
Will you enlarge this, please?	**Wilt u dit vergroten, alstublieft?**	vilt ew dit verrghroatern ahlstewbleeft
When will the photos be ready?	**Wanneer zijn de foto's klaar?**	vahnayr zaiyn der foatoass klaar

Accessories and repairs *Accessoires en reparaties*

I'd like a/an/some...	**Ik wil graag...**	ik vil ghraakh
battery	**een batterij**	ern bahterraiy
cable release	**een draadontspanner**	ern draatontspahnerr
camera case	**een camera etui**	ern kaamerraa aytvee
flash	**een flits**	ern flits
filter	**een filter**	ern filterr
for black and white	**voor zwart-wit**	voar zvahrt-vit
for colour	**voor kleuren**	voar klurrern
lens	**een lens**	ern lehnss
telephoto lens	**telelens**	taylaylehnss
wide-angle lens	**groothoeklens**	ghroathooklehnss
lens cap	**een lensdop**	ern lehnsdop
slide projector	**een diaprojector**	ern deeyaaproayehktor
Can you repair this cine (movie) camera?	**Kunt u dit filmtoestel repareren?**	kurnt ew dit filmtoostehl raypaaraayrern
The film is jammed.	**De film zit vast.**	der film zit vahst
There's something wrong with the...	**Er hapert iets aan...**	ehr haaperrt eets aan
exposure counter	**de opnameteller**	der opnaamertehlerr
film winder	**de terugspoelknop**	der terrurkhspoolknop
flash attachment	**de flits**	der flits
lens	**de lens**	der lehnss
light meter	**de belichtingsmeter**	der berlikhtingsmayterr
rangefinder	**de afstandsmeter**	der ahfstahntsmayterr
self-timing release	**de zelfontspanner**	der zehlfontspahnerr
shutter	**de sluiter**	der slurewterr

NUMBERS, see page 147

Tobacconist's *Sigarenwinkel*

A full range of both local and international makes are available in tobacco shops and supermarkets as well as from vending machines. Holland is especially known for its cigars.

A packet of cigarettes, please.	**Een pakje sigaretten, alstublieft.**	ern pahkyer seeghaarehtern ahlstewbleeft
Do you have any American/English cigarettes?	**Hebt u Amerikaanse/ Engelse sigaretten?**	hehpt ew aamayreekaanser/ ehngerlser seegaarehtern
I'd like a carton.	**Een slof, alstublieft.**	ern slof ahlstewbleeft
Give me a/some..., please.	**Geeft u mij..., alstublieft.**	ghayft ew maiy... ahlstewbleeft
candy	**snoep**	snoop
chewing gum	**kauwgum**	ko^{ow}ghurm
chewing tobacco	**pruimtabak**	prur^{ew}mtaabahk
chocolate	**chocolade**	shoakoalaader
cigarette case	**een sigarettenkoker**	ern seeghaarehternkoakerr
cigarette holder	**een sigarettepijpje**	ern seeghaarehternpaiypyer
cigarettes	**sigaretten**	seeghaarehtern
filter-tipped	**met filter**	meht filterr
without filter	**zonder filter**	zonderr filter
mild/strong	**licht/zwaar**	likht/z√aar
menthol	**menthol**	mehntol
king-size	**extra lang**	ehkstraa lahng
cigarillos	**kleine sigaartjes**	klaiyner seeghaartyerss
cigars	**sigaren**	seeghaarern
hand-rolled	**met de hand gerold**	meht der hahnt gherrolt
lighter	**een aansteker**	ern aanstaykerr
lighter fluid/gas	**benzine/gas voor een aansteker**	behnzeener/ghahss voar ern aanstaykerr
matches	**lucifers**	lewseefehrss
pipe	**een pijp**	ern paiyp
pipe cleaners	**pijpestokers**	paiyperstoakerrss
pipe tobacco	**pijptabak**	paiyptaabahk
light/dark	**lichte/donkere**	likhter/donkerrer
pipe tool	**een pijpestopper**	ern paiyperstopperr
postcard	**een briefkaart**	ern breefkaart
snuff	**snuiftabak**	snur^{ew}ftaabahk
stamps	**postzegels**	postzaygherlss
sweets	**snoep**	snoop
wick	**een lont**	ern lont

Miscellaneous *Diversen*

Souvenirs *Souvenirs*

Typical Dutch souvenirs include wooden clogs, costumed dolls, and pottery from Delft and Makkum. In the higher-price bracket are cut diamonds from Amsterdam, glass and crystal from Leerdam and silverware from Schoonhoven. And don't forget the wide range of edible souvenirs such as Dutch sweets (candies), the best of all are *Haagse hopjes,* not to mention *chocolade hagelslag,* chocolate shavings which children love, and the delicious Frisian *kruidkoek,* a kind of ginger bread. In Belgium, you should look for lace, crystal and porcelain.

I'd like a souvenir from...	**Ik wil graag een souvenir uit...**	ik √il ghraakh ern sooverneer ur^{ew}t
Something typically Dutch/Belgian, please.	**Iets typisch Nederlands/Belgisch, alstublieft.**	eets teepeess nayderrlahnts/behlgheess ahlstewbleeft
I'd like a/some...	**Ik wil graag...**	ik √il ghraakh
(tulip) bulbs	**(tulpen)bollen**	(turlpern)bollern
china	**porselein**	porserrlaiyn
clogs	**klompen**	klompern
copperware	**koperwerk**	koaperr√ehrk
crystal vase	**kristallen vaas**	kristahlern vaass
Delft earthernware	**Delfts aardewerk**	dehlfts aarder√ehrk
(cut) diamonds	**(geslepen) dia-manten**	(gherslaypern) deeyaa-mahntern
dolls in local costumes	**poppen in kleder-dracht**	poppern in klayderr-drahkht
lace	**kant**	kahnt
pewter	**tin**	tin
pottery	**aardewerk**	aarder√ehrk
silverware	**zilverwerk**	zilverr√ehrk
tiles	**tegels**	taygherlss
miniature windmill	**miniatuur molen**	meeneeyaatewr moalern

It's not advisable to take bulbs out of the country yourself because of customs regulations. However, Dutch flower bulb dealers know everything about sending bulbs all over the world.

Records—Cassettes *Grammofoonplaten—Cassettes*

I'd like a...	**Ik wil graag...**	ik √il ghraakh
cassette	**een cassette**	ern kahsehter
video cassette	**een videocassette**	ern veedeeyoakahsehter
compact disc	**een compact disc**	ern kompahkt disk
I'd like 2 blank tapes, please.	**Ik wil graag 2 onbe-speelde bandjes.**	ik √il ghraakh 2 onber-spaylder **bahntyerss**
Do you have any records by...?	**Hebt u platen van...?**	hehpt ew **plaa**tern vahn
Can I listen to this record?	**Kan ik deze plaat even horen?**	kahn ik **dayzer** plaat **ay**vern **hoa**rern
chamber music	**kamermuziek**	kaamerrmewzeek
classical music	**klassieke muziek**	klahseeker mewzeek
folk music	**folkloristische muziek**	folkloaristeesser mewzeek
folk song	**volksliedjes**	volksleetyerss
instrumental music	**instrumentale muziek**	instrewmehntaaler mewzeek
jazz	**jazz**	"jazz"
light music	**lichte muziek**	likhter mewzeek
orchestral music	**orkestmuziek**	orkehstmewzeek

Toys *Speelgoed*

I'd like a toy/ game...	**Ik wil graag speel-goed/een spel...**	ik √il ghraakh spaylghoot/ ern spehl
for a boy	**voor een jongen**	voar ern jongern
for a 5-year-old girl	**voor een meisje van 5 jaar**	voar ern maiysher vahn 5 yaar
(beach) ball	**een (strand)bal**	ern (strahnt)bahl
bucket and spade (pail and shovel)	**een emmer en schepje**	ern ehmerr ehn skhehpyer
building blocks (bricks)	**een bouwdoos**	ern boow doass
card game	**speelkaarten**	spaylkaartern
chess set	**een schaakspel**	ern skhaakspehl
doll	**een pop**	ern pop
electronic game	**een elektronisch spel**	ern aylehktroaneess spehl
roller skates	**rolschaatsen**	rolskhaatsern
snorkel	**een snorkel**	ern snorkerl

Your money: banks—currency

In large towns you can change foreign money at all banks and there's sure to be someone who speaks English.

Opening hours: In Holland, banks are open from 9 a.m. to 4 p.m., Monday to Friday; some banks stay open Thursday or Friday evening until 7 p.m. In Belgium, banks are open Monday to Friday from 9 a.m. to 12.30 p.m. and from 2.30 to 3.30 p.m. (sometimes from 9 a.m. to 4 p.m.).

Monetary unit: In Holland the basic unit of currency is the guilder (*gulden*–**ghurl**dern), abbreviated to *f, fl, gld* or, especially outside the country, *Dfl.* A guilder is divided into 100 *centen* (**sehn**tern).

Coins: 5, 10 and 25 cents; 1, 2½ and 5 guilders
Banknotes: 5, 10, 25, 50, 100, 250 and 1,000 guilders

In Belgium the basic unit of currency is the franc (*frank*—frahnk), abbreviated to *fr, f* or, *Bfr* abroad. A franc is divided into 100 *centimes* (sahn**tee**mern).

Coins: 50 centimes; 1, 5, 10 and 20 francs
Banknotes: 100, 500, 1,000 and 5,000 francs

Credit cards and Eurocheques are accepted in tourist-oriented shops, hotels, restaurants, etc. Traveller's cheques are also widely accepted, although the exchange rate is invariably better at banks.

Where's the nearest bank?	**Waar is de dichtst-bijzijnde bank?**	√aar iss der dikhtst-baiyzaiynder bahnk
Where's the nearest currency exchange office?	**Waar is het dichtst-bijzijnde wissel-kantoor?**	√aar iss heht dikhtst-baiyzaiynder √isserl-kahntoar
Is it open now?	**Is het nu open?**	iss heht new oapern
When does it...?	**Wanneer gaat het...?**	√ahnayr ghaat heht
open	**open**	oapern
close	**dicht**	dikht

At the bank *In de bank*

I'd like to change some dollars/pounds.	**Ik wil graag dollars/ponden wisselen.**	ik √il ghraakh dollahrss/pondern √isserlern
I'd like to cash a traveller's cheque.	**Ik wil graag een reischeque wisselen.**	ik √il ghraakh ern raiysshehk √isserlern
What's the exchange rate?	**Wat is de wissel-koers?**	√aht iss der √isserlkoorss
How much commission do you charge?	**Hoeveel provisie berekent u?**	hoovayl proaveesee berraykernt ew
Can you cash a cheque?	**Kunt u een cheque verzilveren?**	kurnt ew ern shehk verrzilverrern
Can you telex my bank in London?	**Kunt u naar mijn bank in Londen telexen?**	kurnt ew naar maiyn bahnk in londern taylehksern
I have a/an/some...	**Ik heb...**	ik hehp
credit card	**een credit card**	ern "credit card"
Eurocheques	**eurocheques**	urroashehkss
letter of credit	**een kredietbrief**	ern krerdeetbreef
I'm expecting some money from New York. Has it arrived?	**Ik verwacht geld uit New York. Is het al aangekomen?**	ik verr√ahkht ghehlt ur^{ew}t "New York". iss heht ahl aangherkoamern
Please give me... notes (bills) and some small change.	**Geeft u mij... biljetten en wat kleingeld, alstublieft.**	gayft ew maiy... bilyehtern ehn √aht klaiynghehlt ahlstew bleeft
Give me... large notes and the rest in small notes.	**Geeft u mij... in grote coupures en de rest in kleine coupures.**	gayft ew maiy... in ghroater koopewrerss ehn der rehst in klaiyner koopewrerss

Deposits—Withdrawals *Geld storten—Opnemen*

I'd like to...	**Ik wil graag...**	ik √il ghraakh
open an account	**een rekening openen**	ern raykerning oapernern
withdraw... francs/guilders	**... franken/guldens opnemen**	... frahnkern/ghurldernss opnaymern
I'd like to pay this into my account.	**Ik wil dit graag op mijn rekening storten.**	ik √il dit ghraakh op maiyn raykerning stortern

NUMBERS, see page 147

Business terms *Zakelijke uitdrukkingen*

My name is...	**Mijn naam is...**	maiyn naam iss
Here's my card.	**Hier is mijn kaartje.**	heer iss maiyn kaartyer
I have an appointment with...	**Ik heb een afspraak met...**	ik hehp ern ahfspraak meht
Can you give me an estimate of the cost?	**Kunt u mij een opgave van de kosten geven?**	kurnt ew maiy ern opghaaver vahn der kostern ghayvern
What's the rate of inflation?	**Hoe hoog is de inflatie?**	hoo hoakh iss der inflaatsee
Can you provide me with a(n)...	**Kunt u zorgen voor...**	kurnt ew zorghern voar
interpreter	**een tolk**	ern tolk
secretary	**een secretaresse**	ern serkrertaarehser
translater	**een vertaler**	ern verrţaalerr
translation	**een vertaling**	ern verrţaaling
Where should I sign?	**Waar moet ik tekenen?**	√aar moot ik taykernern
Where can I make photocopies?	**Waar kan ik fotocopieën maken?**	√aar kahn ik foatoakoapeeyern maakern

amount	**het bedrag**	heht berdrahkh
balance	**de balans**	der bahlahnss
capital	**het kapitaal**	heht kahpeetaal
contract	**het contract**	heht kontrahkt
discount	**de korting**	der korting
expenses	**de uitgaven**	der ur^{ew}tghaavern
interest	**de rente**	der rehnter
investment	**de investering**	der invehstayring
invoice	**de rekening**	der raykerning
loss	**het verlies**	heht verrleess
mortgage	**de hypotheek**	der heepoatayk
payment	**de betaling**	der bertaaling
percentage	**het percentage**	heht pehrsehntaazher
profit	**de winst**	der √inst
purchase	**de koop**	der koap
sale	**de verkoop**	der vehrkoap
share	**het aandeel**	heht aandayl
transfer	**de overschrijving**	der oaverrskhraiyving
value	**de waarde**	der √aarder

At the post office

In Holland, post offices can be recognized by the letters *PTT (Post, Telegraaf, Telefoon)*. They are generally open from Monday to Friday between 8.30 a.m. and 5.30 p.m. Main offices often have longer hours and are also open on Saturdays from 9 a.m. to noon.

In Belgium, post offices can be identified by the sign *Posterijen/Postes,* and they are generally open from 9 a.m. to 6.p.m., Monday to Friday.

Letterboxes (mailboxes) in Holland and Belgium are painted red and indicate when mail is collected. In Holland, boxes have two slots, one marked *Streekpost* (local region) and the other *Overige bestemmingen* (other destinations).

As well as in the post office, stamps may be bought at newsstands, hotel lobbies, bookshops and from vending machines.

Where's the nearest post office?	**Waar is het dichtstbijzijnde postkantoor?**	√aar iss heht dikhtstbaiyzaiynder postkahntoar
What time does the post office open/close?	**Hoe laat gaat het postkantoor open/dicht?**	hoo laat ghaat heht postkahntoar oapern/dikht
A stamp for this letter/postcard, please.	**Een postzegel voor deze brief/briefkaart, alstublieft.**	ern postzaygherl voar dayzer breef/breefkaart ahlstewbleeft
A...-cent stamp, please.	**Een postzegel van... cent, alstublieft.**	ern postzaygherl vahn... sehnt ahlstewbleeft
What's the postage for a letter to London?	**Hoeveel port moet er op een brief naar Londen?**	hoovayl port moot ehr op ern breef naar londern
What's the postage for a postcard to Los Angeles?	**Hoeveel port moet er op een briefkaart naar Los Angeles?**	hoovayl port moot ehr op ern breefkaart naar "los angeles"
Where's the letter box (mailbox)?	**Waar is de brievenbus?**	√aar iss der breevernburss
I want to send this parcel.	**Ik wil dit pakje verzenden.**	ik √il dit pahkyer verrzehndern

I'd like to send this (by)...	Ik wil dit graag... verzenden.	ik vil dit ghraakh... verrzehndern
airmail	per luchtpost	pehr lurkhtpost
express (special delivery)	per expresse	pehr ehksprehss
registered mail	aangetekend	aanghertaykernt
At which counter can I cash an international money order?	Aan welk loket kan ik een internationale postwissel ver-zilveren?	aan vehlk loakeht kahn ik ern internahsyoanaaler postvisserl verrzilverrern
Where's the poste restante (general delivery)?	Waar is de poste restante?	vaar iss der post rehstahnter
Is there any post (mail) for me? My name is...	Is er post voor mij? Mijn naam is...	iss ehr post voar maiy. maiyn naam iss

POSTZEGELS	STAMPS
PAKJES	PARCELS
POSTWISSELS	MONEY ORDERS

Telegrams *Telegrammen*

In Holland, telegrams are dispatched by the post office. In Belgium, you must go to a *TT (Telefoon/Telegraaf)* office.

I want to send a...	Ik wil graag een... versturen.	ik vil ghraakh ern... verrstewrern
fax/telegram/telex	fax/telegram/telex	fahkss/taylerghrahm/ taylehkss
May I have a form, please?	Mag ik een formulier, alstublieft?	mahkh ik ern formewleer ahlstewbleeft
How much is it per word?	Hoeveel kost het per woord?	hoovayl kost heht pehr voart
How long will a cable to Boston take?	Hoe lang doet een telegram naar Boston erover?	hoolahng doot ern tayler-ghrahm naar "boston" ehroaverr
How much will this telex cost?	Hoeveel kost deze telex?	hoovayl kost dayzer taylehkss

Telephoning *Telefoneren*

The telephone system is entirely automatic in both Holland and Belgium. International or long-distance calls can be made from phone booths, but if you need help in making a call, go to the post office (in Belgium to the *Telefoon/Telegraaf* office) or ask at your hotel. All public phones have directions in English. Area and country codes are also displayed in booths.

Where's the telephone?	**Waar is de telefoon?**	√aar iss der taylerfoan
Where's the nearest telephone booth?	**Waar is de dichtst-bijzijnde telefoon-cel?**	√aar iss der dikhtstbaiy-zaiynder taylerfoansehl
May I use your phone?	**Mag ik uw telefoon gebruiken?**	mahkh ik ew°° taylerfoan gherbrur^ewkern
Do you have a telephone directory for Amsterdam?	**Hebt u een telefoonboek van Amsterdam?**	hehpt ew ern taylerfoan-book vahn ahmsterrdahm
I'd like to call... in England.	**Ik wil graag... in Engeland opbellen.**	ik √il ghraakh... in ehngerlahnt opbehlern
What's the dialling (area) code for...?	**Wat is het net-nummer voor...?**	√aht iss heht nehtnurmerr voar
How do I get the international operator?	**Wat is het nummer voor internationale aanvragen?**	√aht iss heht nurmerr voar interrnahsyoanaaler aanvraaghern

Operator *Telefoniste*

Could you give me the number of...?	**Kunt u mij het num-mer geven van...?**	kurnt ew maiy heht nurmerr ghayvern vahn
I'd like Brussels 23 45 67.	**Ik wil graag Brussel 23 45 67.**	ik √il ghraakh brurserl 23 45 67
Can you help me get this number?	**Kunt u mij helpen om dit nummer te krijgen?**	kurnt ew maiy hehlpern om dit nurmerr ter kraiyghern
I'd like to place a personal (person-to-person) call.	**Ik wil graag een gesprek met voor-bericht.**	ik √il ghraakh ern ghersprehk meht voar-berrikht

NUMBERS, see page 147

| I'd like to reverse the charges (call collect). | **Ik wil graag collect bellen.** | ik √il ghraakh "collect" behlern |

Bad luck *Pech*

Operator, you gave me the wrong number.	**Sorry, u hebt mij verkeerd verbonden.**	"sorry" ew hehpt maiy verrkayrt verrbondern
Operator, we were cut off.	**Sorry, wij werden verbroken.**	"sorry" √aiy √ehrdern verrbroakern
Would you try again later, please?	**Wilt u later nog eens proberen, alstublieft?**	√ilt ew laaterr nokh ayns proabayrern ahlstewbleeft

---

Telephone alphabet *Telefoonalfabet*

A	**Anna**	ahnaa	O	**Otto**	ottoa
B	**Bernard**	behrnahrt	P	**Pieter**	peeterr
C	**Cornelis**	kornayliss	Q	**Quadraat**	k√aadraat
D	**Dirk**	dirk	R	**Rudolf**	rewdolf
E	**Eduard**	aydewahrt	S	**Simon**	seemon
F	**Ferdinand**	fehrdeenant	T	**Teunis**	tur^{ew}niss
G	**Gerard**	ghayrahrt	U	**Utrecht**	ewtrehkht
H	**Hendrik**	hehndrik	V	**Victor**	viktor
I	**Izaak**	eezahk	W	**Willem**	√illerm
J	**Jan**	yahn	X	**Xantippe**	ksahntipper
K	**Karel**	kaarerl	IJ	**IJmuiden**	aiymur^{ew}dern
L	**Lodewijk**	loader√aiyk	Y	**Ypsilon**	eepserlon
M	**Marie**	maaree	Z	**Zaandam**	zaandahm
N	**Nico**	neeko			

Speaking *Spreken*

Hello. This is...	**Hallo. U spreekt met...**	hahloa. ew spraykt meht
I'd like to speak to...	**Ik wil graag... spreken.**	ik √il ghraakh... spraykern
Extension...	**Toestel...**	toostehl
Who's speaking?	**Met wie spreek ik?**	meht √ee sprayk ik
I beg your pardon?	**Wat zegt u?**	√aht zehkht ew
Speak louder/more slowly, please.	**Spreekt u wat harder/langzamer, alstublieft.**	spraykt ew √aht hahrderr/lahngzaamerr ahlstewbleeft

Not there *Afwezig*

When will he/she be back?	**Wanneer komt hij/zij terug?**	√ahnayr komt haiy/zaiy terrurkh
Will you tell him/her I called?	**Wilt u hem/haar zeggen dat ik gebeld heb.**	√ilt ew hehm/haar zehghern daht ik gherbehlt hehp.
My name is...	**Mijn naam is...**	maiyn naam iss
My telephone number is...	**Mijn (telefoon-) nummer is...**	maiyn (taylerfoan-) nurmerr iss
Would you ask him/her to call me?	**Wilt u hem/haar vragen mij terug te bellen?**	√ilt ew hehm/haar vraaghern maiy terrurkh ter behlern
Would you take a message, please?	**Wilt u een bood-schap doorgeven, alstublieft?**	√ilt ew ern boatskhahp doarghayvern ahlstewbleeft

Charges *Kosten*

What was the cost of that call?	**Hoeveel heeft dit gesprek gekost?**	hoovayl hayft dit ghersprehk gherkost
I want to pay for the call.	**Ik wil graag het gesprek betalen.**	ik √il ghraakh heht ghersprehk bertaalern

---

Er is telefoon voor u.	There's a telephone call for you.
Welk nummer belt u?	What number are you calling?
De lijn is bezet.	The line's engaged.
Er is geen gehoor.	There's no answer.
U bent verkeerd verbonden.	You've got the wrong number.
De telefoon is defect.	The phone is out of order.
Een ogenblik.	Just a moment.
Blijft u aan de lijn, alstublieft.	Hold on, please.
Hij/Zij is er momenteel niet.	He's/She's out at the moment.

Telefoon

NUMBERS, see page 147

Doctor

Check that your health insurance policy covers any illness or accident while on holiday. If it doesn't, ask your insurance representative, automobile association or travel agent for details of special health insurance.

General *Algemeen*

Can you get me a doctor?	**Kunt u een dokter roepen?**	kurnt ew ern **dokterr roopern**
Is there a doctor here?	**Is er hier een dokter?**	iss ehr heer ern **dokterr**
I need a doctor, quickly.	**Ik heb snel een dokter nodig.**	ik hehp snehl ern **dokterr** noadikh
Where can I find a doctor who speaks English?	**Waar kan ik een dokter vinden die Engels spreekt?**	√aar kahn ik ern **dokterr** vindern dee **ehng**erliss spraykt
Where's the surgery (doctor's office)?	**Waar heeft de dokter zijn praktijk?**	√aar hayft der **dokterr** zaiyn prahk**taiyk**
What are the surgery (office) hours?	**Hoe laat is het spreekuur?**	hoo laat iss heht **spraykewr**
Could the doctor come to see me here?	**Kan de dokter mij hier komen bezoeken?**	kahn der **dokterr** maiy heer **koamern** berzookern
What time can the doctor come?	**Hoe laat kan de dokter komen?**	hoo laat kahn der **dokterr koamern**
Can you recommend a/an...?	**Kunt u mij... aanbevelen?**	kurnt ew maiy... **aanbervaylern**
general practitioner	**een (huis)arts**	ern (hur^{ew}s)ahrts
children's doctor	**een kinderarts**	ern **kinderrahrts**
eye specialist	**een oogarts**	ern **oakhahrts**
gynaecologist	**een gynaecoloog**	ern gheenaykoa**loakh**
Can I have an appointment...?	**Kan ik... een afspraak maken?**	kahn ik... ern **ahfspraak** maakern
tomorrow	**voor morgen**	voar **morghern**
as soon as possible	**zo snel mogelijk**	zoa snehl **moagherlerk**
When can the doctor see me?	**Wanner kan de doktor mij onderzoeken?**	√ahnayr kahn der **dokterr** maiy onderr**zookern**

CHEMIST'S, see page 107

Parts of the body *Lichaamsdelen*

appendix	de blindedarm	der blinderdahrm
arm	de arm	der ahrm
back	de rug	der rurkh
bladder	de blaas	der blaass
bone	het bot	heht bot
bowel	de darm	der dahrm
breast	de borst	der borst
chest	de borstkas	der borstkahss
ear	het oor	heht oar
eye	het oog	heht oakh
face	het gezicht	heht gherzikht
finger	de vinger	der vingerr
foot	de voet	der voot
genitals	de geslachtsorganen	der gherslahkhtsorghaanern
gland	de klier	der kleer
hand	de hand	der hahnt
head	het hoofd	heht hoaft
heart	het hart	heht hahrt
jaw	de kaak	der kaak
joint	het gewricht	heht gher√rikht
kidney	de nier	der neer
knee	de knie	der knee
leg	het been	heht bayn
lip	de lip	der lip
liver	de lever	der layverr
lung	de long	der long
mouth	de mond	der mont
muscle	de spier	der speer
neck	de nek	der nehk
nerve	de zenuw	der zaynew°°
nervous system	het zenuwstelsel	heht zaynew°°stehlserl
nose	de neus	der nurss
rib	de rib	der rip
shoulder	de schouder	der skho°ʷderr
skin	de huid	der hurᵉʷt
spine	de ruggegraat	der rurgherghraat
stomach	de maag	der maakh
tendon	de pees	der payss
thigh	de dij	der daiy
throat	de hals/de keel	der hahlss/der kayl
thumb	de duim	der durᵉʷm
toe	de teen	der tayn
tongue	de tong	der tong
tonsils	de amandelen	der aamahnderlern
vein	de ader	der aaderr

Accident—Injury   *Ongeval—Verwonding*

There's been an accident.	**Er is een ongeval gebeurd.**	ehr iss ern **ong**hervahl gher**burrt**
My child has had a fall.	**Mijn kind is gevallen.**	maiyn kint iss gher**vah**lern
He/She has hurt his/her head.	**Hij/Zij is gewond aan zijn/haar hoofd.**	haiy/zaiy iss gher**v**ont aan zaiyn/haar hooft
He's/She's unconscious.	**Hij/Zij is bewusteloos.**	haiy/zaiy iss ber**v**usterloass
He's/She's bleeding (heavily).	**Hij/Zij bloedt (erg).**	haiy/zaiy bloot (ehrkh)
He's/She's (seriously) injured.	**Hij/Zij is (ernstig) gewond.**	haiy/zaiy iss (**ehrn**sterkh) gher**v**ont
His/Her arm is broken.	**Zijn/Haar arm is gebroken.**	zaiyn/haar ahrm iss gher**broa**kern
His/Her ankle is swollen.	**Zijn/Haar enkel is gezwollen.**	zaiyn/haar **ehn**kerl iss gherz**v**ollern
I've been stung.	**Ik ben gestoken.**	ik behn gher**stoa**kern
I've got something in my eye.	**Ik heb iets in mijn oog.**	ik hehp eets in maiyn oakh
I've got a/an...	**Ik heb...**	ik hehp
blister	**een blaar**	ern blaar
boil	**een steenpuist**	ern staynpur^{ew}st
bruise	**een kneuzing**	ern knurzing
bump	**een buil**	ern bur^{ew}l
burn	**een brandwond**	ern brahnt**v**ont
cut	**een snijwond**	ern snaiy**v**ont
graze	**een schaafwond**	ern skhaaf**v**ont
insect bite	**een insektenbeet**	ern insehk**tern**bayt
rash	**uitslag**	ur^{ew}tslahkh
sting	**een steek**	ern stayk
swelling	**een zwelling**	ern z**v**ehling
wound	**een wond**	ern **v**ont
Could you have a look at it?	**Kunt u er eens naar kijken?**	kurnt ew ehr ayns naar **kaiy**kern
I can't move my...	**Ik kan mijn... niet bewegen.**	ik kahn maiyn... neet ber**v**ayghern
My... are aching.	**Mijn... doen pijn.**	maiyn doon paiyn
It hurts.	**Het doet pijn.**	heht doot paiyn

Waar doet het pijn?	Where does it hurt?
Wat voor soort pijn is het?	What kind of pain is it?
dof/hevig/bonzend	dull/sharp/throbbing
voortdurend/af en toe	constant/on and off
Het is...	It's...
gebroken/verstuikt	broken/sprained
ontwricht/gescheurd	dislocated/torn
Er moet een röntgenfoto gemaakt worden.	I'd like you to have an X-ray.
U krijgt een gipsverband.	We'll have to put it in plaster.
Het is ontstoken.	It's infected.
Bent u tegen tetanus ingeënt?	Have you been vaccinated against tetanus?
Ik zal u een pijnstiller geven.	I'll give you a painkiller.

Illness *Ziekte*

I'm not feeling well.	**Ik voel mij niet goed.**	ik vool maiy neet ghoot
I'm ill.	**Ik ben ziek.**	ik behn zeek
I'm depressed/tired.	**Ik bin gedeprimeerd/moe.**	ik behn gherdaypreemayrt/moo
I feel...	**Ik voel mij...**	ik vool maiy
dizzy	**duizelig**	dur^{ew}zerlerkh
miserable	**beroerd**	behroort
nauseous	**misselijk**	misserlerk
shivery	**rillerig**	rillerrerkh
I have a temperature (fever).	**Ik heb koorts.**	ik hehp koarts
My temperature is 38 degrees.	**Ik heb 38° koorts.**	ik hehp 38° koarts
I've been vomiting.	**Ik heb overgegeven.**	ik hehp oaverrgherghayvern
I'm constipated/ I've got diarrhoea.	**Ik heb constipatie/ Ik heb diarree.**	ik hehp konsteepaatsee / ik hehp deeyaaray
My... hurts.	**Mijn... doet pijn.**	maiyn... doot paiyn

I've got (a/an)...	**Ik heb...**	ik hehp
asthma	**astma**	ahstmaa
backache	**rugpijn**	rurkhpaiyn
cold	**een verkoudheid**	ern verrko^{ow}thaiyt
cough	**een hoest**	ern hoost
cramps	**krampen**	krahmpern
earache	**oorpijn**	oarpaiyn
hay fever	**hooikoorts**	hoa^{ee}koarts
headache	**hoofdpijn**	hoaftpaiyn
indigestion	**indigestie**	indeeghehstee
nosebleed	**een neusbloeding**	ern nursblooding
palpitations	**hartkloppingen**	hahrtkloppingern
rheumatism	**reumatiek**	rurmaateek
sore throat	**keelpijn**	kaylpaiyn
stiff neck	**een stijve nek**	ern staiyver nehk
stomach ache	**maagpijn**	maakhpaiyn
sunstroke	**een zonnesteek**	ern zonnerstayk
I have difficulties breathing.	**Ik heb ademhalings-problemen.**	ik hehp aadermhaalings-proablaymern
I have chest pains.	**Ik heb pijn in mijn borst.**	ik hehp paiyn in maiyn borst
I had a heart attack ... years ago.	**Ik heb ... jaar geleden een hart-aanval gehad.**	ik hehp ... yaar gherlaydern ern hahrtaanvahl gherhaht
My blood pressure is too high/too low.	**Mijn bloeddruk is te hoog/te laag.**	maiyn blootdruk iss ter hoakh/ter laakh
I'm allergic to...	**Ik ben allergisch voor...**	ik behn ahlehrgheess voar
I'm diabetic.	**Ik ben suikerpatiënt.**	ik behn sur^{ew}kerrpaasyehnt

Women's section *Voor vrouwen*

I have...	**Ik heb...**	ik hehp
period pains	**menstruatiepijn**	mehnstrew√aatseepaiyn
a vaginal infection	**een vaginale infectie**	ern vaagheenaaler infehksee
I'm on the pill.	**Ik ben aan de pil.**	ik behn aan der pil
I haven't had a period for 2 months.	**Ik heb 2 maanden geen menstruatie gehad.**	ik hehp 2 maandern ghayn mehnstrew√aatsee gherhaht
I'm (3 months) pregnant.	**Ik ben (3 maanden) zwanger.**	ik behn (3 maandern) z√ahngerr

DOCTOR

🖙   🗩

Hoelang voelt u zich al zo?	How long have you been feeling like this?
Is dit de eerste keer dat u hier last van hebt?	Is this the first time you've had this?
Ik zal uw temperatuur/ bloeddruk opnemen.	I'll take your temperature/ blood pressure.
Wilt u uw mouw opstropen, alstublieft.	Roll up your sleeve, please.
Wilt u zich (tot uw middel) ontkleden, alstublieft.	Please undress (down to the waist).
Gaat u hier liggen, alstublieft.	Please lie down over here.
Open uw mond.	Open your mouth.
Adem diep.	Breathe deeply.
Hoest u eens.	Cough, please.
Waar doet het pijn?	Where does it hurt?
U hebt...	You've got (a/an)...
een blaasontsteking	cystitis
een blindedarmontsteking	appendicitis
gastritis	gastritis
geelzucht	jaundice
geslachtsziekte	venereal disease
griep	flu
longontsteking	pneumonia
nierstenen	kidney stones
een ontsteking van...	inflammation of...
voedselvergiftiging	food poisoning
Het is (niet) besmettelijk.	It's (not) contagious.
Het is een allergie.	It's an allergy.
Ik zal u een injectie geven.	I'll give you an injection.
Ik heb een bloedmonster/ een monster van uw ontlasting/ een flesje urine van u nodig.	I want a specimen of your blood/stools/urine.
U moet... dagen in bed blijven.	You must stay in bed for... days.
Ik stuur u door naar een specialist.	I want you to see a specialist.
Ik stuur u naar het ziekenhuis voor een algemeen onderzoek.	I want you to go to the hospital for a general check-up.

Prescription—Treatment   *Recept—Behandeling*

This is my usual medicine.	**Gewoonlijk neem ik dit geneesmiddel.**	gher√oanlerk naym ik dit ghernaysmidderl
Can you give me a prescription for this?	**Kunt u mij een recept geven daarvoor?**	kurnt ew maiy ern rersehpt ghayvern daarvoar
Can you prescribe a/an/some...?	**Kunt u mij... voorschrijven?**	kurnt ew maiy... voarskhraiyvern
antidepressant	**een middel tegen neerslachtigheid**	ern midderl tayghern nayrslahkhterkhhaiyt
sleeping pills	**slaappillen**	slaappillern
tranquillizer	**een kalmeringsmiddel**	ern kahlmayringsmidderl
I'm allergic to certain antibiotics/penicillin.	**Ik ben allergisch voor bepaalde antibiotica/penicilline.**	ik behn ahlehrgheess voar berpaalder ahnteebeeoateekaa/pehneeseeleener
I don't want anything too strong.	**Ik wil geen te sterk middel.**	ik √il ghayn ter stehrk midderl
How many times a day should I take it?	**Hoeveel keer per dag moet ik het innemen?**	hoovayl kayr perr dahkh moot ik heht innaymern
Must I swallow them whole?	**Moet ik het heel inslikken?**	moot ik heht hayl inslikkern

👉	👈
Welke behandeling krijgt U?	What treatment are you having?
Welk geneesmiddel neemt u?	What medicine are you taking?
Injectie of pillen?	By injection or orally?
Neem... theelepels van deze medicijn...	Take... teaspoons of this medicine...
Neem een pil met een glas water...	Take one pill with a glass of water...
om de... uur	every... hours
...maal per dag	...times a day
voor/na elke maaltijd	before/after every meal
's morgens/'s avonds	in the morning/at night
bij pijn	if there is any pain
gedurende... dagen	for... days

CHEMIST'S, see page 107

DOCTOR

Fee *Honorarium*

How much do I owe you?	**Hoeveel ben ik u schuldig?**	hoovayl behn ik ew skhurlderkh
May I have a receipt for my health insurance?	**Hebt u een kwitantie voor mijn ziekteverzekering?**	hehpt ew ern kveetahnsee voar maiyn zeekterverrzaykerring
Can I have a medical certificate?	**Kunt u mij een medisch attest geven?**	kurnt ew maiy ern maydeess ahtehst ghayvern
Would you fill in this health insurance form, please?	**Kunt u dit verzekeringsformulier invullen, alstublieft?**	kurnt ew dit verrzaykerringsformewleer invurlern ahlstewbleeft

Hospital *Ziekenhuis*

Please notify my family.	**Waarschuw mijn familie, alstublieft.**	√aarskhew⁰⁰ maiyn faameelee ahlstewbleeft
What are the visiting hours?	**Wat zijn de bezoekuren?**	√aht zaiyn der berzookewrern
When can I get up?	**Wanneer mag ik opstaan?**	√ahnayr mahkh ik opstaan
When will the doctor come?	**Wanneer komt de dokter?**	√ahnayr komt der dokterr
I'm in pain.	**Ik heb pijn.**	ik hehp paiyn
I can't eat/sleep.	**Ik kan niet eten/slapen.**	ik kahn neet aytern/slaapern
Where is the bell?	**Waar is de bel?**	√aar iss der behl

male nurse	**de verpleegkundige**	der verrplaykhkurndergher
nurse	**de verpleegster**	der verrplaykhsterr
patient	**de patiënt(e)**	der paasyehnt(er)
anaesthetic	**de narcose**	der nahrkoazer
blood transfusion	**de bloedtransfusie**	der bloottrahnsfewzee
injection	**de injectie**	der inyehksee
operation	**de operatie**	der oaperraatsee
bed	**het bed**	heht beht
bedpan	**de ondersteek**	der onderrstayk
thermometer	**de thermometer**	der tehrmoamayterr

Dokter

Dentist *Tandarts*

Can you recommend a good dentist?	**Kunt u een goede tandarts aanbevelen?**	˙ kurnt ew ern **ghooder tahntahrts aan**bervaylern
Can I make an (urgent) appointment to see Dr...?	**Kan ik (zo snel mogelijk) een afspraak maken met dokter...?**	kahn ik (zoa snehl moagherlerk) ern **ahf**spraak **maa**kern meht **dokter**
Couldn't you make it earlier?	**Kan het echt niet eerder?**	kahn heht ehkht neet ayrderr
I have a broken tooth.	**Ik heb een afgebroken tand.**	ik hehp ern **ahf**gherbroakern tahnt
I have toothache.	**Ik heb kiespijn.**	ik hehp **kees**paiyn
I have an abscess.	**Ik heb een abces.**	ik hehp ern ahp**sehss**
This tooth hurts.	**Deze tand doet pijn.**	**day**zer tahnt doot paiyn
at the top	**bovenin**	**boa**vernin
at the bottom	**onderin**	**onder**rin
at the front	**voorin**	**voar**in
at the back	**achterin**	**ahkh**terrin
Can you fix it temporarily?	**Kunt u een provisorische behandeling doen?**	kurnt ew ern proaveesoa-reesser berhahnderling doon
I don't want it pulled out.	**Ik wil niet laten trekken.**	ik √il neet **laa**tern **treh**kern
Could you give me an anaesthetic?	**Kunt u mij een verdoving geven?**	kurnt ew maiy ern verr-**doa**ving **ghay**vern
I've lost a filling.	**Ik heb een vulling verloren.**	ik hehp ern **vur**ling verr**loa**rern
My gums...	**Mijn tandvlees...**	maiyn **tahnt**vlayss
are very sore	**is zeer pijnlijk**	iss zayr **paiyn**lerk
are bleeding	**bloedt**	bloot
I've broken my dentures.	**Ik heb mijn gebit gebroken.**	ik hehp maiyn gher**bit** gherbroakern
Can you repair my dentures?	**Kunt u mijn gebit repareren?**	kurnt ew maiyn gher**bit** raypaarayrern
When will they be ready?	**Wanneer is het klaar?**	√ah**nnayr** iss heht klaar

Reference section

Where do you come from? *Waar komt u vandaan?*

I'm from...	Ik kom uit...	ik kom ur^ew^t
Africa	**Afrika**	aafreekaa
Asia	**Azië**	aazeeyer
Australia	**Australië**	oastraaleeyer
Europe	**Europa**	urroapaa
North America	**Noord-Amerika**	noart aamayreekaa
South America	**Zuid-Amerika**	zur^ew^t aamayreekaa
Austria	**Oostenrijk**	oasternraiyk
Belgium	**België**	behlgheeyer
Canada	**Canada**	kahnaadaa
China	**China**	sheenaa
Denmark	**Denemarken**	daynermahrkern
England	**Engeland**	ehngerlahnt
Finland	**Finland**	finlahnt
France	**Frankrijk**	frahnkraiyk
Germany	**Duitsland**	dur^ew^tslahnt
Great Britain	**Groot-Brittannië**	groat brittahneeyer
Greece	**Griekenland**	ghreekernlahnt
Holland	**Holland**	hollahnt
Hungary	**Hongarije**	hongahraiyer
India	**India**	indeeyaa
Ireland	**Ierland**	eerlahnt
Israel	**Israël**	israaehl
Italy	**Italië**	eetaaleeyer
Japan	**Japan**	yaapahn
Luxembourg	**Luxemburg**	lewksermburrkh
Morocco	**Marokko**	maarokkoa
Netherlands	**Nederland**	nayderrlahnt
New Zealand	**Nieuw-Zeeland**	nee^oo^zaylahnt
Norway	**Noorwegen**	noar√ayghern
Portugal	**Portugal**	portewghahl
Russia	**Rusland**	rurslahnt
Scotland	**Schotland**	skhotlahnt
South Africa	**Zuid-Afrika**	zur^ew^t aafreekaa
Spain	**Spanje**	spahnyer
Sweden	**Zweden**	z√aydern
Switzerland	**Zwitserland**	z√itserrlahnt
Turkey	**Turkije**	turrkaiyyer
United States	**Verenigde Staten**	vehraynerghder **staa**tern
Wales	**Wales**	√aylss

Numbers *Getallen*

0	**nul**	nurl
1	**een**	ayn
2	**twee**	t√ay
3	**drie**	dree
4	**vier**	veer
5	**vijf**	vaiyf
6	**zes**	zehss
7	**zeven**	zayvern
8	**acht**	ahkht
9	**negen**	nayghern
10	**tien**	teen
11	**elf**	ehlf
12	**twaalf**	t√aalf
13	**dertien**	dehrteen
14	**veertien**	vayrteen
15	**vijftien**	vaiyfteen
16	**zestien**	zehsteen
17	**zeventien**	zayvernteen
18	**achttien**	ahkhteen
19	**negentien**	nayghernteen
20	**twintig**	t√interkh
21	**eenentwintig**	aynernt√interkh
22	**tweeëntwintig**	t√ayyernt√interkh
23	**drieëntwintig**	dreeyernt√interkh
24	**vierentwintig**	veerernt√interkh
25	**vijfentwintig**	vaiyfernt√interkh
26	**zesentwintig**	zehsernt√interkh
27	**zevenentwintig**	zayvernernt√interkh
28	**achtentwintig**	ahkhternt√interkh
29	**negenentwintig**	nayghernernt√interkh
30	**dertig**	dehrterkh
31	**eenendertig**	aynerndehrterkh
32	**tweeëndertig**	t√ayyerndehrterkh
33	**drieëndertig**	dreeyerndehrterkh
40	**veertig**	vayrterkh
41	**eenenveertig**	aynernvayrterkh
42	**tweeënveertig**	t√ayyernvayrterkh
43	**drieënveertig**	dreeyernvayrterkh
50	**vijftig**	vaiyfterkh
51	**eenenvijftig**	aynernvaiyfterkh
52	**tweeënvijftig**	t√ayyernvaiyfterkh
53	**drieënvijftig**	dreeyernvaiyfterkh
60	**zestig**	zehsterkh
61	**eenenzestig**	aynernsehsterkh
62	**tweeënzestig**	t√ayyernsehsterkh

63	**drieënzestig**	dreeyernsehsterkh
70	**zeventig**	zayvernterkh
71	**eenenzeventig**	aynernsayvernterkh
72	**tweeënzeventig**	t√ayyernsayvernterkh
73	**drieënzeventig**	dreeyernsayvernterkh
80	**tachtig**	tahkhterkh
81	**eenentachtig**	aynerntahkhterkh
82	**tweeëntachtig**	t√ayyerntahkhterkh
83	**drieëntachtig**	dreeyerntahkhterkh
90	**negentig**	nayghernterkh
91	**eenennegentig**	aynernnayghernterkh
92	**tweeënnegentig**	t√ayyernnayghernterkh
93	**drieënnegentig**	dreeyernnayghernterkh
100	**honderd**	honderrt
101	**honderd één**	honderrt ayn
102	**honderd twee**	honderrt t√ay
110	**honderd tien**	honderrt teen
120	**honderd twintig**	honderrt t√interkh
130	**honderd dertig**	honderrt dehrterkh
140	**honderd veertig**	honderrt vayrterkh
150	**honderd vijftig**	honderrt vayfterkh
160	**honderd zestig**	honderrt sehsterkh
170	**honderd zeventig**	honderrt sayvernterkh
180	**honderd tachtig**	honderrt tahkhterkh
190	**honderd negentig**	honderrt nayghernterkh
200	**tweehonderd**	t√ayhonderrt
300	**driehonderd**	dreehonderrt
400	**vierhonderd**	veerhonderrt
500	**vijfhonderd**	vaiyfhonderrt
600	**zeshonderd**	zehshonderrt
700	**zevenhonderd**	zayvernhonderrt
800	**achthonderd**	ahkhthonderrt
900	**negenhonderd**	nayghernhonderrt
1000	**duizend**	dur^{ew}zernt
1100	**elfhonderd**	ehlfhonderrt
1200	**twaalfhonderd**	t√aalfhonderrt
2000	**tweeduizend**	t√aydur^{ew}zernt
2001	**tweeduizend een**	t√aydur^{ew}zernt ayn
3000	**drieduizend**	dreedur^{ew}zernt
4000	**vierduizend**	veerdur^{ew}zernt
5000	**vijfduizend**	vaiyfdur^{ew}zernt
10,000	**tienduizend**	teendur^{ew}zernt
50,000	**vijftigduizend**	vaiyfterghdur^{ew}zernt
100,000	**honderdduizend**	honderrtdur^{ew}zernt
1,000,000	**een miljoen**	ayn milyoon
1,000,000,000	**een miljard**	ayn milyahrt

first	eerste	ayrster
second	tweede	t√ayder
third	derde	dehrder
fourth	vierde	veerder
fifth	vijfde	vaifder
sixth	zesde	zehsder
seventh	zevende	zayvernder
eighth	achtste	ahkhster
ninth	negende	nayghernder
tenth	tiende	teender

| once/twice | eenmaal/tweemaal | aynmaal/t√aymaal |
| three times | driemaal | dreemaal |

a half	een helft	ern hehlft
half a...	een halve...	ern hahlver
half of...	de helft van...	der hehlft vahn
half (adj.)	half, halve	hahlf hahlver
a quarter/one third	een kwart/een derde	ern k√ahrt/ayn dehrder
a pair of...	een paar...	ern paar
a dozen	een dozijn	ern doazaiyn

| one per cent | een procent | ayn proasehnt |
| 3.4% | 3,4% | dree kommah veer proasehnt |

1981	negentien eenentachtig	nayghernteen aynehntahkhterkh
1992	negentien tweeënnegentig	nayghernteen t√ayehnnaygharnterkh
2003	tweeduizend drie	t√aydur^(ew)zernt dree

Year and age   *Jaar en leeftijd*

year	jaar	yaar
leap year	schrikkeljaar	skhrikkerlyaar
decade	decennium	daysehneeyurm
century	eeuw	ay^(oo)

this year	dit jaar	dit yaar
last year	vorig jaar	voarikh yaar
next year	volgend jaar	volghernt yaar
each year	elk jaar	ehlk yaar

2 years ago	2 jaar geleden	t√ay yaar gherlaydern
in one year	over een jaar	oaverr ayn yaar
in the eighties	in de jaren 80	in der yaarern tahkhterkh

| the 16th century | de 16e eeuw | der zehsteender ay^(oo) |
| in the 20th century | in de 20e eeuw | in der t√interkhster ay^(oo) |

How old are you?	**Hoe oud bent u?**	hoo o^{ow}t behnt ew
I'm 30 years old.	**Ik ben 30 jaar.**	ik behn **dehrterkh** yaar
He/She was born in 1960.	**Hij/Zij is in 1960 geboren.**	haiy/zaiy iss in **nayghernteen zehsterkh** gherboarern
What is his/her age?	**Wat is zijn/haar leeftijd?**	√aht iss zaiyn/haar **layftaiyt**
Children under 16 are not admitted.	**Kinderen onder de 16 jaar worden niet toegelaten.**	**kinderrern onderr** der **zehsteen** yaar √ordern neet **toogherlaatern**

Seasons *Jaargetijden*

spring/summer	**lente/zomer**	**lehnter**/**zoamerr**
autumn/winter	**herfst/winter**	**hehrfst**/√**interr**
in spring	**in de lente**	in der **lehnter**
during the summer	**gedurende de zomer**	gherdewrender der **zoamerr**
in autumn	**in de herfst**	in der **hehrfst**
during the winter	**gedurende de winter**	gherdewrender der √**interr**
high season	**hoogseizoen**	**hoakh**saiyzoon
low season	**voorseizoen/ naseizoen**	**voar**saiyzoon/**naa**saiyzoon

Months *Maanden*

January	**januari***	yahnew√**aari**
February	**februari**	faybrew√**aari**
March	**maart**	maart
April	**april**	ah**pril**
May	**mei**	maiy
June	**juni**	**yew**nee
July	**juli**	**yew**lee
August	**augustus**	o^{ow}**ghurs**turss
September	**september**	sehp**tehm**berr
October	**oktober**	ok**toa**berr
November	**november**	noa**vehm**berr
December	**december**	day**sehm**berr
in September	**in september**	in sehp**tehm**berr
since October	**sinds oktober**	sints ok**toa**berr
the beginning of January	**begin januari**	berg**hin** yahnew√**aari**
the middle of February	**midden februari**	**middern** faybrew√**aaree**
the end of March	**eind maart**	aiynt maart

---

* The names of months aren't capitalized in Dutch.

Days and Date   *Dagen en datum*

What day is it today?	**Welke dag is het vandaag?**	**✓ehl**ker dahkh iss heht vahn**daakh**
Sunday	**zondag***	**zon**dahkh
Monday	**maandag**	**maan**dahkh
Tuesday	**dinsdag**	**dins**dahkh
Wednesday	**woensdag**	**✓oons**dahkh
Thursday	**donderdag**	**don**derr**dahkh**
Friday	**vrijdag**	**vraiy**dahkh
Saturday	**zaterdag**	**zaa**terr**dahkh**
It's...	**Het is...**	heht iss
July 1	**1 juli**	ayn **yew**lee
March 10	**10 maart**	teen maart
in the morning	**'s morgens**	s**mor**ghernss
during the day	**overdag**	**oa**verr**dahkh**
in the afternoon	**'s middags**	s**mid**dahkhss
in the evening	**'s avonds**	**saa**vonts
at night	**'s nachts**	s**nahkhts**
the day before yesterday	**eergisteren**	ayr**ghis**terrern
yesterday	**gisteren**	**ghis**terrern
today	**vandaag**	vahn**daakh**
tomorrow	**morgen**	**mor**ghern
the day after tomorrow	**overmorgen**	**oa**verr**mor**ghern
the day before	**de vorige dag**	der **voa**rergher dahkh
the next day	**de volgende dag**	der **volg**hernder dahkh
two days ago	**twee dagen geleden**	t✓ay **daa**ghern gherl**ay**dern
in three days' time	**over drie dagen**	**oa**verr dree **daa**ghern
last week	**vorige week**	**voa**rergher ✓ayk
next week	**volgende week**	**volg**hernder ✓ayk
for a fortnight (two weeks)	**gedurende twee weken**	gherde**wrer**rider t✓ay **✓ay**kern
birthday	**de verjaardag**	der verr**yaar**dahkh
day off	**de vrije dag**	der **vraiy**yer dahkh
holiday	**de feestdag**	der **fayst**dahkh
holidays/vacation	**de vakantie**	der vaa**kahn**see
week	**de week**	der ✓ayk
weekend	**het weekend**	heht **✓ee**kehnt
working day	**de werkdag**	der **✓ehrk**dahkh

---

* The names of days aren't capitalized in Dutch.

Public holidays *Openbare feestdagen*

National holidays in Holland (NL) and Belgium (B):

January 1	**Nieuwjaarsdag**	New Year's Day	NL	B
April 30	**Koninginnedag**	Queen's Birthday	NL	
May 1	**Dag van de Arbeid**	Labour Day		B
May 5	**Bevrijdingsdag***	Liberation Day	NL	
July 21	**Nationale Feestdag**	National Day		B
August 15	**Maria Hemelvaart**	Assumption Day		B
November 1	**Allerheiligen**	All Saints Day		B
November 11	**Wapenstil-standsdag**	Armistice Day		B
December 25	**Kerstmis**	Christmas	NL	B
December 26	**Kerstmis**	St. Stephen's Day	NL	
Movable dates:	**Goede Vrijdag**	Good Friday	NL	
	Paasmaandag	Easter Monday	NL	B
	Hemelvaartsdag	Ascension Thursday	NL	B
	Pinkstermaandag	Whit Monday	NL	B

* official holiday once every five years

Greetings and wishes *Groeten en wensen*

Merry Christmas!	**Vrolijk Kerstfeest!**	vroalerk kehrstfayst
Happy New Year!	**Gelukkig Nieuwjaar!**	gherlurkgherkerkh nee°°yaar
Happy Easter!	**Vrolijk Pasen!**	vroalerk paasern
Happy birthday!	**Gelukgewenst met uw verjaardag!**	gherlurkgher√ehnst meht ew°° verryaardahkh
I/We wish you all the best!	**Mijn/Onze beste wensen!**	maiyn/onzer behster √ehnsern
Congratulations!	**Hartelijk gefeli-citeerd!**	hahrterlerk gherfaylee-seetayrt
Good luck/ All the best!	**Veel geluk!**	vayl gherlurk
Have a good trip!	**Goede reis!**	ghoo°der raiyss
Have a good holiday!	**Prettige vakantie!**	prehtergher vaakahnsee
Best regards from...	**Hartelijke groeten van...**	hahrterlerker ghrootern vahn
My regards to...	**Mijn groeten aan...**	maiyn ghrootern aan

What time is it?   *Hoe laat is het?*

Excuse me. Can you tell me the time?	**Pardon. Kunt u mij zeggen hoe laat het is?**	pahrdon. kurnt ew maiy zehghern hoo laat heht iss
It's...	**Het is ...**	heht iss
five past one	**vijf over een***	vaiyf oaverr ayn
ten past two	**tien over twee**	teen oaverr tⱱay
a quarter past three	**kwart over drie**	kⱱahrt oaverr dree
twenty past four	**tien voor half vijf/ twintig over vier**	teen voar hahlf vaiyf/ tⱱinterkh oaverr veer
twenty-five past five	**vijf voor half zes**	vaiyf voar hahlf zehss
half past six	**half zeven****	hahlf zayvern
twenty-five to seven	**vijf over half zeven**	vaiyf oaverr hahlf zayvern
twenty to eight	**tien over half acht/ twintig voor acht**	teen oaverr hahlf ahkht/ tⱱinterkh voar ahkht
a quarter to nine	**kwart voor negen**	kⱱahrt voar napghern
ten to ten	**tien voor tien**	teen voar teen
five to eleven	**vijf voor elf**	vaiyf voar ehlf
twelve o'clock (noon/midnight)	**12 uur ('s middags/ 's nachts)**	12 ewr (smiddahkhss/ snahkhss)
in the morning	**'s morgens**	smorgherss
in the afternoon	**'s middags**	smiddahkhss
in the evening	**'s avonds**	saavontss
The train leaves at...	**De trein vertrekt om...**	der traiyn verrtrehkt om
13.04 (1.04 p.m.)	**dertien uur vier**	dehrteen ewr veer
0.40 (0.40 a.m.)	**nul uur veertig**	nurl ewr vayrterkh
in five minutes	**in vijf minuten**	in vaiyf meenewtern
in a quarter of an hour	**in een kwartier**	in ern kⱱahrteer
half an hour ago	**een half uur geleden**	ern hahlf ewr gherlaydern
about two hours	**ongeveer twee uur**	onghervayr tⱱay ewr
more than 10 minutes	**meer dan 10 minuten**	mayr dahn 10 meenewtern
a few seconds	**enkele seconden**	ehnkerler serkondern
The clock is fast/ slow.	**De klok loopt voor/ achter**	der klok loapt voar/ ahkhterr
early/late	**vroeg/laat**	vrookh/laat
on time	**op tijd**	op taiyt

* In everyday conversation, time is expressed as shown here. However, official time uses a 24-hour clock which means that after noon hours are counted from 13 to 24.
** Note that the Dutch say "half to" the following hour and not "half past" the preceding hour; in this example "half past six" is expressed in Dutch "half to seven".

Common abbreviations   *Gangbare afkortingen*

afd.	afdeling	department
afz.	afzender	from...
A.N.W.B.	Algemene Nederlandse Wielrijdersbond	Dutch Touring Club
a.s.	aanstaande	next
a.u.b.	alstublieft	please
b.g.	begane grond	ground floor
B.T.W.	Belasting Toegevoegde Waarde	VAT/value added tax (sales tax)
b.v.	bijvoorbeeld	for example
blz.	bladzijde	page
C.S.	Centraal Station	Central Station
d.w.z.	dat wil zeggen	i.e.
E.H.B.O.	Eerste Hulp bij Ongelukken	first-aid organization
enz.	enzovoort	etc.
G.G.D.	Gemeentelijke Genees-kundige Dienst	local ambulance service
GWK-bank	grenswisselkantoren	frontier exchange offices
Hr.	heer	Mr.
inl.	inlichtingen	information office
j.l.	jongstleden	last
K.A.C.B.	Koninklijke Automobiel Club van België	Royal Belgian Automobile Club
K.N.A.C.	Koninklijke Nederlandse Automobiel Club	Royal Dutch Automobile Club
Mej.	mejuffrouw	Miss
Mevr. (Mw.)	mevrouw	Mrs.
n.C.	na Christus	A.D.
N.J.H.C.	Nederlandse Jeugdherberg Centrale	Dutch Youth Hostels Organization
n.m.	namiddag	p.m.
nr.	nummer	number
N.S.	Nederlandse Spoorwegen	Dutch Railway
N.V.	naamloze vennootschap	Ltd./Inc.
p.a.	per adres	care of
str.	straat	street
s.v.p.	s'il vous plaît	please
t.e.m.	tot en met	up to and including
v.C.	voor Christus	B.C.
v.m.	voormiddag	a.m.
V.T.B.	Vlaamse Toeristenbond	Flemish Tourist Association
VVV	Vereniging voor Vreemdelingenverkeer	Dutch tourist information office
z.o.z.	zie ommezijde	please turn page

Signs and notices *Borden en opschriften*

Bellen, a.u.b.	Please ring
Bezet	Occupied
Binnen zonder kloppen	Enter without knocking
Dames	Ladies
Deur sluiten	Close the door
Duwen	Push
Fietspad	Cycle path
Geopend van... tot...	Open from... to...
Gereserveerd	Reserved
Gesloten	Closed
Heren	Gentleman
Hoogspanning	High voltage
Informatie	Information
Ingang	Entrance
Inlichtingen	Information office
Kassa	Cashier's (cash desk)
Koud	Cold
Levensgevaar	Danger of death
Lift	Lift (elevator)
Mannen	Men
Natte verf	Wet paint
Niet aanraken, a.u.b.	Do not touch
Niet-roken	No smoking
Niet storen	Do not disturb
Nooduitgang	Emergency exit
Open	Open
Pas op	Caution
Pas op voor de hond	Beware of the dog
Privé	Private
Privéweg	Private road
Roken	Smoking
Te huur	For hire/For rent/To let
Te koop	For sale
Trekken	Pull
Uitgang	Exit
Uitverkocht	Sold out
Uitverkoop	Sales
Verboden toegang	No entrance
Voetgangers	Pedestrians
Vol	Full
Voor honden verboden	Dogs not allowed
Vrij	Vacant
Vrije toegang	Admission free
Warm	Hot
's Zondags gesloten	Closed on Sundays

Emergency *In geval van nood*

Call the police	**Roep de politie**	roop der poaleetsee
Consulate	**Consulaat**	konsewlaat
DANGER	**GEVAAR**	ghervaar
Embassy	**Ambassade**	ahmbahsaader
FIRE	**BRAND**	brahnt
Gas	**Gas**	ghahss
Get a doctor	**Roep een dokter**	roop ern dokterr
Go away	**Ga weg**	ghaa √ehkh
HELP	**HELP**	hehlp
Get help quickly	**Haal snel hulp**	haal snehl hurlp
I'm ill	**Ik ben ziek**	ik behn zeek
I'm lost	**Ik ben verdwaald**	ik behn verrd√aalt
Leave me alone	**Laat mij met rust**	laat maiy meht rurst
LOOK OUT	**PAS OP**	pahss op
Poison	**Vergif**	verrghif
POLICE	**POLITIE**	poaleetsee
Stop that man/ women	**Houd die man/ vrouw tegen**	ho°°w dee mahn/ vro°°w tayghern
STOP THIEF	**HOUD DE DIEF**	ho°°w der deef

Emergency telephone numbers *Alarmnummers*			
		Belgium	Netherlands
Ambulance	**Ambulance**	900	06–11
Fire	**Brandweer**	900	06–11
Police	**Politie**	901	06–11

Lost property—Theft *Gevonden voorwerpen—Diefstal*

Where's the...?	**Waar is ...?**	√aar iss
lost property (lost and found) office	**het bureau voor gevonden voorwerpen**	heht bewroa voar ghervondern voar√ehrpern
police station	**het politiebureau**	heht poaleetseebewroa
I want to report a theft.	**Ik wil aangifte doen van een diefstal.**	ik √il aanghifter doon vahn ern deefstahl
My... has been stolen.	**Mijn... is gestolen.**	maiyn... iss gherstoalern
I've lost my...	**Ik heb... verloren.**	ik hehp... verrloarern
handbag	**mijn handtas**	maiyn hahnttahss
passport	**mijn paspoort**	maiyn pahspoort
wallet	**mijn portefeuille**	maiyn porterfur°°w yer

CAR ACCIDENTS, see page 78

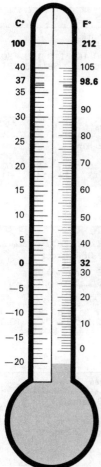

Conversion tables

Centimetres and inches

To change centimetres into inches, multiply by .39.

To change inches into centimetres, multiply by 2.54.

	in.	feet	yards
1 mm.	0.039	0.003	0.001
1 cm.	0.39	0.03	0.01
1 dm.	3.94	0.32	0.10
1 m.	39.40	3.28	1.09

	mm.	cm.	m.
1 in.	25.4	2.54	0.025
1 ft.	304.8	30.48	0.305
1 yd.	914.4	91.44	0.914

(32 metres = 35 yards)

Temperature

To convert centigrade into degrees Fahrenheit, multiply centigrade by 1.8 and add 32.

To convert degrees Fahrenheit into centigrade, subtract 32 from Fahrenheit and divide by 1.8.

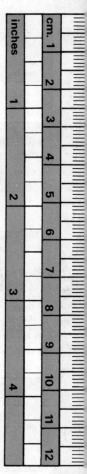

Kilometres into miles

1 kilometre (km.) = 0.62 miles

km.	10	20	30	40	50	60	70	80	90	100	110	120	130
miles	6	12	19	25	31	37	44	50	56	62	68	75	81

Miles into kilometres

1 mile = 1.609 kilometres (km.)

miles	10	20	30	40	50	60	70	80	90	100
km.	16	32	48	64	80	97	113	129	145	161

Fluid measures

1 litre (l.) = 0.88 imp. quart or = 1.06 U.S. quart

1 imp. quart = 1.14 l.	1 U.S. quart = 0.95 l.
1 imp. gallon = 4.55 l.	1 U.S. gallon = 3.8 l.

litres	5	10	15	20	25	30	35	40	45	50
imp. gal.	1.1	2.2	3.3	4.4	5.5	6.6	7.7	8.8	9.9	11.0
U.S. gal.	1.3	2.6	3.9	5.2	6.5	7.8	9.1	10.4	11.7	13.0

Weights and measures

1 kilogram or kilo (kg.) = 1000 grams (g.)

100 g. = 3.5 oz.	½ kg. = 1.1 lb.
200 g. = 7.0 oz.	1 kg. = 2.2 lb.

1 oz. = 28.35 g.
1 lb. = 453.60 g.

CLOTHING SIZES, see page 115/YARDS AND INCHES, see page 112

Basic grammar

Dutch is a Germanic language spoken throughout Holland and, under the name of Flemish, by about 5 million Belgians. The following concise outline of some essential features of Dutch grammar will be of help to you in understanding and speaking the language.

Articles

Dutch nouns are either common gender (originally separate masculine and feminine) or neuter.

1) **Definite article (the)**

   The definite article in Dutch is either **de** or **het**. **De** is used with roughly two thirds of all common-gender singular nouns as well as with all plural nouns, while **het** is mainly used with neuter singular nouns and all diminutives:

de straat the street   **het huis** the house   **het katje** the kitten

2) **Indefinite article (a; an)**

   The indefinite article is **een** for both genders, always unstressed and pronounced like *an* in the English word "another". As in English there is no plural. When it bears accent marks (**één**) it means "one" and is pronounced rather like a in "late", but a pure vowel, not a diphthong.

een man	a man	**een vrouw**	a woman	**een kind**	a child
mannen	men	**vrouwen**	women	**kinderen**	children

Plural

The most common sign of the plural in Dutch is an **-en** ending:

krant	newspaper	**woord**	word	**dag**	day
kranten	newspapers	**woorden**	words	**dagen**	days

a) In nouns with a double vowel, one vowel is dropped when **-en** is added:

uur	hour	**boot**	boat	**jaar**	year
uren	hours	**boten**	boats	**jaren**	years

b) most nouns ending in **-s** or **-f** change this letter into **-z** and **-v** respectively, when **-en** is added:

prijs	the price	**brief**	letter
prijzen	prices	**brieven**	letters

Another common plural ending in Dutch is **-s**. Nouns ending in an unstressed **-el, -em, -en, -aar** as well as **-je** (diminutives) take an **-s** in the plural:

tafel/		**winnaar/**	winner(s)
tafels	table(s)	**winnaars**	
deken/		**kwartje/**	
dekens	blanket(s)	**kwartjes**	25-cent piece(s)

Some exceptions:

stad/steden	town(s)	**auto/auto's**	car(s)
schip/schepen	ship(s)	**paraplu/**	umbrella(s)
kind/kinderen	child(ren)	**paraplu's**	
ei/eieren	egg(s)	**foto/foto's**	photo(s)
		musicus/musici	musician(s)

Adjectives

When the adjective stands immediately before the noun, it usually takes the ending **-e**:

de jonge vrouw	the young woman
een prettige reis	a pleasant trip
aardige mensen	nice people

However, no ending is added to the adjective in the following cases:

1) When the adjective follows the noun:

De stad is groot.	The city is big.
De zon is heet.	The sun is hot.

2) When the noun is neuter singular and preceded by **een**
(a/an), or when the words **elk/ieder** (each), **veel** (much),
zulk (such) and **geen** (no) precede the adjective:

een wit huis	a white house
elk goed boek	each good book
veel vers fruit	much fresh fruit
zulk mooi weer	such good weather
geen warm water	no hot water

Demonstrative adjectives (this/that):

this	**deze**	(with nouns of common gender)
	dit	(with nouns of neuter gender)
that	**die (daar)**	(with nouns of common gender)
	dat	(with nouns of neuter gender)
these	**deze**	(with all plural nouns)
those	**die (daar)**	(with all plural nouns)

Deze stad is groot.   This city is big.
Dat huis is wit.   That house is white.

Personal pronouns

Subject		**Object**	
I	**ik**	me	**mij** or **me**
you	**jij** or **je** (fam.)*	you	**jou** or **je** (fam.)*
you	**u** (pol.)**	you	**u** (pol.)**
he	**hij**	him	**hem**
she	**zij** or **ze**	her	**haar**
it	**het**	it	**het**
we	**wij** or **we**	us	**ons**
you	**jullie** (fam.)*	you	**jullie** (fam.)*
they	**zij** or **ze**	them	**hen**

The versions **je**, **ze**, **we** and **me** may be used in unstressed positions.

 * The familiar **jij** or **je** (singular) and **jullie** (plural) and their associated forms are used
only when talking to familiars, friends and children.

** When addressing people you don't know well, use **u** (and its associated form **uw**)
in both singular and plural.

Possessive adjectives

my	**mijn**
your	**jouw** (fam.)*
your	**uw** (pol.)**
his	**zijn**
her	**haar**
its	**zijn**
our	**ons** (with singular neuter nouns)
	onze (with singular nouns of common gender and all plurals)
your	**jullie** (fam.)*
their	**hun**

Verbs

First a few handy irregular verbs. If you learn only these, or even only the "I" and polite "you" forms of them, you'll have made a useful start.

1) The indispensible verbs **hebben** (to have) and **zijn** (to be) in the present:

I have	**ik heb**	I am	**ik ben**
you have	**jij hebt***	you are	**jij bent***
you have	**u hebt****	you are	**u bent****
he/she/it has	**hij/zij/het heeft**	he/she/it is	**hij/zij/het is**
we have	**wij hebben**	we are	**wij zijn**
you have	**jullie hebben***	you are	**jullie zijn***
they have	**zij hebben**	they are	**zij zijn**

2) Some more useful irregular verbs (in the present):

Infinitive		**willen** (to want)	**kunnen** (can)	**gaan** (to go)	**doen** (to do)	**weten** (to know)
I	**ik**	**wil**	**kan**	**ga**	**doe**	**weet**
you	**jij***	**wilt**	**kunt**	**gaat**	**doet**	**weet**
you	**u****	**wilt**	**kunt**	**gaat**	**doet**	**weet**
he	**hij**	**wil**	**kan**	**gaat**	**doet**	**weet**
she	**zij**	**wil**	**kan**	**gaat**	**doet**	**weet**
it	**het**	**wil**	**kan**	**gaat**	**doet**	**weet**
we	**wij**	**willen**	**kunnen**	**gaan**	**doen**	**weten**
you	**jullie***	**willen**	**kunnen**	**gaan**	**doen**	**weten**
they	**zij**	**willen**	**kunnen**	**gaan**	**doen**	**weten**

3) Infinitive and verb stem:

In Dutch verbs, the infinitive generally ends in **-en**: **noemen** (to name).

As the verb stem is usually the base for forming tenses, you need to know how to obtain it. The general rule is: the infinitive less **-en**:

infinitive: **noemen**   stem: **noem**

4) Present and past tenses:

First find the stem of the verb (see under 3 above).
Then add the appropriate endings, where applicable, according to the models given below for present and past tenses.

Note: in forming the past tense, the **-de/-den** endings shown in our example are added after most verb stems. However, if the stem ends in **p, t, k, f, s,** or **ch,** add **te/-ten** instead.

Present tense		Past tense	
ik noem	I name	**ik noemde**	I named
jij noemt*	you name	**jij noemde***	you named
u noemt* *	you name	**u noemde*** *	you named
hij/zij/het noemt	he/she/it names	**hij/zij/het noemde**	he/she/it named
wij noemen	we name	**wij noemden**	we named
jullie noemen*	you name	**jullie noemden***	you named
zij noemen	they name	**zij noemden**	they named

5) Past perfect (e.g.: "I have built"):

This tense is generally formed, as in English, by the verb "to have" **(hebben)** (see page 162) + the past participle.

To form the past participle, start with the verb stem, and add **ge-** to the front of it and **-d** or **-t** to the end:

---

*/** See footnote, page 161

infinitive:	**bouwen** (to build)
verb stem:	**bouw**
past participle:	**gebouwd**

The past participle must be placed *after* the object of the sentence:

| **Ik heb een huis gebouwd.** | I have built a house. |

Note: Verbs prefixed by **be-, er-, her-, ont-** and **ver-** do not take **ge-** in the past participle.

Instead of **hebben,** the verb **zijn** (to be) is used with verbs expressing motion (if the destination is specified or implied) or a change of state:

| **Wij zijn naar Parijs gevlogen.** | We have flown to Paris. |
| **Hij is rijk geworden.** | He has become rich. |

Negatives

To put a verb into the negative, place **niet** (not) after the verb, or after the direct object if there is one:

| **Ik rook.** | I smoke. | **Ik heb de kaartjes.** | I have the tickets. |
| **Ik rook niet.** | I don't smoke. | **Ik heb de kaartjes niet.** | I don't have the tickets. |

Questions

In Dutch, questions are formed by placing the subject after the verb:

| **Hij reist.** | He travels. | **Ik betaal.** | I pay. |
| **Reist hij?** | Does he travel? | **Betaal ik?** | Do I pay? |

Questions are also introduced by the following **interrogative pronouns:**

Wie (who)	Who says so?	**Wie zegt dat?**
	Whose house is that?	**Van wie is dat huis?**
Wat (what)	What does he do?	**Wat doet hij?**
Waar (where)	Where is the hotel?	**Waar is het hotel?**
Hoe (how)	How are you?	**Hoe gaat het met u?**

Dictionary
and alphabetical index

English–Dutch

c common	*nt* neuter	*pl* plural

a een 159
abbreviation afkorting *c* 154
able, to be kunnen 162
about *(approximately)* ongeveer 78, 153
above boven 15, 62, 85
abscess abces *nt* 145
absorbent cotton watten *c/pl* 108
accept, to aannemen 61, 102
accessories accessoires *c/pl* 115, 125
accident ongeval *nt* 78, 139
accommodation accommodatie *c* 22
account rekening *c* 130
ache, to pijn doen 139
adaptor verloopstekker *c* 118
address adres *nt* 21, 31, 79, 102
adhesive tape plakband *nt* 104
admission toegang *c* 82, 155
admitted toegelaten 150
adult volwassene *c* 82
Africa Afrika 146
after na 15, 77, 150
afternoon middag *c* 151, 153
again weer 96
age leeftijd *c* 149, 150
ago geleden 149, 151, 153
agriculture landbouw *c* 83
air bed luchtbed *nt* 106
airmail per luchtpost 133
air mattress luchtbed *nt* 106
airplane vliegtuig *nt* 65
airport luchthaven *c* 16, 19, 21, 65
aisle seat plaats aan het gangpad *c* 65
alarm clock wekker *c* 121
alcohol alcohol *c* 37, 59
alcoholic alcoholisch 58
all alles 103
allergic allergisch 141, 143
allergy allergie *c* 142

allowed toegestaan 84
alphabet alfabet *nt* 9, 135
also ook 15
alter, to *(garment)* vermaken 116
amazing verbazingwekkend 84
ambulance ambulance *c* 156; ziekenauto *c* 79
American Amerikaans 105, 126
American Amerikaan(se) *c* 93
American plan vol pension *nt* 24
amount bedrag *nt* 61, 131
amplifier versterker *c* 118
anaesthetic narcose *c* 144; verdoving *c* 145
analgesic pijnstillend middel *nt* 108
and en 15
animal dier *nt* 85
ankle enkel *c* 139
another nog een 57
answer antwoord *nt* 12; *(phone)* gehoor *nt* 136
antibiotic antibioticum *nt* 143
antidepressant middel tegen neerslachtigheid *nt* 143
antique antiek *nt* 83
antique shop antiekwinkel *c* 98
antiseptic antiseptisch 108
any enige 15
anyone iemand 12
anything iets 17, 101, 103, 113
anywhere ergens 89
aperitif aperitief *nt* 56
appendicitis blindedarm-ontsteking *c* 142
appendix blindedarm *c* 138
appetizer voorgerecht *nt* 41
apple appel *c* 52, 64
apple juice appelsap *nt* 59
appointment afspraak *c* 30, 131, 137, 145
April april (c) 150
architect architect *c* 83

area gebied *nt* 85; *(of town)* wijk *c* 81

area code netnummer *nt* 134

arm arm *c* 138, 139

around *(approximately)* omstreeks 31

arrangement arrangement *nt* 20

arrival aankomst *c* 16, 25, 65

arrive, to aankomen 65, 68, 70

art kunst *c* 83

art gallery kunstgalerij *c* 98

artificial kunstmatig 37

artificial light kunstlicht *nt* 124

artificial sweetener zoetstof *c* 37

artist kunstenaar *c* 83

art museum museum voor beeldende kunst *nt* 81

ashtray asbak *c* 36

Asia Azië 146

ask, to vragen 25, 60, 76, 136

asparagus asperge *c* 49

aspirin aspirine *c* 108

assorted gevarieerd 41

at te 15

at least minstens 24

at once onmiddellijk 31

auction veiling *c* 81

August augustus *(c)* 150

aunt tante *c* 93

Australia Australië 146

automatic automatisch 124

autumn herfst *c* 150

awful afschuwelijk 84, 94

B

baby baby *c* 24, 110

babysitter babysitter *c* 27

back rug *c* 138

backache rugpijn *c* 141

backpack rugzak *c* 106

bacon (ontbijt)spek *nt* 38

bacon and eggs spiegeleieren met (ontbijt)spek 38

bad slecht 14, 95

bag tas *c* 17, 18, 103

baggage bagage *c* 18, 26, 31, 71

baggage cart bagagewagentje *nt* 18, 71

baggage checking inschrijven bagage *c* 71

baggage locker bagagekluis *c* 18, 67, 71

baked (in de oven) gebakken 45

baker's bakker *c* 98

balance *(finance)* balans *c* 131

balcony balkon *nt* 23

ball *(inflated)* bal *c* 128

ballet ballet *nt* 88

ball-point pen ballpoint *c* 104

banana banaan *c* 52, 64

bandage verband *nt* 108

Band-Aid pleister *c* 108

bangle armband *c* 121

bank *(finance)* bank *c* 98, 129, 130

banknote (bank)biljet *nt* 130

bar *(room)* bar *c* 33

barber's herenkapper *c* 30, 98

bath bad *nt* 23, 25

bathing cap badmuts *c* 115

bathing hut badhokje *nt* 91

bathrobe badjas *c* 115

bathroom badkamer *c* 27

bath towel badhanddoek *c* 27

battery batterij *c* 118, 125; *(car)* accu *c* 75, 78

be, to zijn 13, 14, 162

beach strand *nt* 91

beach ball strandbal *c* 128

bean boon *c* 49

beard baard *c* 31

beautiful mooi 14, 84

beauty salon schoonheidssalon *c* 30, 98

bed bed *nt* 24, 144

bed and breakfast overnachting met ontbijt *c* 24

bedpan ondersteek *c* 144

beef rundvlees *nt* 46; runder- 46; osse- 46

beefsteak biefstuk *c* 46

beer bier *nt* 56, 57, 64; pils *c/nt* 56

before voor 15, 143

begin, to beginnen 86

beginning begin *nt* 150

behind achter 15, 77

Belgian Belgisch 18, 55

Belgium België 146

bell bel *c* 144

below onder 15, 62, 85

belt ceintuur *c* 116

berth couchette *c* 69, 71

better beter 14, 95, 101

between tussen 15

bicycle fiets *c* 74, 90

big groot 14, 25, 101, 117

bill rekening *c* 31, 61, 102; *(banknote)* biljet *nt* 130

billion *(Am.)* miljard *nt* 148

binoculars verrekijker *c* 123

bird vogel *c* 85

DICTIONARY

Woordenboekje

cafeteria cafetaria *c* 33
cake koek *c* 63; taart *c* 53, 63
cake shop banketbakkerij *c* 98
calculator rekenmachientje *nt* 105
calendar kalender *c* 104
call *(phone)* gesprek *nt* 134, 136
call, to *(give name)* noemen 11; *(phone)* (op)bellen 134, 136; *(summon)* roepen 60, 79, 156
camera fototoestel *nt* 124
camera case camera etui *c* 125
camera shop fotozaak *c* 98
camp, to kamperen 32
camp bed veldbed *nt* 106
camping camping *c* 32
camping equipment kampeeruitrusting *c* 106
camp site kampeerterrein *nt* 32
can *(container)* blik *nt* 119
can *(be able to)* kunnen 13, 162
Canada Canada 146
Canadian Canadees (-dese) *c* 93
canal gracht *c* 81
canal tour rondvaart door de grachten *c* 74
cancel, to annuleren 65
candle kaars *c* 120
candy snoep *nt* 126
candy store snoepwinkel *c* 98
can opener blikopener *c* 120
cap pet *c* 115
capital *(finance)* kapitaal *nt* 131
capsule *(medical)* capsule *c* 108
car auto *c* 19, 20, 32, 75, 76, 78; *(train)* rijtuig *nt* 66, 70, 71; wagen *c* 66, 70, 71
carafe karaf *c* 57
carat karaat *nt* 121
caravan caravan *c* 32
carbon paper carbonpapier *nt* 104
card kaart *c* 93, 131
card game speelkaarten *c/pl* 128
cardigan gebreid vest *nt* 115
car ferry veerboot *c* 74
car hire autoverhuur *c* 20
car park parkeerplaats *c* 77
car rental autoverhuur *c* 20
carrot wortel *c* 49
carry, to dragen 71
cart wagentje *nt* 18, 71
carton slof *c* 17, 126
cartridge *(camera)* cassette *c* 124
case koker *c* 123, 126

cash, to verzilveren 130, 133
cash desk kassa *c* 103, 155
cassette cassette *c* 127
cassette recorder cassette recorder *c* 118
castle kasteel *nt* 81
catalogue catalogus *c* 82
cathedral kathedraal *c* 81
Catholic katholiek 84
cauliflower bloemkool *c* 49
caution pas op 79, 155
cave grot *c* 81
CD-player CD-speler *c* 118
celery selderij *c* 49
cemetery kerkhof *nt* 81
centimetre centimeter *c* 111
centre centrum *c* 19, 21, 76, 81
century eeuw *c* 149
ceramics keramiek *c* 83
cereal cornflakes *c/pl* 38
chain *(jewellery)* ketting *c* 121
chain bracelet schakelarmband *c* 121
chair stoel *c* 106
change *(money)* kleingeld *nt* 130; wisselgeld *nt* 61, 77
change, to veranderen 65; verwisselen 75, 123; *(money)* wisselen 18, 130; *(trains)* overstappen 68, 69, 73
changing room paskamer *c* 114
chapel kapel *c* 81
charcoal houtskool *c* 106
charge kosten *c/pl* 28, 136; tarief *nt* 20
charge, to berekenen 24, 130
charm *(trinket)* gelukshangertje *nt* 121
charm bracelet bedelarmband *c* 121
cheap goedkoop 14, 24, 25, 101
check cheque *c* 130; *(restaurant)* rekening *c* 61
check, to controleren 75
check in, to *(airport)* inchecken 65
check out, to vertrekken 31
check-up *(medical)* onderzoek *nt* 142
cheers! proost! 58
cheese kaas *c* 38, 64
cheese shop kaaswinkel *c* 98
chemist's apotheek *c* 98, 107
cheque cheque *c* 130
cherry kers *c* 52

DICTIONARY

chess schaak *nt* 93
chess set schaakspel *nt* 128
chest borst *c* 141; borstkas *c* 138
chewing gum kauwgum *c* 126
chewing tobacco pruimtabak *c* 126
chicken kip *c* 48, 62
child kind *nt* 24, 60, 82, 91, 93, 139
children's ... kinder- 115
children's doctor kinderarts *c* 137
China China 146
china porselein *nt* 127
china shop porseleinwinkel *c* 98
chips patates frites *c/pl* 50, 62; *(Am.)* chips *c/pl* 64
chives bieslook *nt* 53
chocolate chocolade *c* 119, 126; *(drink)* chocolademelk *c* 38, 59
chocolate bar reep chocolade *c* 64
chop *(meat)* karbonade *c* 46; kotelet *c* 46
Christmas Kerstmis *c* 152, Kerstfeest *nt* 152
chromium chroom *nt* 122
church kerk *c* 81, 84
cigar sigaar *c* 126
cigarette sigaret *c* 17, 95, 126
cigarette holder sigarettepijpje *nt* 126
cigarillo klein sigaartje *nt* 126
cigarette lighter aansteker *c* 126
cinema bioscoop *c* 86, 96
circle *(theatre)* balkon *nt* 87
city stad *c* 81; 160
city centre stadscentrum *nt* 81
classical klassiek 128
clean schoon 60
clean, to schoonmaken 75
cleansing cream reinigings-crème *c* 109
cloakroom garderobe *c* 87
clock klok *c* 121, 153
clock-radio radiowekker *c* 118
clogs klompen *c/pl* 127
close, to dichtgaan 11, 82, 107, 129, 132
closed gesloten 155
cloth linnen *nt* 118
clothes kleren *c/pl* 29, 115
clothes peg/pin wasknijper *c* 120
clothing kleding *c* 111
cloud wolk *c* 94
coach *(bus)* bus *c* 72

coach terminal busstation *nt* 72
coat jas *c* 115
coffee koffie *c* 38, 59, 64
coffee house koffieshop *c* 33
coin munt *c* 83
cold koud 14, 25, 38, 60, 94, 155
cold *(illness)* verkoudheid *c* 107, 141
cold cuts vleeswaren *c/pl* 64
collar kraag *c* 116
collect call collect bellen *nt* 135
colour kleur *c* 111, 112, 124, 125
colour chart kleurenkaart *c* 30
colourfast kleurecht 113
colour rinse kleurspoeling *c* 30
colour shampoo kleurshampoo *c* 110
comb kam *c* 110
come, to komen 36, 92, 95, 137
comedy blijspel *nt* 86
commission *(fee)* provisie *c* 130
compact disc compact disc *c* 128
compartment *(train)* coupé *c* 70; compartiment *nt* 70
compass kompas *nt* 106
complaint klacht *c* 60
concert concert *nt* 88
concert hall concertgebouw *nt* 81, 88
condom condoom *nt* 108
conductor *(orchestra)* dirigent *c* 88
conference room vergaderzaal *c* 19
confirm, to bevestigen 65
confirmation bevestiging *c* 23
congratulation felicitatie *c* 152
connection verbinding *c* 65; *(transport)* aansluiting *c* 68
connect, to verbinden 28
constipation constipatie *c* 140
consulate consulaat *nt* 156
contact lens contactlens *c* 123
contagious besmettelijk 142
contain, to bevatten 37
contraceptive voorbehoeds-middel *nt* 108
contract contract *nt* 131
control controle *c* 16
cookie beschuitje/koekje *nt* 64
cooking facilities kook-gelegenheid *c* 32
cool box koelbox *c* 106
copper koper *nt* 122, 127
cordless snoerloos 118

Woordenboekje

DICTIONARY

Woordenboekje

corkscrew kurketrekker *c* 120
corn *(Am.)* maïs *c* 49; *(foot)* likdoorn *c* 108
corner hoek *c* 21, 36, 77
corn plaster likdoornpleister *c* 108
cosmetics cosmetica *c* 109
cost kosten *c/pl* 131, *(expenses)* onkosten *c/pl* 20
cost, to kosten 11, 24, 80, 136
cot kinderbed *nt* 24
cotton katoen *c* 113
cotton wool watten *c/pl* 108
couchette couchette *c* 69
couchette car ligrijtuig *nt* 66, 70
cough hoest *c* 107, 141
cough, to hoesten 142
cough drops hoestpastilles *c/pl* 108
cough syrup hoestsiroop *c* 108
counter loket *c* 133
country land *nt* 92, 146
countryside platteland *nt* 85
court house gerechtshof *nt* 81
cousin *(male)* neef *c* 93; *(female)* nicht *c* 93
crab krab *c* 41, 44
cramp kramp *c* 141
crayfish *(river)* rivierkreeft *c* 44
crayon tekenstift *c* 104
cream room *c* 53, 59; *(toiletry)* crème *c* 108, 110
crease resistant kreukvrij 113
credit krediet *nt* 130
credit card credit card *c* 20, 31, 61, 102, 130
crisps chips *c/pl* 64
crockery serviesgoed *nt* 120
cross kruis *nt* 121
crossing *(maritime)* overtocht *c* 74
crossroads kruispunt *nt* 77
cruise cruise *c* 74
crystal kristal *nt* 122, 127
cucumber komkommer *c* 49, 64
cuff link manchetknoop *c* 121
cuisine keuken *c* 35
cup kopje *nt* 36, 59, 120
curler haarroller *c* 110
currant krent *c* 119
currency valuta *c* 129
currency exchange office wisselkantoor *nt* 18, 67, 98, 129
current stroming *c* 91
curtain gordijn *nt* 28

customs douane *c* 16, 102
cut *(wound)* snijwond *c* 139
cut, to *(with scissors)* knippen 30
cut off, to *(interrupt)* verbreken 135
cut glass geslepen glas *nt* 122
cuticle remover nagelriem remover *c* 109
cutlery bestek *nt* 120, 121
cycling fietsen *nt* 89
cyclist fietser *c* 79
cystitis blaasontsteking *c* 142

D
daffodil narcis *c* 85
dairy melkwinkel *c* 98
dance, to dansen 88, 96
danger gevaar *nt* 155, 156
dangerous gevaarlijk 91
dark donker 25, 101, 111, 112
date *(day)* datum *c* 25, 151; *(appointment)* afspraak *c* 95; *(fruit)* dadel *c* 52
daughter dochter *c* 93
day dag *c* 20, 24, 32, 80, 151, 152
daylight daglicht *nt* 124
day off vrije dag *c* 151
decaffeinated cafeïnevrij 38, 59
December december *(c)* 150
decision beslissing *c* 25, 102
deck *(ship)* dek *nt* 74
deck chair ligstoel *c* 106
declare, to *(customs)* aangeven 17
deep diep 142
deep fried gefrituurd 45
delicatessen delicatessenzaak *c* 98
delicious heerlijk 61
deliver, to bezorgen 102
delivery bezorging *c* 102
dentist tandarts *c* 98, 145
denture gebit *nt* 145
department afdeling *c* 83, 100
department store warenhuis *nt* 98
departure vertrek *nt* 65
deposit *(down payment)* waarborgsom *c* 20
deposit, to *(in bank)* storten 130
depressed gedeprimeerd 140
depression neerslachtigheid *c* 143
dessert dessert *nt* 37; nagerecht *nt* 53

detour *(traffic)* omleiding *c* 79
diabetic diabeticus *c* 37;
suikerpatiënt(e) *c* 141
dialling code netnummer *nt* 134
diamond diamant *c* 121, 127
diaper luier *c* 110
diarrhoea diarree *c* 140
dictionary woordenboek *nt* 104
diesel diesel *c* 75
diet dieet *nt* 37
difficult moeilijk 14
difficulty moeilijkheid *c* 28, 102;
probleem *c* 141
dining car restauratiewagen *c* 68,
71
dining room eetzaal *c* 27
dinner diner *nt* 27, 34, 94
direct rechtstreeks 65
direct, to de weg wijzen 13
direction richting *c* 76
directory *(phone)* telefoonboek *nt*
134
disabled invaliden *pl* 82
disc disc *c* 124, 128
discotheque discotheek *c* 88, 96
discount korting *c* 131
disease ziekte *c* 142
dish schotel *c* 39, 40; *(food)*
gerecht *nt* 36, 37
dish detergent afwasmiddel *nt*
120
dish of the day dagschotel *c* 39,
40
disinfectant ontsmettingsmiddel
nt 108
dislocated ontwricht 140
display case vitrine *c* 100
dissatisfied niet tevreden 103
district *(of town)* wijk *c* 81
diversion *(traffic)* omleiding *c* 79
dizzy duizelig 140
do, to doen 162
doctor dokter *c* 79, 98, 137, 144,
145, 156; arts *c* 137
doctor's office praktijk *c* 137
dog hond *c* 155
doll pop *c* 127, 128
dollar dollar *c* 18, 102, 130
door deur *c* 8
double dubbel 58
double bed tweepersoonsbed *nt*
23
double room tweepersoons-
kamer *c* 19, 23
down neer 15

downstairs beneden 15
downtown stadscentrum *nt* 81
dozen dozijn *nt* 149
draught beer bier van het vat *nt*
56
drawing paper tekenpapier *nt*
104
drawing pin punaise *c* 104
dress jurk *c* 115
dressing gown kamerjas *c* 115
drink drankje *nt* 56, 58, 59, 60;
glaasje *nt* 95
drink, to drinken 35, 36, 37, 59
drinking water drinkwater *nt* 32
drip, to druppelen 28
drive, to rijden 21, 76
driving licence rijbewijs *nt* 20, 79
drop *(liquid)* druppel *c* 108
drugstore apotheek *c* 98, 107
dry droog 30, 57, 110
dry cleaner's stomerij *c* 29, 98
dry shampoo droogshampoo *c*
110
duck eend *c* 48
dummy *(baby's)* fopspeen *c* 110
dune duin *c* 76
during tijdens 15; gedurende 150
Dutch Nederlands 11, 12, 95
duty *(customs)* invoerrecht *nt* 17
duty-free shop duty-free winkel *c*
19
dye, to verven 30
dyke dijk *c* 76

E
each elk 125, 149, 161
ear oor *nt* 138
earache oorpijn *c* 141
ear drops oordruppels *c/pl* 108
early vroeg 14, 31
earring oorbel *c* 121
earthernware aardewerk *nt* 127
east oost 77
Easter Pasen *c* 152
easy gemakkelijk 14
eat, to eten 36, 37, 144
eel paling *c* 43, 44, 45
egg ei *nt* 38, 42, 64
eight acht 147
eighteen achttien 147
eighty tachtig 148
elastic elastisch 108
Elastoplast pleisters *c/pl* 108
electric(al) elektrisch 118

electrical appliance elektrisch apparaat *nt* 118
electrical goods shop elektriciteitszaak *c* 98
electricity elektriciteit *c* 32
electronic elektronisch 128
elevator lift *c* 27, 100, 155
eleven elf 147
embankment kade *c* 81
embassy ambassade *c* 156
emergency noodgeval *nt* 156
emergency exit nooduitgang *c* 27, 99, 155
emery board kartonnen nagelvijl *c* 109
empty leeg 14
end eind *nt* 150
engaged *(phone)* bezet 136
engagement ring verlovingsring *c* 121
engine *(car)* motor *c* 78
England Engeland 146
English Engels 12, 82, 84, 104
English Engels(e) *c* 93
enjoyable prettig 31
enjoy, to genieten 61, 96
enlarge, to vergroten 125
enough genoeg 15
enquiry inlichting *c* 68
entrance ingang *c* 67, 99; *(admission)* toegang *c* 155
entrance fee toegangsprijs *c* 82
envelope enveloppe *c* 27, 104
equipment uitrusting *c* 91, 106
eraser gummetje *nt* 104
escalator roltrap *c* 100
estimate *(cost)* opgave *c* 131
Europe Europa 146
evening avond *c* 87, 95, 96, 151
evening dress avondkleding *c* 88; *(woman's)* avondjurk *c* 115
event gebeurtenis *c* 89
everything alles 61
examine, to onderzoeken 137
exchange, to ruilen 103
exchange rate wisselkoers *c* 130
excursion excursie *c* 80
excuse, to kwalijk nemen 11
exercise book schrift *nt* 104
exhaust pipe uitlaatpijp *c* 78
exhibition tentoonstelling *c* 81
exit uitgang *c* 67, 99, 155; *(cars)* uitrit *c* 79
expect, to verwachten 130
expenses uitgaven *c/pl* 131

expensive duur 14, 19, 24, 101
exposure *(photography)* opname *c* 124
exposure counter opnameteller *c* 125
express per expresse 133
expression uitdrukking *c* 10, 100
expressway autosnelweg *c* 76
extension *(phone)* toestel *nt* 135
extension cord/lead verleng-snoer *nt* 118
extra extra 20, 27
eye oog *nt* 138, 139
eyebrow pencil wenkbrauw-potlood *nt* 109
eye drops oogdruppels *c/pl* 108
eye shadow oogschaduw *c* 109
eyesight gezichtsscherpte *c* 123
eye specialist oogarts *c* 137

F
fabric *(cloth)* stof *c* 112, 113
face gezicht *nt* 138
face pack gezichtsmasker *nt* 30
face powder poeder *c* 109
factory fabriek *c* 81
fair jaarmarkt *c* 81
fall *(autumn)* herfst *c* 149
fall, to vallen 139
family familie *c* 144; gezin *nt* 93
fantastic fantastisch 84
far ver 11, 14, 100
fare tarief *nt* 69; *(ticket)* kaartje *nt* 68, 73
farm boerderij *c* 76
fast snel 124
fat *(meat)* vet *nt* 37
father vader *c* 93
faucet kraan *c* 28
fax fax *c* 133
February februari *(c)* 150
fee *(doctor's)* honorarium *nt* 144
feeding bottle zuigfles *c* 110
feel, to *(physical state)* voelen 140, 142
felt-tip pen viltstift *c* 105
ferry veerboot *c* 74
fever koorts *c* 140
few weinig 14; *(a few)* enkele 14; een paar 16; 24
field veld *nt* 76, 85
fifteen vijftien 147
fifty vijftig 147
file *(tool)* vijl *c* 109
fill in, to invullen 26, 144

filling *(tooth)* vulling *c* 145
filling station benzinestation *nt* 75
film film *c* 86, 124, 125
filter filter *c* 125
filter-tipped met filter 126
fine arts beeldende kunst *c* 83
find, to vinden 10, 12, 100
fine *(OK)* uitstekend 10; prima 25
finger vinger *c* 138
finish, to eindigen 86
fire brand *c* 156
fire lighter aansteekblokjes *nt/pl* 106
first eerste 68, 69, 149
first-aid kit verbandtrommel *c* 108
first class eerste klas *c* 69
first name voornaam *c* 25
fish vis *c* 44, 45
fish, to vissen 90
fishing tackle visgerei *nt* 106
fishmonger's vishandel *c* 98
fit, to passen 114, 115
five vijf 147
fix, to repareren 75
fizzy *(mineral water)* met koolzuur 59
flash *(photography)* flits *c* 125
flashlight zaklantaarn *c* 106
flat plat 117
flat *(apartment)* appartement *nt* 22
flat tyre lekke band *c* 75, 78
flatware bestek *nt* 120
flea market vlooienmarkt *c* 81
Flemish Vlaams 55
flight vlucht *c* 65
floor verdieping *c* 23
florist's bloemist *c* 98
flour meel *nt* 37
flower bloem *c* 85
flower market bloemenmarkt *c* 81
flower, to bloeien 85
flu griep *c* 142
fluid vloeistof *c* 75, 123
foam rubber schuimrubber *nt* 106
fog mist *c* 94
folding chair klapstoel *c* 106
folding table vouwtafel *c* 106
folk music folkloristische muziek *c* 128
follow, to volgen 77

food eten *nt* 60; voeding *c* 110;
(dish) gerecht *nt* 37
food poisoning voedsel-
vergiftiging *c* 142
foot voet *c* 138
football voetbal *c* 89
foot cream voetcrème *c* 109
for voor 15
forbidden verboden 155
foreign buitenlands 12
foreigner buitenlander (-dse) *c* 12
forget, to vergeten 60
fork vork *c* 36, 60, 120
form *(document)* formulier *nt* 25, 26, 133, 144
fortnight twee weken *c/pl* 151
forty veertig 147
forwarding address volgende adres *nt* 31
foundation cream basiscrème *c* 109
fountain fontein *c* 81
fountain pen vulpen *c* 105
four vier 147
fourteen veertien 147
frame *(for glasses)* montuur *nt* 123
franc frank *c* 18
France Frankrijk 146
free vrij 14, 70, 96, 155
French bean sperzieboon *c* 49
French fries patates frites *c/pl* 50
fresh vers 52, 53, 60
Friday vrijdag *c* 151
fried gebakken 45, 47
fried egg spiegelei *nt* 38
friend vriend(in) *c* 95
from van 15
frost vorst *c* 94
fruit fruit *nt* 52, 53; vrucht *c* 52
fruit juice vruchtesap *nt* 37, 38
fruit salad vruchtensalade *c* 52
frying pan koekepan *c* 120
full vol 14
full board vol pension *nt* 24
full insurance all risk verzekering *c* 20
fur coat bontjas *c* 115
furniture meubels *nt/pl* 83
furrier's bontzaak *c* 98

G
gallery galerij *c* 98
game spel *nt* 128; *(food)* wild *nt* 48
garage garage *c* 26, 78

garden(s) tuin(en) *c* 76, 81, 85
garlic knoflook *c* 51
gas gas *nt* 126, 156
gasoline benzine *c* 75
gauze verbandgaas *nt* 108
gem edelsteen *c* 121
general algemeen 27, 100
general delivery poste restante 133
general practitioner (huis)arts *c* 137
genitals geslachtsorganen *nt/pl* 138
gentleman heer *c* 155
genuine *(real)* echt 118, 121
Germany Duitsland 146
get, to *(obtain)* krijgen 11, 32, 89, 107; *(find)* vinden 19; *(order)* bestellen 21, 31; *(phone)* verbinden 28; roepen 137
get back, to *(return)* terugkomen 80; terug zijn 21
get off, to uitstappen 73
get past, to passeren 70
get to, to komen naar 19, 70, 76
get up, to opstaan 144
gherkin augurk *c* 64
gift cadeau *nt* 17
gin and tonic gin tonic *c* 58
girdle step-in *c* 115
girl meisje *nt* 111, 128
girlfriend vriendin *c* 93
give, to geven 13, 131, 135
gland klier *c* 138
glass glas *nt* 36, 57, 58, 59, 60
glasses bril *c* 123
glasses case brillekoker *c* 123
gloomy somber 84
glove handschoen *c* 115
glue lijm *c* 105
go away! ga weg! 156
go, to gaan 96, 162
go back, to teruggaan 77
go out, to uitgaan 96
gold goud *nt* 121, 122
golden gouden 112
gold plated verguld 122
golf course golfterrein *nt* 90
good goed 10, 14, 101
good afternoon goedemiddag 10
goodbye tot ziens 10
good evening goedenavond 10
Good Friday Goede Vrijdag *c* 152
good morning goedemorgen 10
good night goedenacht 10

goods goederen *nt/pl* 16
goose gans *c* 48
gram gram *nt* 119
grammar book grammatica *c* 105
grape druif *c* 52, 59
grapefruit grapefuit *c* 52, 64
gravy saus *c* 50
gray grijs 112
graze schaafwond *c* 139
greasy vet 30, 110
Great Britain Groot-Brittannië 146
green groen 112
green bean sperzieboon *c* 49
greengrocer's groenteman *c* 98
greeting groeten *c/pl* 152
grey grijs 112
grilled gegrild 45; geroosterd 45
grocer's kruidenier *c* 98, 119
groundsheet grondzeil *nt* 106
group groep *c* 82
grow, to kweken 85
guesthouse pension *nt* 19, 22
guide gids *c* 80
guidebook reisgids *c* 82, 104, 105
guilder gulden *c* 101, 103
gum *(teeth)* tandvlees *nt* 145
gynaecologist gynaecoloog *c* 137

H
hair haar *nt* 30, 110
haircut knippen *nt* 30
hairdresser kapper *c* 27, 30, 98
hair dryer haardroger *c* 118
hair dye haarverf *c* 110
hairgrip schuifspeldje *nt* 110
hair lotion haarwater *nt* 110
hairpin haarspeld *c* 110
hair slide haarspeld *c* 110
hair spray haarlak *c* 30
half half 149
half helft *c* 149
half an hour een half uur *nt* 153
half board half pension *nt* 24
half price halve prijs *c* 69
hall porter portier *c* 26
ham ham *c* 38, 62, 64, 119
hammer hamer *c* 120
hand hand *c* 138
handbag handtas *c* 115, 156
hand cream handcrème *c* 109
handicrafts kunstnijverheid *c* 83
handkerchief zakdoek *c* 115
hanger kleerhanger *c* 27

happy gelukkig 152
harbour haven *c* 74, 81
hard hard 123
hard-boiled *(egg)* hardgekookt 38
hardware store ijzerhandel *c* 98
hare haas *c* 48
hat hoed *c* 115
have, to hebben 141, 162
hay fever hooikoorts *c* 107, 141
hazelnut hazelnoot *c* 52
he hij 161
head hoofd *nt* 138, 139
headache hoofdpijn *c* 107, 141
headphones koptelefoon *c* 118
head waiter gerant *c* 60
health food shop reformwinkel *c* 98
health insurance ziekte-verzekering *c* 144
heart hart *nt* 138
heart attack hartaanval *c* 141
heated verwarmd 90
heating verwarming *c* 23, 28
heavy zwaar 14, 101
heel hiel *c* 117
hello hallo 10, 135
help hulp *c* 156
help, to helpen 13, 71, 100, 134; *(oneself)* zichzelf bedienen 119
her haar 162
herbs kruiden *nt/pl* 51
herb tea kruidenthee *c* 59
here hier 14
herring haring *c* 41, 44
hi hallo 10
high hoog 141
high tide vloed *c* 91
high season hoogseizoen *nt* 150
hike, to trekken 74
hill heuvel *c* 76
hire verhuur *c* 20
hire, to huren 19, 20, 74, 90, 91
his zijn 162
history geschiedenis *c* 83
hitchhike, to liften 74
hold on! *(phone)* blijft u aan de lijn! 136
hole gat *nt* 29
holiday feestdag *c* 151, 152
holiday cottage vakantiehuisje *nt* 22
holidays vakantie *c* 16, 151
Holland Holland 112, 146
home address huisadres *nt* 31
home-made eigengemaakt 40

home town woonplaats *c* 25
honey honing *c* 38
hope, to hopen 96
horseback riding paardrijden *nt* 89
horse racing paardenrennen *nt* 89
horticulture tuinbouw *c* 83
hospital ziekenhuis *nt* 99, 144
hot warm 14, 25, 38, 59, 94, 155
hotel hotel *nt* 19, 21, 22, 26
hotel directory/guide hotelgids *c* 19
hotel reservation hotel-reservering *c* 19; *(booking office)* hotelbemiddeling *c* 67
hot-water bottle kruik *c* 27
hour uur *nt* 80, 90, 143, 153
house huis *nt* 83
household article huishoudelijk artikel *nt* 120
how hoe 11
how far hoever 11, 76
how long hoelang 11, 24, 76
how many hoeveel 11
how much hoeveel 11, 24, 102
hundred honderd 148
hungry honger 13, 35
hunting jagen *nt* 90
hurry, to be in a haast hebben 21
hurt, to pijn doen 139, 140, 145; *(to be)* gewond zijn 139
husband man *c* 93
hydrofoil draagvleugelboot *c* 74

I
I ik 161
ice ijs *nt* 94
ice cream ijs *nt* 53, 64
ice cube ijsblokje *nt* 27
iced tea ijsthee *c* 59
ice hockey ijshockey *c* 89
ice pack koelelement *nt* 106
ill ziek 140, 156
illness ziekte *c* 140
important belangrijk 13
imported geïmporteerd 112
impressive indrukwekkend 84
in in 15
included inbegrepen 20, 31, 40, 61, 80; inclusief 24
India India 146
indigestion indigestie *c* 141
indoor binnen- 90
inexpensive goedkoop 124

infected ontstoken 140
infection infectie c 141
inflammation ontsteking c 142
inflation inflatie c 131
influenza griep c 142
information informatie c 67
information desk informatiebalie c 19
information office inlichtingen-bureau nt 69, 154
injection injectie c 142, 144
injure, to verwonden 139
injured gewond 79, 139
injury verwonding c 139
ink inkt c 105
inquiry inlichting c 68
insect bite insektenbeet c 107
insect repellent insektenwerend middel nt 108
insect spray insektenspray c 106
inside binnen 15
instant coffee instant koffie c 64
instead of in plaats van 37
insurance verzekering c 20, 71, 144
insurance company verzekerings-maatschappij c 79
interest (finance) rente c 131
interested, to be belangstelling hebben 83
interesting interessant 84
international internationaal 134
interpreter tolk c 131
intersection kruispunt nt 77
introduce, to voorstellen 92
introduction (social) kennis-making c 92
investment investering c 131
invitation uitnodiging c 94
invite, to uitnodigen 94
invoice rekening c 131
iodine jodium c 108
Ireland Ierland 146
Irish Ier(se) c 93
iron (for laundry) strijkijzer nt 118
iron, to strijken 29
ironmonger's ijzerhandel c 99
Israel Israël 146
it het 161
its zijn 162; haar 162

J
jacket jasje nt 115
jam (preserves) jam c 38, 119
jam, to klemmen 28, 125

January januari (c) 150
Japan Japan 146
jar (container) pot c 119
jaundice geelzucht c 142
jaw kaak c 138
jeans spijkerbroek c 115
jewel box bijouteriekistje nt 121
jeweller's juwelier c 99, 121
joint gewricht nt 138
journey rit c 72
juice sap nt 37, 38, 59
July juli (c) 150
June juni (c) 150
just (only) slechts 37; alleen 100

K
keep, to behouden 61
kerosene petroleum c 106
key sleutel c 27
kidney nier c 46, 138
kidney stones nierstenen c/pl 142
kilo(gram) kilo(gram) c 119
kilometre kilometer c 20, 78
kind vriendelijk 95
kind (type) soort nt 140
knee knie c 138
knife mes nt 36, 60, 120
know, to kennen 113; weten 16, 24, 96, 162

L
label etiket nt 105
lace kant c 113, 127
lady dame c 155
lake meer nt 90
lamb (meat) lamsvlees nt 46; lams- 46
lamp lamp c 29, 106, 118
landmark oriënteringspunt nt 76
language taal c 12, 159
lantern lantaarn c 106
large groot 20, 101, 117, 130
last laatste 14, 68; vorige 151
late laat 14, 70
laugh, to lachen 95
launderette wasserette c 99
laundry (place) wasserij c 29, 99; (clothes) was c 29
laxative laxeermiddel nt 108
lead (metal) lood nt 75
leather leer nt 117
leave, to vertrekken 31, 68, 69, 73, 80; weggaan 95; (leave behind) achterlaten 20, 71; (deposit) deponeren 26

leave alone, to met rust laten 96, 156
left links 21, 62, 69, 77
left-luggage office bagagedepot nt 67, 71
leg been nt 138
lemon citroen c 38, 52, 59, 64
lemonade limonade c 59
lens lens c 123, 125; *(spectacle)* (brille)glas nt 123
lentil linze c 49
less minder 14
lesson les c 90
let, to *(hire out)* te huur 155
letter brief c 132
letter box brievenbus c 132
letter of credit kredietbrief c 130
library bibliotheek c 81, 99
licence *(driving)* rijbewijs nt 20
lie down, to gaan liggen 142
life belt reddingsboei c 74
life boat reddingsboot c 74
life guard *(beach)* reddings-brigade c 91
life jacket reddingsvest nt 74
lift *(elevator)* lift c 27, 100, 155
light licht 14, 53, 56, 101, 111, 112
light licht nt 28, 124; *(for cigarette)* vuurtje nt 95
light bulb (gloei)lamp c 28, 75
lighter aansteker c 126
lighter fluid/gas benzine voor aansteker c 126
light meter belichtingsmeter c 125
like, to houden van 61; *(please)* bevallen 25, 92, 102; *(want)* willen 13, 20, 23, 95, 111; *(fancy)* zin hebben 96
line lijn c 73
linen *(cloth)* linnen nt 113
lip lip c 138
lipsalve lippenpommade c 109
lipstick lippenstift c 109
liqueur likeur c 58
liquid *(fluid)* vloeistof c 123
liquor store slijterij c 99
listen, to horen 128
litre liter c 75, 119
little *(a little)* een beetje 14
live, to leven 83; *(reside)* wonen 83
liver lever c 48, 138
lobster kreeft c 41, 43, 44
local van de streek 36

local train stoptrein c 66, 69
long lang 60, 114
long-sighted verziend 123
look, to kijken 100, 123, 139
look for, to zoeken 13
look out! pas op! 156
loose *(clothes)* wijd 114
lose, to verliezen 123, 145, 156
loss verlies nt 131
lost, to be verdwaald zijn 13, 156
lost and found office/lost property office bureau voor gevonden voorwerpen nt 67, 99, 156
lot *(a lot)* veel 14
loud *(voice)* hard 135
lovely prachtig 94
low laag 141
lower onder 69
low tide eb c 91
low season *(early)* voorseizoen nt 150; *(late)* naseizoen nt 150
luck geluk nt 152
luggage bagage c 18, 26, 31, 71
luggage insurance bagage-verzekering c 71
luggage locker bagagekluis c 18, 67, 71
luggage trolley bagagewagentje nt 18, 71
lunch lunch c 27, 34, 80, 94
lung long c 138

M
machine machine c 113
magazine tijdschrift nt 105
magnificent prachtig 84
magnifying glass vergrootglas nt 123
maid kamermeisje nt 26
mail post c 28, 133
mail, to posten 28
mailbox brievenbus c 132
main hoofd- 40; belangrijkste 80
main course hoofdgerecht nt 40
make, to maken 112, 122
make up, to *(prepare)* klaar-maken 71, 107; opmaken 28
man man c 155, 156; heer c 114
manager directeur c 26
man's ... heren- 115
many veel 11, 14
map (land)kaart c 76, 105
March maart (c) 150
market markt c 81, 99

marmalade marmelade *c* 38
married getrouwd 93
mashed potatoes aardappel-
purée *c* 50
mass *(church)* mis *c* 84
match *(matchstick)* lucifer *c* 106,
126; *(sport)* wedstrijd *c* 89
matinée matinee *c* 87
mattress matras *c* 106
May mei *(c)* 150
may *(can)* mogen 13
meal maaltijd *c* 24, 143
mean, to betekenen 11, 25
means middel *nt* 74
measure, to meten 113
meat vlees *nt* 46, 60
meatball gehaktbal *c* 46
mechanic monteur *c* 78
mechanical pencil vulpotlood *nt*
105
medical certificate medisch
attest *nt* 144
medicine geneeskunde *c* 83;
(drug) geneesmiddel *nt* 143
medium *(meat)* net gaar
gebakken 47
medium-sized middelgroot 20
meet, to kennismaken 92;
ontmoeten 96
mend, to repareren 29, 75
menu menu *nt* 36, 37, 39, 40;
(printed) (spijs)kaart *c* 36, 39;
(menu)kaart *c* 36, 39, 40
message boodschap *c* 28, 136
metre meter *c* 111
mezzanine *(theatre)* balkon *nt* 87
middle midden *nt* 69, 87, 150
midnight twaalf uur 's nachts 153
mild *(light)* licht 126
mileage aantal kilometers *nt* 20
milk melk *c* 38, 59, 64
mill molen *c* 76
milliard miljard *nt* 148
million miljoen *nt* 148
mineral water mineraalwater *nt*
40, 59
minister *(religion)* dominee *c* 84
minute minuut *c* 21, 153
mirror spiegel *c* 114, 123
miscellaneous diversen 127
Miss juffrouw *c* 10, 154
miss, to ontbreken 18, 29, 60
miserable beroerd 140
mistake vergissing *c* 31, 60; fout *c*
102

mixed gemengd 49
modified American plan half
pension *nt* 24
moisturizing cream
vochtinbrengende crème *c* 109
moment ogenblik *nt* 12, 136
monastery klooster *nt* 81
Monday maandag *c* 151
money geld *nt* 18, 129, 130
money order postwissel *c* 133
month maand *c* 16, 150
monument monument *nt* 81
moon maan *c* 94
moped bromfiets *c* 74
more meer 14, 37
morning morgen *c* 31, 151, 153
mosque moskee *c* 84
mother moeder *c* 93
motorbike motorfiets *c* 74
motorboat motorboot *c* 91
motorway autosnelweg *c* 76
moustache snor *c* 31
mouth mond *c* 138
mouthwash mondwater *nt* 108
move, to bewegen 139
movie film *c* 86
movies bioscoop *c* 86, 96
Mr. mijnheer *c* 10, 154
Mrs. mevrouw *c* 10, 154
much veel 11, 14
mug mok *c* 120
muscle spier *c* 138
museum museum *nt* 81
mushroom champignon *c* 49
music muziek *c* 128
musical musical *c* 86
mussel mossel *c* 41, 44
must *(have to)* moeten 23, 31, 95
mustard mosterd *c* 64
my mijn 162

N
nail spijker *c* 120; *(human)* nagel *c*
109
nail brush nagelborstel *c* 109
nail file nagelvijl *c* 109
nail polish nagellak *c* 109
nail polish remover nagellak
remover *c* 109
nail scissors nagelschaartje *nt*
109
name naam *c* 23, 25, 79, 92, 133
napkin servet *c* 36, 105
nappy luier *c* 110
narrow nauw 117

DICTIONARY

nationality nationaliteit *c* 25, 93
nauseous misselijk 140
near dichtbij 14, 19
nearby/near here in de buurt 32, 77, 84
nearest dichtstbijzijnde 75, 132
neat *(drink)* puur 58
neck nek *c* 30, 138
necklace halsketting *c* 121
need, to nodig hebben 29, 90, 117, 137
needle naald *c* 27
negative negatief *nt* 124, 125
nephew neef *c* 93
nerve zenuw *c* 138
nervous system zenuwstelsel *nt* 138
Netherlands Nederland 146
never nooit 15
new nieuw 14, 117
newspaper krant *c* 104, 105
newsstand kiosk *c* 19, 67, 104
New Year Nieuwjaar *nt* 152
New Zealand Nieuw-Zeeland 146
next volgende 14, 65, 68, 77, 151
next time volgende keer 95
next to naast 15, 77
nice aardig 160, mooi 94
niece nicht *c* 93
night nacht *c* 10, 24, 151
nightclub nachtclub *c* 88
night cream nachtcrème *c* 109
nightdress/-gown nachtjapon *c* 115
nine negen 147
nineteen negentien 147
ninety negentig 148
no nee 10
noisy lawaaierig 25
nonalcoholic alcoholvrij 39, 59
none geen 15
nonsmoking niet-roken 70, 155
non-smoking area niet-roken gedeelte *nt* 36
noon twaalf uur 's middags 153
north noord 77
North America Noord-Amerika 146
nose neus *c* 138
nosebleed neusbloeding *c* 141
nose drops neusdruppels *c/pl* 108
not niet 15, 164
note *(banknote)* biljet *nt* 130
notebook notitieboekje *nt* 105
note paper briefpapier *nt* 105

nothing niets 15, 16, 17
notice *(sign)* opschrift *nt* 155
notify, to waarschuwen 144
November november *(c)* 150
now nu 15
number nummer *nt* 25, 134, 135; getal *nt* 147
nurse verpleegster *c* 144, *(male)* verpleegkundige *c* 144
nursery *(plants)* kwekerij *c* 85
nut *(fruit)* noot *c* 52

O

occupation *(profession)* beroep *nt* 25
occupied bezet 14, 155
o'clock uur *nt* 153
October october *(c)* 150
office bureau *nt* 67, 99; kantoor *nt* 98, 132
often dikwijls 85
oil olie *c* 37, 75, 110
oily *(greasy)* vet 30, 110
ointment zalf *c* 108
old oud 14, 150
old town oude stad *c* 81
on op 15
once eenmaal 149
one een 147
one-way ticket enkele reis *c* 65, 69
one-way traffic eenrichtings-verkeer *nt* 79
on foot te voet 76
onion ui *c* 49
only slechts 15; alleen 24
on time op tijd 68, 153
open open 11, 14, 82, 107, 129
open, to openen 17, 130
open-air museum openlucht museum *nt* 81
open-air pool buitenbad *nt* 90
opening hours openingstijden *c/pl* 82
opera opera *c* 88
opera house opera *c* 81, 88
operation operatie *c* 144
operator telefoniste *c* 134
operetta operette *c* 88
opposite tegenover 77
optician opticiën *c* 99, 123
or of 15
orange sinaasappel *c* 52, 64
orange juice sinaasappelsap *nt* 59

Woordenboekje

orchestra orkest nt 88; *(seats)* zaal c 87
order, to *(goods, meal)* bestellen 36, 60, 102, 103
other andere 58, 74
our onze 161
out of order defect 136
out of stock niet in voorraad 103
outlet *(electric)* stopcontact nt 27
outside buiten 15, 36
oval ovaal 101
overdone *(meat)* te gaar 60
overheat, to *(engine)* koken 78
overnight *(stay)* vannacht 24
overtake, to inhalen 79
owe, to schuldig zijn 144
oyster oester c 41, 44

P

pacifier *(baby's)* fopspeen c 110
packet pakje nt 119, 126
pail emmer c 128
pain pijn c 140, 141, 143, 144
painkiller pijnstiller c 140
paint, to schilderen 83
paintbox verfdoos c 105
painter schilder c 83
pair paar nt 115, 117, 149
pajamas pyjama c 116
palace paleis nt 81
palpitation hartklopping c 141
pancake pannekoek c 33, 53
panties slipje nt 115
pants *(trousers)* lange broek c 115
panty hose panty c 116
paper papier nt 105
paperback pocketboek nt 105
paper napkin papieren servet nt 105
paper towel huishoudrol c 120
paraffin *(fuel)* petroleum c 106
parcel pakje nt 132, 133
parents ouders c/pl 93
park park nt 81
park, to parkeren 26, 77
parking parking c 77, 79
parking lot parkeerplaats c 77
parking meter parkeermeter c 77
parliament building parlements-gebouw nt 81
parsley peterselie c 51
part deel nt 138
party *(social gathering)* feestje nt 95

pass, to *(driving)* inhalen 79
passport paspoort nt 16, 17, 25, 26, 156
passport photo pasfoto c 124
pass through, to doorreizen 16
pasta meelspijzen c/pl 50
pastry gebak nt 63
pastry shop banketbakkerij c 99
patch, to verstellen 29
path pad nt 76
patient patiënt(e) c 144
pattern patroon nt 111
pay, to betalen 31, 61, 100, 102
payment betaling c 131
pea doperwt c 49
peach perzik c 52
pear peer c 52
pearl parel c 122
pedestrian voetganger c 79
peg *(tent)* haring c 106
pen pen c 105
pencil potlood nt 105
pendant hanger c 121
penknife zakmes nt 120
pensioner gepensioneerde c 82
people mensen c/pl 92
pepper peper c 37, 38, 64
per cent procent c 149
percentage percentage nt 131
per day per dag 20, 32, 90
perfume parfum nt 109
perhaps misschien 15
per hour per uur 77, 90
period *(monthly)* menstruatie c 141
permanent wave permanent c 30
permit vergunning c 90
person persoon c 32
personal persoonlijk 17
personal call/person-to-person call gesprek met voorbericht nt 134
petrol benzine c 75, 78
pewter tin nt 127
pharmacy apotheek c 99, 107
photo foto c 124, 125, 160
photocopy fotokopie c 131
photograph, to fotograferen 82
photographer fotograaf c 99
photography fotografie c 124
phrase uitdrukking c 12
phrase book taalgids c 105
pick, to plukken 85
pick up, to *(person)* afhalen 80, 96

pickles augurken *c/pl* 64
picnic picknick *c* 64
picture *(painting)* schilderij *nt* 83; *(photo)* foto *c* 84
picture-book prentenboek *nt* 105
piece stuk *nt* 17, 63, 119
pier pier *c* 74
pill pil *c* 108, 141, 143
pillow kussen *nt* 27
pin speld *c* 109, 110, 121
pineapple ananas *c* 52
pink rose 112
pipe pijp *c* 126
pipe cleaner pijpestoker *c* 126
place plaats *c* 25, 76
place of birth geboorteplaats *c* 25
plane vliegtuig *nt* 65
plant plant *c* 85
plaster gipsverband *nt* 140; *(sticky)* pleister *c* 108
plastic bag plastic zak *c* 120
plate bord *nt* 36, 60, 120
platform *(station)* perron *nt* 67, 68, 69, 70
play *(theatre)* stuk *nt* 86
play, to spelen 86, 88, 89, 93
playground speelplaats *c* 32
playing card speelkaart *c* 105
please alstublieft 10, 154
pliers nijptang *c* 120
plimsoll gymnastiekschoen *c* 117
plug *(electric)* stekker *c* 29, 118
plum pruim *c* 52
pneumonia longontsteking *c* 142
pocket zak *c* 116
pocket calculator zakrekenmachientje *nt* 105
pocketknife zakmes *nt* 120
pocket watch zakhorloge *nt* 121
point, to aanwijzen 12
poison vergif *nt* 108, 156
poisoning vergiftiging *c* 142
pole *(tent)* stok *c* 106
police politie *c* 78, 79, 156
police station politiebureau *nt* 99, 156
pond vijver *c* 76
pork varkens(vlees) *nt* 46
port haven *c* 74; *(wine)* port *c* 56
portable draagbaar 118
porter kruier *c* 18, 26, 71
portion portie *c* 37, 60
possible mogelijk 137
post *(mail)* post *c* 28, 133

post, to posten 28
postage port *c* 132
postage stamp postzegel *c* 28, 126, 132, 133
postcard briefkaart *c* 105, 132
poste restante poste restante 133
post office postkantoor *nt* 132
pot potje *nt* 59
potato aardappel *c* 50
pottery aardewerk *nt* 127; *(craft)* pottenbakken *nt* 83
poultry gevogelte *nt* 48
pound pond *nt* 18, 102, 119, 130
powder poeder *c* 109
powder compact poederdoos *c* 121

prawn garnaal *c* 41, 44
prefer, to liever hebben 49, 101
pregnant zwanger 141
premium *(gasoline)* super 75
prepare, to klaarmaken 107
prescribe, to voorschrijven 143
prescription recept *nt* 108, 143
press, to *(iron)* persen 29
press stud drukknoop *c* 116
pressure druk *c* 141; spanning *c* 75

pretty aardig 84
price prijs *c* 40, 69, 124
priest priester *c* 84
print *(photo)* afdruk *c* 125
private privé 80, 155
processing *(photo)* ontwikkelen *nt* 125
profit winst *c* 131
programme programma *nt* 87
pronounce, to uitspreken 12
pronunciation uitspraak *c* 6
propelling pencil vulpotlood *nt* 105
Protestant protestant 84
provide, to zorgen voor 131
prune pruimedant *c* 52
public holiday openbare feestdag *c* 152
pull, to trekken 145, 155
pullover pullover *c* 116
pump pomp *c* 106
puncture lekke band *c* 75
purchase koop *c* 131
pure zuiver 113
push, to duwen 155
put, to zetten 24
pyjamas pyjama *c* 116

Q
quail kwartel *c* 48
quality kwaliteit *c* 112
quantity hoeveelheid *c* 14
quarter kwart *nt* 149
quarter of an hour kwartier *nt*
153
question vraag *c* 11
quick(ly) snel 14, 36, 137, 156
quiet rustig 23, 25

R
rabbi rabbi *c* 84
rabbit konijn *nt* 48
race wedstrijd *c* 89
race course/track renbaan *c* 89
racket *(sport)* racket *nt* 90
radio radio *c* 23, 28, 118
railway spoorwegen *c/pl* 154
railway station station *nt* 21, 67
rain regen *c* 94
rain, to regenen 94
raincoat regenjas *c* 116
raisin rozijn *c* 52
rangefinder afstandsmeter *c* 125
rare *(meat)* niet gaar 47; rood 60
rash uitslag *c* 139
raspberry framboos *c* 52
rate tarief *nt* 20; *(of exchange)*
koers *c* 18, 130
razor scheermes *nt* 109
razor blade scheermesje *nt* 109
reading lamp leeslamp *c* 27
ready klaar 29, 31, 117, 123, 125
real *(genuine)* echt 118, 121
rear achter 69, 75
receipt kwitantie *c* 102, 103, 144
reception receptie *c* 23
receptionist receptionist *c* 26
recommend, to aanbevelen 35,
36, 80, 145
record *(disc)* grammofoonplaat *c*
128
record player platenspeler *c* 118
rectangular rechthoekig 101
red rood 112
reduction reductie *c* 24, 82
refill *(pen)* vulling *c* 105
refund *(to get a)* geld
terug(krijgen) 103
regards groeten *c/pl* 152
register, to *(luggage)* inschrijven
71; *(mail)* aantekenen 133
registered mail aangetekend 133

registration inschrijven *nt* 25
registration form aanmeldingsformulier *nt* 25
regular *(petrol)* normaal 75
religion godsdienst *c* 83
religious service kerkdienst *c* 84
rent, to huren 19, 20, 74, 90, 91
rental verhuur *c* 20
repair reparatie *c* 125
repair, to repareren 29, 117, 118
repeat herhalen 12
report, to *(a theft)* aangeven 156
reservation reservering *c* 19, 65,
69
reserve, to reserveren 19, 23, 36,
69, 87, 155
restaurant restaurant *nt* 32, 34,
35, 67
return ticket retour *nt* 65, 69
return, to *(come back)*
terugkomen 80; terug zijn 21;
(give back) teruggeven 103
reverse-charge call collect
bellen *nt* 135
rheumatism reumatiek *c* 141
rib rib *c* 138
ribbon lint *nt* 105
rice rijst *c* 50
right *(correct)* juist 14; goed 76;
(direction) rechts 21, 62, 69, 77
ring *(jewellery)* ring *c* 121
river rivier *c* 76
road weg *c* 76, 77
road assistance wegenwacht *c*
78
road map wegenkaart *c* 105
road sign verkeersbord *nt* 79
roasted gebraden 47
roast beef rosbief *c* 46
roll broodje *nt* 38, 64
roller skates rolschaatsen *c/pl*
128
roll film rolfilm *c* 124
room kamer *c* 19, 23, 24, 25;
(space) plaats *c* 32
room number kamernummer *nt*
26
rope touw *nt* 106
rosé rosé *c* 57
round rond 101
round *(golf)* ronde *c* 90
round-trip ticket retour *nt* 65, 69
route weg *c* 85
rowing boat roeiboot *c* 91
royal koninklijk 73

rubber (eraser) gummetje nt 105; (material) rubber nt 117
rubber band elastiekje nt 105
rucksack rugzak c 106
ruin ruïne c 82
ruler (for measuring) lineaal c 105

S

safe (free from danger) veilig 91
safe kluis c 26
safety pin veiligheidsspeld c 109
sailing zeilen nt 89
sailing boat zeilboot c 91
salad salade c 42; sla c 49
sale verkoop c 131; (bargains) uitverkoop c 100, 155
sales tax B.T.W. c 24, 61, 102, 154
salmon zalm c 44
salt zout nt 37, 38, 64
salty zout 60
same dezelfde 117
sand zand nt 91
sandal sandaal c 117
sandwich sandwich c 64
sandwich shop broodjeswinkel c 33, 62
sanitary napkin/towel maandverband nt 108
Saturday zaterdag c 151
sauce saus c 50
saucepan pan c 120
saucer schoteltje nt 120
sausage saucijsje nt 46; worst c 64
scarf sjaal c 16
scenic schilderachtig 85
scissors schaar c 109, 120
Scotland Schotland 146
scrambled egg roerei nt 38
screwdriver schroevedraaier c 120
sculptor beeldhouwer c 83
sculpture beeldhouwkunst c 83
sea zee c 23, 74
seafood schaal- en schelpdieren nt/pl 44
sea level zeespiegel c 85
season jaargetijde nt 150; seizoen nt 150
seat plaats c 69, 70, 87
seat belt veiligheidsgordel c 75
second tweede 149
second seconde c 153
second class tweede klas c 69
second hand secondewijzer c 122

second-hand shop tweedehandswinkel c 99
secretary secretaresse c 27, 131
see, to zien 23, 80, 96
seed zaad nt 85
self-adhesive zelfklevend 105
sell, to verkopen 100
send, to sturen 78, 102; (send off) verzenden/versturen 132, 133
send up, to naar boven laten brengen 26
senior citizen gepensioneerde c 82
sentence zin c 12
separately apart 61
September september (c) 150
serious ernstig 139
service dienst c 98; bediening c 23, 24, 61, 100; (church) (kerk)dienst c 84
serviette servet nt 36
set menu menu van de dag nt 36
setting lotion haarversteviger c 30, 110
seven zeven 147
seventeen zeventien 147
seventy zeventig 148
sew, to naaien 29
shade schaduw c 85; (colour) tint c 111
shampoo shampoo c 30, 110
shape vorm c 103
share (finance) aandeel nt 131
shave, to zich scheren 31
shaver scheerapparaat nt 27, 118
shaving cream scheercrème c 110
she zij 161
sherbet sorbet c 53
ship schip nt 74, 160
shirt overhemd nt 116
shoe schoen c 117
shoelace schoenveter c 117
shoemaker's schoenmaker c 99
shoe polish schoenpoets c 117
shoe shop schoenenwinkel c 99
shop winkel c 98, 99
shopping winkelen nt 97
shopping area winkelwijk c 82; winkelbuurt c 100
shopping centre winkelcentrum nt 99
shop window etalage c 100, 111
short kort 30, 114

DICTIONARY

Woordenboekje

shorts short c 116
short-sighted bijziend 123
shoulder schouder c 138
shovel schepje nt 128
show voorstelling c 87, 88
show, to laten zien 13, 76, 100
shower douche c 23, 32
shower gel doucheschuim nt 110
shrimp garnaal c 44
shrink, to krimpen 113
shrub heester c 85
shut dicht 14
shutter (window) luik nt 29; (camera) sluiter c 125
sick (ill) ziek 140, 156
sickness (illness) ziekte c 140
side zijkant c 30
sideboards/-burns bakkebaard c 31
side dish bijgerecht nt 40
sight bezienswaardigheid c 80
sightseeing sightseeing nt 80
sightseeing tour sightseeing toer c 80
sign (notice) bord nt 77, 79, 155
sign, to (onder)tekenen 26, 131
signature handtekening c 25
signet ring zegelring c 121
silk zijde c 113
silver (colour) zilver 112
silver zilver c 121, 122
silver plated verzilverd 122
silverware zilverwerk nt 121, 127
simple eenvoudig 124
since sedert 15, 150
sing, to zingen 88
single enkel 65, 69; (unmarried) ongetrouwd 93
single cabin eenpersoonscabine c 74
single room eenpersoonskamer c 19, 23
single ticket enkele reis c 65, 69
sister zuster c 93
sit down, to gaan zitten 95
six zes 147
sixteen zestien 147
sixty zestig 147
size formaat nt 124; (clothes) maat c 113, 114, 117
skate schaats c 90
skate, to schaatsen 90
skating schaatsenrijden nt 89
skating rink ijsbaan c 90
skin huid c 138

skirt rok c 116
sky hemel c 94
sleep, to slapen 144
sleeping bag slaapzak c 106
sleeping car slaapwagen c 68, 70
sleeping pill slaappil c 143
sleeve mouw c 115
slice plak c 119; (bread) snede c 38
slide (photo) dia c 124
slide film diafilm c 124
slide projector diaprojector c 125
slip (underwear) onderjurk c 116
slipper pantoffel c 117
slow(ly) langzaam 12, 14, 21, 135
small klein 14, 25, 101, 117, 130
smoke, to roken 70, 95
smoked gerookt 45, 47
smoking roken nt 155
snack snack c 62
snack bar snackbar c 67
snap fastener drukknoop c 116
sneakers gymnastiekschoen c 117
snow sneeuw c 94
snow, to sneeuwen 94
snuff snuiftabak c 126
soap zeep c 27, 110
soccer voetbal c 89
sock sok c 116
socket (electric) stopcontact nt 27
soft zacht 123
soft-boiled (egg) zacht gekookt 38
soft drink frisdrank c 59
sold out uitverkocht 87, 155
sole (fish) tong c 44; (shoe) zool c 117
soloist solist c 88
some wat 15
someone iemand 95
something iets 29, 36, 107, 112
somewhere ergens 87
son zoon c 93
song liedje nt 128
soon spoedig 15
sorbet sorbet nt 53
sore (painful) pijnlijk 141, 145
sorry (to be) spijten 11, 16, 103; sorry! 11
sort (kind) soort c/nt 119
soup soep c 43
south zuid 77
South Africa Zuid-Afrika 146
South America Zuid-Amerika 146

souvenir souvenir *c* 127
souvenir shop souvenirwinkel *c* 99
sow, to zaaien 85
spade schepje *nt* 128
spanner moersleutel *c* 120
spare tyre reservewiel *nt* 75
spark(ing) plug bougie *c* 75
sparkling mousserend 47
speak, to spreken 12, 84, 135
speaker *(loudspeaker)* luidspreker *c* 118
special speciaal 20, 37
specialist specialist *c* 142
speciality specialiteit *c* 40
specimen *(medical)* monster *nt* 142
spell, to spellen 12
spend, to uitgeven 101
spice specerij *c* 64
spinach spinazie *c* 49
spine ruggegraat *c* 138
sponge spons *c* 110
spoon lepel *c* 36, 60, 120
sport sport *c* 89
sporting goods shop sportzaak *c* 99
sports event sportgebeurtenis *c* 89
sportswear sportkleding *c* 116
sprain, to verstuiken 140
spring *(season)* lente *c* 150
square vierkant 101
square *(town)* plein *nt* 82
stadium stadion *nt* 82
staff *(personnel)* personeel *nt* 26
stain vlek *c* 29
stainless steel roestvrij staal *nt* 120
stalls *(theatre)* zaal *c* 87
stamp *(postage)* postzegel *c* 28, 126, 132, 133
staple nietje *nt* 105
star ster *c* 94
start, to beginnen 80; starten 78
starter *(meal)* voorgerecht *nt* 41
station station *nt* 21, 67, 70, 73
stationer's kantoorboekhandel *c* 99, 104
statue standbeeld *nt* 82
stay verblijf *nt* 31
stay, to blijven 16, 19, 24; *(reside)* logeren 93
steak biefstuk *c* 46
steal, to stelen 156
steamed gestoomd 45

steamer stoomboot *c* 74
stewed gestoofd 45, 47
stiff stijf 141
still *(mineral water)* zonder koolzuur 59
sting steek *c* 139
sting, to steken 139
stitch, to naaien 29; stikken 117
stock voorraad *c* 103
stock exchange beurs *c* 82
stocking kous *c* 116
stomach maag *c* 138
stomach ache maagpijn *c* 141
stone steen *c* 122
stools ontlasting *c* 142
stop, to stoppen 21, 68, 70, 72
stop thief! houd de dief! 156
store *(shop)* winkel *c* 98, 99
straight *(drink)* puur 58
straight ahead rechtdoor 21, 77
strange vreemd 84
strawberry aardbei *c* 54, 55
street straat *c* 25, 77
streetcar tram *c* 72
street map plattegrond *c* 19, 105
string touw *nt* 105
strong zwaar 126, 143
student student *c* 82, 93
study, to studeren 93
stuffed gevuld 41, 45
sturdy stevig 101
styling gel haargel *c* 110
subway *(railway)* metro *c* 73
suede suède *c* 117
sugar suiker *c* 37, 64
suit *(man's)* kostuum *nt* 116; *(woman's)* mantelpak *nt* 116
suitcase koffer *c* 18
summer zomer *c* 150
sun zon *c* 85, 94
sunburn zonnebrand *c* 107
Sunday zondag *c* 151
sunglasses zonnebril *c* 123
sunshade *(beach)* parasol *c* 91
sun-tan cream zonnebrandcrème *c* 110
sun-tan oil zonnebrandolie *c* 110
super *(petrol)* super 75
superb groots 84
supermarket supermarkt *c* 99
supplement toeslag *c* 69
suppository zetpil *c* 108
surcharge toeslag *c* 40
surgery *(consulting room)* praktijk *c* 137

surname (familie)naam *c* 25
suspenders *(Am.)* bretels *c/pl* 116
swallow, to inslikken 143
sweater trui *c* 116
sweet zoet 60
sweet *(confectionery)* snoep *nt* 64, 126
sweet corn maïs *c* 49
sweetener zoetstof *c* 37
sweet pepper paprika *c* 49
sweet shop snoepwinkel *c* 99
swelling zwelling *c* 139
swim, to zwemmen 89, 90
swimming zwemmen *nt* 89, 91
swimming pool zwembad *nt* 32, 90
swimming trunks zwembroek *c* 116
swimsuit badpak *nt* 116
switch *(electric)* schakelaar *c* 29
switch on, to aandoen 118
switchboard operator telefoniste *c* 26
swollen gezwollen 139
synagogue synagoge *c* 84
synthetic synthetisch 113

T

table tafel *c* 36, 106; *(list)* tabel *c* 157
tablet *(medical)* tablet *nt* 108
tailor's kleermaker *c* 99
tail pipe uitlaatpijp *c* 78
take, to nemen 25, 73, 77, 102; *(time)* duren 60, 72, 74, 102; *(bring)* brengen 18, 21, 96
take away, to *(carry)* meenemen 62
talcum powder talkpoeder *c* 110
tampon tampon *c* 108
tap *(water)* kraan *c* 28
tap beer bier van het vat *nt* 56
tape *(music)* bandje *nt* 128, *(adhesive)* plakband *nt* 104
taste, to smaken 60
tax belasting *c* 32
tax-free shop duty-free winkel *c* 19
taxi taxi *c* 18, 19, 21, 31, 67
taxi rank/stand taxistandplaats *c* 21
tea thee *c* 38, 59, 64
teashop tearoom *c* 34
teaspoon theelepeltje *nt* 120, 143
tea towel theedoek *c* 120

telegram telegram *nt* 133
telegraph office postkantoor *nt* 99, 133
telephone telefoon *c* 28, 79, 134
telephone, to *(call)* telefoneren 134
telephone booth telefooncel *c* 134
telephone call (telefoon)gesprek *nt* 136; telefoon *c* 136
telephone directory telefoonboek *nt* 134
telephone number (telefoon)nummer *nt* 134, 136
telephoto lens telelens *c* 125
television televisie *c* 23, 28, 118
telex telex *c* 133
telex, to telexen 130
tell, to zeggen 13, 153
tell the way, to de weg wijzen 76
temperature temperatuur *c* 91, 142; *(fever)* koorts *c* 140
temporary provisorisch 145
ten tien 147
tendon pees *c* 138
tennis tennis *c* 89
tennis court tennisbaan *c* 90
tennis racket (tennis)racket *nt* 90
tent tent *c* 32, 106
tent peg haring *c* 106
tent pole tentstok *c* 106
terrace terras *nt* 36
terrifying vreselijk 84
than dan 15
thank, to danken 10, 96
that dat 11, 100, 161; die 161
the de 159; het 159
theatre schouwburg *c* 82; theater *nt* 86
theft diefstal *c* 156
their hun 162
then dan 15
there daar 14; er 14
thermometer thermometer *c* 108, 144
these deze 62, 117, 161
they zij 161
thief dief *c* 156
thigh dij *c* 138
thin dun 112
think, to *(believe)* geloven 31, 61; denken 94
thirsty, to be dorst hebben 13, 35
thirteen dertien 147
thirty dertig 147

DICTIONARY

this dit 11, 100, 161; deze 161
those die (daar) 161
thousand duizend 148
thread draad *c* 27
three drie 147
throat hals *c* 138; keel *c* 138, 141
throat lozenge keelpastille *c* 108
through door 15
through train doorgaande trein *c* 68, 69
thumb duim *c* 138
thumbtack punaise *c* 105
thunder donder *c* 94
thunderstorm onweer *nt* 94
Thursday donderdag *c* 151
ticket kaartje *nt* 69, 72, 73, 87, 89; *(air ticket)* ticket *c* 65
ticket office loket *nt* 67
tie stropdas *c* 116
tie clip dasclip *c* 121
tie pin dasspeld *c* 122
tight *(close-fitting)* nauw 114
tights maillot *c* 116
tile tegel *c* 127
time tijd *c* 80, 153; *(occasion)* keer *c* 95, 142, 143; maal 143
timetable *(trains)* spoorboekje *nt* 68
tin *(container)* blik *nt* 119
tin opener blikopener *c* 120
tinted gekleurd 123
tint, to tinten 30
tired moe 13, 140
tissue *(handkerchief)* papieren zakdoek *c* 110
to naar 15
tobacco tabak *c* 126
tobacconist's sigarenwinkel *c* 99, 126
today vandaag 29, 151
toe teen *c* 138
toilet paper toiletpapier *nt* 110
toiletry toiletartikelen *nt/pl* 109
toilets toiletten *nt/pl* 27, 32, 37, 67
toilet water eau de toilette *c* 110
tomato tomaat *c* 49
tomato juice tomatesap *nt* 59
tomb graf *nt* 82
tomorrow morgen 29, 94, 96, 151
tongue tong *c* 46, 138
tonight vanavond 86, 87, 88, 96
tonsils amandelen *c/pl* 138
too te 15, 19, 114; *(also)* ook 15, 75
tool gereedschap *nt* 120

too much te veel 15
tooth tand *c* 145
toothache kiespijn *c* 145
toothbrush tandenborstel *c* 110
toothpaste tandpasta *c* 110
torch *(flashlight)* zaklantaarn *c* 116
torn gescheurd 140
tough *(meat)* taai 60
tour toer *c* 74, 80; rondvaart *c* 74
tourist toerist *c* 40
tourist office verkeersbureau *nt* 80; VVV *c* 22, 80, 154
tourist tax verblijfsbelasting *c* 32
towards naar 15
towel handdoek *c* 110
tower toren *c* 82
town stad *c* 19, 88, 160
town hall stadhuis *nt* 82
tow truck takelwagen *c* 78
toy speelgoed 128
toy shop speelgoedwinkel *c* 99
track *(railway)* spoor *nt* 67, 69
tracksuit trainingspak *nt* 116
traffic verkeer *nt* 79
traffic jam file *c* 79
traffic light stoplicht *nt* 77, 79
trailer caravan *c* 32
train trein *c* 66, 68, 69, 70
tram tram *c* 72
tranquillizer kalmeringsmiddel *nt* 143
transfer *(finance)* overschrijving *c* 131
transformer transformator *c* 118
translate, to vertalen 12
translation vertaling *c* 131
translator vertaler *c* 131
transport vervoer *nt* 74
travel, to reizen 65, 93
travel agency reisbureau *nt* 99
travel guide reisgids *c* 105
traveller's cheque reischeque *c* 18, 61, 102, 130
travel sickness reisziekte *c* 107
treatment behandeling *c* 143
tree boom *c* 85
tremendous enorm 84
trim, to *(a beard)* bijknippen 31
trip reis *c* 92, 152; rit *c* 72; *(boat)* tocht *c* 74
trolley wagentje *nt* 18, 71
trousers lange broek *c* 116
trout forel *c* 44
try, to proberen 58, 135

Woordenboekje

try on, to aanpassen 114
tube tube *c* 119
Tuesday dinsdag *c* 151
tulip tulp *c* 85
tumbler bekerglas *nt* 120
turkey kalkoen *c* 48
turn, to *(change direction)* afslaan 21, 77
tweezers pincet *nt* 110
twelve twaalf 147
twenty twintig 147
twice tweemaal 149
twin beds lits-jumeaux *nt/pl* 23
two twee 147
typewriter schrijfmachine *c* 27
typically typisch 127
typing paper schrijfmachine-papier *nt* 105
tyre band *c* 75

U

ugly lelijk 14, 84
umbrella paraplu *c* 116
uncle oom *c* 93
unconscious bewusteloos 139
under onder 15
underdone *(meat)* niet gaar 47, 60; rood 47
underground *(railway)* metro *c* 73
underpants onderbroek *c* 116
undershirt hemd *nt* 116
understand, to begrijpen 12, 16
underwear onderkleding *c* 116
undress, to ontkleden 142
United States Verenigde Staten 146
university universiteit *c* 82
unleaded loodvrij 75
until tot 15
up op 15
upper boven 69
upset stomach indigestie *c* 107
upstairs boven 15, 69
urgent dringend 13
urine urine *c* 142
use gebruik *nt* 17, 108
use, to gebruiken 78
useful nuttig 15
usual gewoonlijk 143

V

vacancy kamer vrij *c* 22, 23
vacant vrij 14, 22
vacation vakantie *c* 151
vaccinate, to inenten 140

vacuum flask thermosfles *c* 120
vaginal infection vaginale infectie *c* 141
valid geldig 73
valley dal *nt* 76
value waarde *c* 131
value-added tax B.T.W. *c* 24, 102
vanilla vanille *c* 53
vase vaas *c* 127
VAT *(sales tax)* B.T.W. *c* 154
veal kalfsvlees *nt* 46; kalfs- 46
vegetable groente *c* 49
vegetable store groentewinkel *c* 99
vegetarian vegetarisch 37
vein ader *c* 138
venereal disease geslachtsziekte *c* 142
venison reebout *c* 48
very zeer 15
vest hemd *nt* 116; *(Am.)* vest *nt* 116
veterinarian dierenarts *c* 99
video camera videocamera *c* 124
video cassette videocassette *c* 118, 124, 128
video recorder videorecorder *c* 118
view *(panorama)* uitzicht *nt* 23, 25
village dorp *nt* 76
vinegar azijn *c* 37
visit bezoek *nt* 92
visiting hours bezoekuren *nt/pl* 144
visit, to bezoeken 80, 85; *(a place)* bezichtigen 84
vitamin pill vitaminepil *c* 108
voltage voltage *nt* 27, 118
vomit, to overgeven 140

W

waffle wafel *c* 63
waistcoat vest *nt* 116
wait, to wachten 108
wait for, to wachten op 21, 95
waiter kelner *c* 26; ober *c* 26, 36
waiting room wachtkamer *c* 67
waitress serveerster *c* 26; juffrouw *c* 26, 36
wake, to wekken 27, 71
Wales Wales 146
walk, to lopen 76; wandelen 74
wall muur *c* 76
wallet portefeuille *c* 156
walnut walnoot *c* 52

Nederlandse inhoudsopgave